'What does torture and brutality feel like to those at the receiving end? What are the factors which lead victims to narrate their experience afterwards or to keep silent? In what ways does masculinity restrict or fashion the ways in which narration occurs? What is the link between storytelling and propaganda? Lisa White's findings from her interviews with republican male prisoners in Northern Ireland provide us with fascinating, complex and informative answers to those questions. This book will be of great value to anyone interested in how people seek to come to terms with the legacy of political violence and conflict.'
Bill Rolston, Emeritus Professor, University of Ulster, UK

'Through a tenacious reading of the stories of men detainees during the Northern Ireland "Troubles", the author upsets conventional preoccupations with truth claiming (with all that this implies for exclusion and privileging hierarchies of victimhood). By contrast, this book shows how and why "truth-sharing" should be the basis for communicative action and political healing. This book is essential reading for all students of conflict studies, transitional justice and victimisation.'
Mary Corcoran, Senior Lecturer in Criminology, Keele University, UK

Transitional Justice and Legacies of State Violence

As politicians, public bodies and non-Governmental organisations continue to profess an interest in making peace with the past, this highly original study explores the motivation, significance and legacy of 'making public' experiences of state violence in Northern Ireland.

Based on a synthesis of documentary material with the findings from a series of contemporary interviews, this timely book uncovers the reasoning behind many Republican former detainees' accounts of state violence and torture. It examines the aims of those who 'went public' during the conflict and discusses the meaning they attached to their stories and the various responses to them. It also identifies some of the risks involved in criticising the violence of the British State and illuminates the ways in which 'truths' are often contested in Northern Ireland – both during the conflict and in the years which have followed. A unique piece of interdisciplinary work, the study disentangles and evaluates the discourses presented by former detainees and makes an innovative and interesting contribution to knowledge about transitional justice and legacies of state violence.

The book is suitable for social science scholars interested in human rights, state violence, criminology and transitional justice, as well as those seeking to understand more about experiences of imprisonment and the legacy of the Northern Ireland conflict.

Lisa White is a Senior Lecturer in Criminology at the University of Lincoln. Her interests include state violence, imprisonment and human rights.

Routledge studies in crime and society

1 **Sex Work**
Labour, mobility and sexual services
Edited by JaneMaree Maher, Sharon Pickering and Alison Gerard

2 **State Crime and Resistance**
Edited by Elizabeth Stanley and Jude McCulloch

3 **Collective Morality and Crime in the Americas**
Christopher Birkbeck

4 **Talking Criminal Justice**
Language and the just society
Michael J. Coyle

5 **Women Exiting Prison**
Critical essays on gender, post-release support and survival
Bree Carlton and Marie Segrave

6 **Collective Violence, Democracy and Protest Policing**
David R. Mansley

7 **Prostitution in the Community**
Attitudes, action and resistance
Sarah Kingston

8. **Surveillance, Capital and Resistance**
Michael McCahill and Rachel L. Finn

9 **Crime, Community and Morality**
Simon Green

10 **Flexible Workers**
Labour, regulation and the political economy of the stripping industry
Teela Sanders and Kate Hardy

11 **Histories of State Surveillance in Europe and Beyond**
Edited by Kees Boersma, Rosamunde van Brakel, Chiara Fonio and Pieter Wagenaar

12 **Rape, Victims and Investigations**
Experiences and perceptions of law enforcement officers responding to reported rapes
Shana L. Maier

13 **Understanding Gender Based Violence**
National and international contexts
Edited by Nadia Aghtaie and Geetanjali Gangoli

14 **Queer Sex Work**
Edited by Mary Laing, Katy Pilcher and Nicola Smith

15 **Criminology and War**
Transgressing the borders
Edited by Sandra Walklate and Ross McGarry

16 **Transitional Justice and Legacies of State Violence**
Talking about torture in Northern Ireland
Lisa White

Transitional Justice and Legacies of State Violence
Talking about torture in Northern Ireland

Lisa White

LONDON AND NEW YORK

First published 2015
by Routledge
2 Park Square, Milton Park, Abingdon, Oxfordshire OX14 4RN

Simultaneously published in the USA and Canada
by Routledge
711 Third Avenue, New York, NY 10017

First issued in paperback 2016

Routledge is an imprint of the Taylor & Francis Group, an informa business

© 2015 Lisa White

The right of Lisa White to be identified as author of this work has been
asserted by her in accordance with sections 77 and 78 of the Copyright,
Designs and Patents Act 1988.

All rights reserved. No part of this book may be reprinted or reproduced or
utilised in any form or by any electronic, mechanical, or other means, now
known or hereafter invented, including photocopying and recording, or in
any information storage or retrieval system, without permission in writing
from the publishers.

British Library Cataloguing in Publication Data
A catalogue record for this book is available from the British Library

Library of Congress Cataloging-in-Publication Data
White, Lisa,
Transitional justice and legacies of state violence : talking about torture in
Northern Ireland / Lisa White. – First Edition.
   pages cm. – (Routledge studies in crime and society ; 16)
   1. Political violence–Northern Ireland–History–20th century.
   2. Northen Ireland–History, Military. 3. Torture–Northern Ireland–
History–20th century. I. Title.
   DA990.U46W465 2014
   941.60824–dc23   2014034879

ISBN 13: 978-1-138-28854-6 (pbk)
ISBN 13: 978-0-415-82624-2 (hbk)

Typeset in Times New Roman
by Wearset Ltd, Boldon, Tyne and Wear

Contents

Acknowledgements		x
1	Introduction	1
2	The history of state violence in Northern Ireland	26
3	Defining experiences of state violence in detention	49
4	Revealing as healing?	60
5	The masculinity of 'making public'	80
6	Former detainees' narratives as 'propaganda'	100
7	Discourse, denial and dehumanisation	126
8	Seeking accountability for state violence	160
9	The problems and possibilities of talking about violence	186
	Index	198

Acknowledgements

In completing this book, I owe a great deal of thanks to Professor Peter Shirlow for his advice and good humour and to Professor Shadd Maruna for his patience and understanding. Together they supervised the original thesis on which this book is based. I would also like to thank Ms. Ruth Jamieson and Professor Kieran McEvoy for their early comments when the project was still in its infancy. Professor Phil Scraton and Professor Kevin Bean were also immensely influential in offering good advice and inspiration. The staff at Linenhall Library in Belfast, Belfast Central Newspaper Library, Special Collections Section at Queen's University and Great Central Warehouse at the University of Lincoln also deserve praise for their role in helping me locate the documentary material from the 1970s and 1980s which laid the foundations for this book. My deepest gratitude also goes to Laurence McKeown, Jim Auld, PJ McClean, Tommy McKearney, Liam Shannon, Richard O'Rawe, Michael Culbert, Harry Murray and Interviewees 'P' and 'F' for their interest, enthusiasm and participation in the project.

I am continually thankful for the support of academic colleagues at the University of Lincoln who have provided a listening ear for my arguments and anxieties. In particular Liam McCann, Dr Andrea Beckmann, Kate Strudwick, Jill Jameson, Jan Gordon, Sue Bond-Taylor, Joe Heslop and Dr Kelvin Jones have always been willing to engage with my ideas, and I have found this immensely beneficial. Dr Yassin M'Boge, Dr Marian Duggan, Dr Mark Brunger, Dr Smita Kheria, Clare McCann, Julie McBride and Neil Graffin have also been influential in offering the social support which prevented the research process from being an isolating experience. Deirdre MacAliskey played an important role in motivating me towards overcoming obstacles, and Fabio Tartarini's enthusiasm, interest and meaningful words of encouragement helped bring the book to its conclusion. The 'working lunches' helped too.

A number of sections in this book draw on my previously published research. Chapter 7 develops ideas originally published in Papers from the British Criminology Conference. Many thanks to the British Society of Criminology (BSC) for allowing its inclusion here and for granting the paper 'The BSC Postgraduate Paper Prize' for 2010. The original reference is: White, L. (2010) 'Discourse, Denial and Dehumanisation: Former detainees' experiences of narrating state

Acknowledgements xi

violence in Northern Ireland', Papers from the British Criminology Conference, Vol. 10, 3–18, available at: www.britsoccrim.org/volume10/2010_PBCC_full. pdf. I am also grateful to Palgrave MacMillan for allowing me to build on elements of White, L. (2012) 'Masculinities, Pain and Power: "Gendering" Experiences of "Truth Sharing"' first published in Shepherd, L.J. and Åhäll, L. (eds) *Gender, Agency and Political Violence*. Basingstoke: Palgrave. Thank you to Laura and Linda for offering me the opportunity to publish my work on Northern Ireland in their text.

Lastly, thanks must go to my family, especially Pat for sparking my interest in the Northern Ireland conflict, Chris for his motivation and drive, and Jordan for his laughter and endless patience with computers. This book is a result of their continued faith, love and support.

1 Introduction

Based on research with Republican former detainees,[1] this book explores the motivation, significance and legacy of bringing private memories of state violence into the contested public history of the Northern Ireland conflict.[2] To do this, the text first examines how former detainees define the state violence they experienced whilst in detention. Second, it analyses the popular discourses around 'healing' and the extent to which these motivated former detainees 'go public' with their experiences. Third, it explores former detainees' perceptions of gendered concepts of hegemonic masculinity and the impact such perceptions may or may not have had on their decision to narrate their experiences of violence. Fourth, the book discusses the extent to which former detainees perceived their narratives to be significant as political propaganda for the Republican movement in Northern Ireland. The consequences of official discourse are then explored from the perspective of those whose accounts challenged the imagery of an impartial and liberal state. Finally, the book presents an overview of previous attempts to hold the British State to account for its violence in Northern Ireland. In sum, the book argues that the presentation of experiences of conflict is a complex act which emerges out of a synthesis of personal and collective motivations, takes on a significance for former detainees that can in itself become challenging, and often leads to consequences that are far from homogeneous in terms of form and scale. Through its original synthesis of literature, documentary analysis and qualitative interview data, the book disentangles and evaluates the discourses presented by former detainees about state violence. It investigates the production of these contested narratives of victimisation and analyses just what those who 'go public' may desire from those who 'hear' their stories. The research contributes to an enhanced knowledge about the production, significance, ownership and effects of narratives of state violence at the individual and societal level.

Within the context of the conflict in Northern Ireland, the existence of a wide range of public accounts, testimonies, narratives and memoirs describing personal experiences of violence appear to suggest that 'going public' with accounts may be a valuable and possibly even a necessary exercise for those who have experienced harm. The meaning of 'going/making public' remains dynamic and flexible, in order to reflect the diversity and range of opportun-

2   *Introduction*

ities which have been utilised by survivors and their families to bring their experiences into the public domain. It may refer to newspaper articles featuring survivors' accounts, to television interviews or to the publication of memoirs and everything in between. It may also refer to localised storytelling projects. In the absence of any overarching truth-sharing mechanism in Northern Ireland, a number of storytelling projects have developed to try to enable survivors of state violence to 'make public' their stories and record the history of the conflict as they have experienced it. These projects are listed in Kelly (2005, 2007) but a few illustrative examples are discussed here. In 1999, a community-based truth-sharing initiative was established by Falls Community Council to record the experiences of the conflict as felt by those living in nationalist West Belfast (Kelly 2005: 54). The project coordinators of 'Dúchas: Living History' felt that state violence against the local community had been framed as legitimate and that the narratives of those most affected had been replaced by the official discourse, which further facilitated a lack of trust in the British State and its institutions. Similarly, in South Fermanagh, Fírinne (Truth) began a storytelling project aimed at recording people's experiences of state violence in the region, which lies on the border with the Republic of Ireland. The organisation felt that it was important to document experiences of state violence, 'for posterity and have them acknowledged, not just within their community, but the wider community, particularly to highlight the sanctioned policy by the state' (Kelly 2005: 68).

These projects are an attempt to respond to the legacy of state violence by recording the stories of those affected by this facet of the conflict. Possibly the most well known is the Ardoyne Commemoration Project (ACP) which 'was established in 1998 to document the stories of Ardoyne residents in North Belfast who lost their lives as a result of the conflict between 1969 and 1998' (Kelly 2005: 32). The resulting book *Ardoyne: The Untold Truth* was designed to enable the community in Ardoyne to tell their story of the conflict in their own way (Kelly 2005; Lundy and McGovern 2006). People wanted 'an opportunity to "set the record straight", to "tell their story" [and] challenge the hierarchy of victims' (ACP 2002: 3). The participation of the Ardoyne community was of vital importance to the project, partly in order to ensure that people's narratives of suffering were not misrepresented and that survivors retained a sense of ownership over their narratives which, as Kelly (2005) recognises, had not always been the case in the past. Narratives were recorded, then returned to participants to ensure all details were correct and approved, before consent was sought for publication (ACP 2002; Kelly 2005; Lundy and McGovern 2005, 2006). The ACP is an example of a community-based initiative and a 'bottom up' approach which took place amidst a 'lack of interest amongst dominant political actors in developing formal mechanisms' (Lundy and McGovern 2008: 285). Such community-based initiatives are undoubtedly of value. They provide space for the 'airing' of subjugated narratives and can help to foster a sense of shared experience which enables social movements to develop and/or strengthen. They also can be an opportunity for intra-group

Introduction 3

discussion and reflection, particularly around the difficult 'taboo' questions – such as the treatment of suspected informers in Ardoyne (Lundy and McGovern 2008). Community-based initiatives might also form early building blocks to help people develop confidence in the benefits of wider truth sharing (Aiken 2010). When referring to victims and survivors of state violence, community-based approaches also function so as to illustrate the 'view from below'. For Gormally and McEvoy (2009: 12), this denotes 'a "resistant" or "mobilising" character to the actions of community, civil society and other non-state actors in their opposition to powerful political, social or economic forces'.

That said, any discussion of storytelling must avoid over-romanticising community-based approaches to the legacy of state violence. If only one community (or section of the community) takes part, it risks reducing those communities to symbols of suffering. Individual stories can become lost in the overarching narrative of community experience and a falsely homogeneous portrayal of the legacy of state violence might be produced. These approaches might also be limited in their ability to gain and impart information (and possibly achieve a sense of acknowledgement) from other communities, including from the 'security community'[3] whose role in the conflict is often downplayed or diminished within the official discourse (Lundy and McGovern 2001). If projects become overly insular and inward looking, they risk only 'preaching to the converted' (Gormally and McEvoy 2009). Furthermore, as Lundy and McGovern (2008) recognise, even the most conscientious of community-based approaches sometimes reflect the structural inequalities of wider society, with men's experiences of the conflict tending to dominate. Care must be taken so that the experiences of women and the conflict's impact upon people with disabilities (McEvoy 2013) do not drop out of community-based approaches or the wider discourse of transitional justice itself (Ní Aoláin 2009; Bell 2009). The relative absence of women's narratives of state violence during the conflict is particularly pronounced in regards to female detainees and their stories of life in Armagh during the conflict, although there are some exceptions (see e.g. Aretxaga 1997; Corcoran 2006a, 2006b).

In addition, the very meaning of 'community-based' approach is difficult to define. It might refer to the way in which a project emerges and operates and/or to projects which receive a level of state funding but still retain a sense of being in and of 'the community'. As Gormally and McEvoy (2009) suggest, groups may also 'start out' as being 'single identity' and linked to only one community, but move later to work with others. Others begin with an understanding of truth sharing across communities being built into their *raison d'être*. This can be clearly seen in the work of groups such as 'Towards Understanding and Healing', an organisation whose members include 'ex-members of non-state armed groups, Republican and Loyalist, ex-members of the state security forces – RUC, UDR/RIR, regular British Army regiments – and those who have suffered from violence from any of these sources from the two main communities here and in Britain and the Republic' (Gormally and McEvoy 2009: 29). The sharing of experiences is an important part of their work. Alongside the work of

4   *Introduction*

organisations like the multiple-community 'Healing Through Remembering', these groups offer one potential way of responding to the legacy of state violence through truth sharing.

Storytelling about state violence in detention

Storytelling has become a popular way of responding to the legacy of the conflict, but what is sometimes marginalised within the transitional justice discourses emerging from Northern Ireland is the existence of truth sharing *during* conflict itself. The existence of these primary materials shows that there has been a constant dissemination of narratives *throughout* what might have appeared at times to be an intractable, violent conflict, rather than simply after its apparent cessation. As shown in Chapter 2 state violence in Northern Ireland took a range of forms. It included the use of violence against detainees by the Royal Ulster Constabulary (RUC),[4] the British Army and the Prison Service of Northern Ireland. Many former detainees first gave their accounts to local lawyers, who were permitted to distribute their narratives to the Association for Legal Justice[5] and related civil society organisations who would publish and distribute them. Some of those interviewed for this book had given their narratives of state violence to other political activists, for example, those working for *An Phoblacht*, which merged with *Republican News* in 1979. This magazine has been the official paper of armed Republicanism and has remained broadly sympathetic to the Provisional Irish Republican Army (PIRA hereafter 'IRA'). Others gave their accounts to journalists from local newspapers, such as *The Tyrone Democrat*. Some former detainees' accounts also featured in publications with far wider circulations, including *The Irish Times*, and British newspapers, such as *The Sunday Times*. Similar accounts featured in the publications of international human rights-based non-governmental organisations (NGOs), including Amnesty International. Finally, many personal accounts of state violence appear in the collected memoirs of former prisoners released towards the apparent end of the armed conflict, including biographical-type memoirs like texts such as *Nor Meekly Serve Thy Time* (Campbell *et al.* 1994, 2006), *Out of Time* (McKeown 2001) and *Blanketmen* (O'Rawe 2005). These texts contain detailed narratives about experiences of imprisonment, often as edited by groups of former prisoners themselves. Other accounts by former detainees can be found in histories of the conflict written by journalists (Taylor 1980, 1998, 2002) or by academic researchers (e.g. Feldman 1991; English 2003).

These accounts underpin this entire book and examples feature in Chapter 2, which explores the extent of state violence in Northern Ireland. Their existence created the spark from which this research emerged. Why did male former detainees choose (or experience sufficient pressure) to 'go public' with their stories? What did they gain by doing so? What did they lose? How did they experience 'going public' and its consequences? What do they feel has been the personal legacy of their narrative? These questions are rarely discussed in former

Introduction 5

detainees' narratives of state violence themselves. Although based within criminology in its study of state violence and victimhood, the book also touches upon a range of disciplines, including law, social psychology and the political sciences. As such, it shares some foundations with Stanley's (2002, 2005, 2009) work on survivor identity, Hayner's (2002) discussions of truth and Cohen's (2001) study of denial.

Methodology

In order to carry out the research, a list of existing literature featuring former detainees' narratives of state violence experienced during detention was located during an extensive review of historical literature about the conflict. This review utilised the vast newspaper archives, civil society pamphlets, television and media sources contained in the Linenhall Library in Belfast and the Special Collections at Queen's University. Other documentary material could be found in the published memoirs of former detainees (e.g. McKeown 2001). From this collected material, a list containing named detainees who had previously 'gone public' (and done so under their own name) was drawn up. Personal contacts were asked to help locate those on the list who might wish to participate in the research project, thus enabling prospective snowball sampling. Access to the sample was dependent on trust and good practice, and the complex workings of a series of inter-relationships both professional and personal, which slowly led to a 'snowball effect' (Silverman 2005). In addition to these networks, former prisoner groups including Coiste n-Iarchimí[6] were also used to locate former detainees from the list of those who had previously made public accounts of state violence. These groups acted as gatekeepers to the research project, sometimes controlling access and sometimes initiating the first contact with former detainees.

There are, however, problems with involving 'gatekeeper' organisations. They might close down access to those who are critical of the organisation, or whose views the organisation finds problematic. They may also misrepresent the research project or its aims. Possible participants may understand the project as the gatekeeper's own and may make decisions to/not to participate based upon this understanding. Although not the case in the research for this book, 'gatekeeper' organisations may also bring pressure to influence the findings of any resulting report, or otherwise bargain with the researcher for access to participants (Hughes 2000). In this instance, organisations such as Coiste helped locate possible participants from my list of former detainees who had made public their experiences and did not ask for anything in return.

Ten former detainees agreed to participate. Others on the list were found to have since died or were difficult to access. One possible interviewee did not wish to participate in the study and hinted that due to his current circumstances he could find the process difficult – even with mechanisms in place to minimise harm. Another former detainee felt that his own experiences were not 'worth' any discussion, but was keen to help find other possible participants. The

6   *Introduction*

language of 'truth sharing' was chosen in order to reflect the possible significance of audience in the production of narratives by former detainees and this was later evidenced in discussions with participants (and forms a key finding of the book). The sample was not limited by age, race, class or other structural forces, but was instead contingent only on gender and on an experience of 'making public' an account of state violence in relation to the detention system of Northern Ireland. Women were excluded from the sample. This is not to minimise their involvement in the conflict or their experiences of state violence, such as those detailed by Murray (1998). Rather, by restricting the sample only to male former detainees, it was felt that concepts such as masculinities and their role in 'truth sharing' could be explored in greater depth.

Eight out of the ten interviewees were happy to be identified and waived their rights to anonymity. Most are well known within the political and civil society sphere of Northern Ireland. In regards to the content of their original narrative testimony, Jim, Liam and PJ's refer to internment, whereas Tommy, Interviewee 'F', Richard and Michael's public accounts primarily concerned later interrogation practices. Laurence, Interviewee 'P' and Harry's testimonies mostly concerned experiences of imprisonment, although it would be misleading to portray any of these periods as mutually exclusive. At the time of the fieldwork, nine out of the ten volunteers defined themselves as 'Republican' or, to quote Tommy, as 'having a Republican outlook on things'. The remaining respondent, Interviewee PJ, defined himself as being a 'civil rights activist' keen to participate in the research. This is not to collapse differences between the various strands of civil rights activism, nationalism and/or Republicanism, but merely to reflect that most accounts of state violence experienced whilst in detention were produced by Republican former detainees.

Although they took part in extensive conversations early in the life of the study, the voices of other Republican groups (including the Irish National Liberation Army, hereafter 'INLA') are largely absent, partly because of a relative dearth of original testimonies – the result of historical differences of emphasis within the paramilitary organisations themselves. This may change in the future, as organisations seek to record their own history (see e.g. Irish Socialist Republican Forum's call for prison stories). With the exception of a few testimonies of state violence experienced by Loyalists which feature in Crawford (1999) and the allusions made to Protestant allegations of ill-treatment in Castlereagh in May/June 1977 (Taylor 1980: 182), detailed public narratives by Loyalist prisoners about state violence experienced during detention are difficult to find.

By choosing to research with Republicans, I was able to triangulate existing and accessible narratives around state violence, and build upon levels of trust already present in personal networks. Research within personal networks, for example, with the friends of mutual friends, brings with it its own ethical problems. Though it is useful in terms of building trust and rapport, the nature of personal relationships may mean that participants take part in research out of a sense of obligation. Equally this means of access may also lead to a form of bias in the results and social desirability in the responses. Such things are, however, difficult to measure within such a small scale project. Furthermore, as the research is exploratory in nature and not directed towards achieving a conclusion that is applicable to *all* former detainees at *all* times, it is thought that a synthesis of purposeful and snowball sampling has proved most useful in achieving the research aims and in enabling access to willing volunteers.

Former detainees took part in a series of tape-recorded interviews about the motivation behind their original testimony which described violence in detention. They were also asked questions about the language they would use to define their experiences and the extent to which a need for healing underpinned their 'making public'. The interviews also explored ways in which their sense of 'masculinity' may have shaped their narrative, and whether or not they felt they had had a propagandist intention in publicising their account of state violence. Lastly, they discussed in depth their attitudes towards the British State's response to their original allegations. Using the Ardoyne Commemorative Project (2002) and Smyth and Fay (2000) as a model, the completed transcripts were returned to participants, in order to enable them to make any edits and to grant their approval for the use of those transcripts in publications. Only two participants chose to edit their transcripts and these changes were essentially points of clarification and/or addition, rather than extensive deletions or changes. This (along with the rest of the research process) was designed to allow former detainees as much ownership over the testimonies as possible, so that 'the issue of what [was to] be disclosed [remains] under the control of the interviewee' (Jamieson and Grounds 2002: 10). Returning transcripts to interviewees was an important aspect of the continuous process of informed consent, in that it enabled participants to remove or add details to their transcripts before they became part of this book. All gatekeepers and potential volunteers were informed of the limits to anonymity before agreeing to participate and were reminded of this again after the data collection was complete. Only two former detainees wished to remain anonymous and their transcripts have been assigned a random alphabetical code ('P' and 'F' respectively). Their original narrative of their experience of state violence can be found in the public domain, but – unlike the other narratives – does not appear in this book because of the risk of identifying aspects which might lead to the loss of anonymity for 'P' and 'F'.

Chapter outlines

Chapter 2 provides an introduction to the conflict in Northern Ireland and features the original 'truth sharing' narratives of a selection of former detainees. The very term 'Northern Ireland' itself remains contentious. It refers to six of the nine counties of the province of Ulster, which were retained as a region of the United Kingdom (UK) following partition in 1921. The six counties contained a roughly two-thirds Protestant majority, many of whom wished to maintain constitutional links with the UK. According to McKittrick and McVea (2001: 5) 'the boundaries of the Northern Ireland which came into being in 1921 were

8 *Introduction*

essentially worked out between Westminster and the Ulster Unionist party'. Thus, at its birth in 1921, the borders of Northern Ireland were gerrymandered to preserve Protestant power in the North (Farrell 1976, 1983). Many nationalists refuse to recognise the partition of Ireland and instead refer to the place as 'the North' or the 'Six Counties'. The mostly nationalist Catholic minority were discriminated against in a range of social policy areas, including voting, housing and employment. In the late 1960s, the increased strength of feeling about the denial of civil rights to over one-third of the population contributed to the creation of the Northern Ireland Civil Rights Association (NICRA). NICRA did not seek Irish unification but called for the inclusion of Catholic citizens in the social, political and economic life of Northern Ireland. Its original membership had a minority of Protestants, although this was to decline in later years.

In 1968, a banned NICRA march in Derry was violently broken up by the predominantly Protestant Royal Ulster Constabulary (RUC) and its auxiliary wing, the 'B-Specials'. This wing operated as a violent, quasi-paramilitary force dedicated to the 'internal security' of Northern Ireland. Later the following year, rioting took place across Northern Ireland and the RUC seemingly allowed Loyalists to attack Catholic areas. The British Army was deployed, initially under the guise of restoring 'order'. The conflict that followed led to the deaths of almost 4,000 people from a range of jurisdictions, injured 50,000 people and resulted in high levels of trauma and poor mental health across generations (Shirlow and Murtagh 2006).

A number of broad perspectives exist regarding the conflict's causes and consequences. For Republicans, the conflict was constructed within an anti-colonial ideology which sought the cessation of Britain's presence in Ireland. Inequality and discrimination were highlighted as features of a violent and illegitimate state, one committed to sectarian actions in order to bolster Northern Ireland's constitutional link with the UK. Some Republicans became involved in paramilitary violence in organisations such as the Official Irish Republican Army (OIRA), Provisional Irish Republican Army (IRA) and the Irish National Liberation Army (INLA). Such groups are thought to be responsible for the deaths of approximately 2,057 people, 52 per cent of which were members of the 'security community' (Punch 2012). Though there were some ideological differences between the various Republican groups, all wished to see the creation of a united Ireland, the withdrawal of British forces and an end to British involvement in the governing of the Six Counties. For Loyalists on the other hand, the conflict was understood as a mixed sectarian/civil war scenario in which they feared the consequences of British withdrawal (both militarily and politically) and the possible creation of a united Ireland. They cast Republicans and Catholics alike as threats to the cohesion and integrity of the Union, and some took part in paramilitary violence, under the guise of the Ulster Volunteer Force (UVF), Ulster Freedom Fighters (UFF) and Ulster Defence Association (UDA).[7] They are thought to be responsible for the deaths of approximately 1,019 people – 85 per cent of whom came from a 'civilian' background. Because of the ways in which the conflict in Northern Ireland was managed, membership of paramilitary organisations was

Introduction 9

often hidden in order to avoid the attention of opposing paramilitary groups and/ or the security community. This may mean that the status of some of the dead might hide a degree of ambiguity, although paramilitary groups would often 'claim' their dead and memorialise them. What is clear, however, is that approximately one in ten of those killed during the conflict were direct victims of state violence. Of these 363 people, some 52 per cent were thought to be 'civilians'. Despite such acts of violence, the British State invoked the idea that it was a peacekeeping, neutral and honest broker between 'two tribes' whose supposed atavism reflected a complicated and divisive history (Darby 1997). In addition to causing these deaths, the security community's role also included the passing on of private information to Loyalist paramilitary 'death squads' (Sluka 1999; Rolston 2005), who then carried out the killing of those the security community felt were too sympathetic to the Republican cause. The State's role is therefore central to the conflict and it would be reasonable to believe that there is still more to be 'made public' about its involvement, particularly around the use of informers. State violence also took place along a spectrum ranging from on-street harassment, house searches and raids through to interrogation, detention and the violence both of and during incarceration. Although precise figures are unknown, Shirlow and McEvoy (2008) estimate that 15,000 Republicans and between 5,000 and 10,000 Loyalists were imprisoned during the conflict. Although not an extensive history, Chapter 2 of this book traces the nature of violence against Republican prisoners and internees. It uses former detainees' original narratives to provide the reader with something of the context of state violence in Northern Ireland. As such, the chapter presents the necessary historical background required to understand and analyse former detainees' narratives and their experiences of 'making public' private memories.

By further incorporating details from a series of interviews with former detainees, Chapter 3 explores the lived experience of legal definitions around torture, and inhuman or degrading treatment. The literature concerning torture is extensive and debates about how to define the harms caused by agents of states appear repeatedly within critical criminology (see Green and Ward 2004; Kretzmer 2007; Coleman *et al.* 2009). The related human rights discourses about state violence and its legacy are of increasing relevance in a 'globalising' twenty-first century. There is a growing understanding and partial acceptance by many political actors of the importance of human rights as a theoretical instrument on which to base policy and also as a means of holding others to account for violations, evidenced in part by the continuing development of a body of international law, treaty organisations, international ad hoc tribunals, and the International Criminal Court. Although these developments are not without problems and their powers should not be overstated (Mahoney 2007; Nickel 2007), their evidence increased awareness of the value and importance of 'human rights' across different states, even if only as a theoretical concept or rhetorical device.

Within this rights-based discourse, one of the most fundamental protections involves freedom from torture. Article 5 of the Universal Declaration of Human

10   *Introduction*

Rights (1948) states that 'no one should be subjected to torture or to cruel, inhuman or degrading treatment or punishment'. This pronouncement has itself been incorporated into a central element of the International Covenant on Civil and Political Rights in 1966. The prohibition of torture also features in regional instruments such as in Article 3 of the European Convention for the Protection of Human Rights and Fundamental Freedoms (1950) and its related protocols. Furthermore, the centrality of the prohibition in international law is also evidenced by a series of treaties that take the prevention and regulation of torture as their sole focus. For example, the United Nations Convention Against Torture and Other Cruel, Inhuman or Degrading Treatment or Punishment (1984) has been followed by a dedicated Inter-American Convention to Prevent and Punish Torture (1985) and also by the European Convention for the Prevention of Torture and Inhuman or Degrading Treatment or Punishment (1987). Thus, freedom from torture is amongst the rights deemed most well established as core human rights. What is missing, however, from such discourses, is the meaning that survivors of these events give to their own experiences.[8] Chapter 3 therefore explores the ways in which former detainees construct the meaning of state violence. It particularly examines the language of torture and brutality, synthesising the legal definitions found in official discourse with the lived experiences of those who have made public their accounts.

The deep desire to tell stories about personal experiences of state violence – including torture – is evidenced by the vast array of published accounts, memoirs, poetry, art, cultural artefacts and other communicative tools which facilitate and assist 'truth sharing'. After living through the violence of the Holocaust, Primo Levi (1987: 15) passionately asserted that 'the need to tell our story … has taken on the character of an immediate and violent impulse'. This desire to 'tell their story' is reflected in the array of narratives available from a vast range of different conflict settings and across diverse cultures, suggesting that the need of some who have experienced violence to have their voices heard remains powerful. This book is focused primarily upon those former detainees from the conflict in Northern Ireland who have previously 'gone public' with their accounts. Those who took part discussed the reasons why they 'went public' and the significance and consequences which have emerged as a result of their public utterances. The research direction was partially influenced by early, entirely unstructured discussions with potential participants These pre-interviews are perhaps better understood as 'little chats' and were designed as a rapport building exercise. They also were an attempt to gain greater knowledge of the field before commencing the research project itself. These participants' words (or unexpected omissions) directed the research project towards new avenues for exploration under the broad analytical rubric of narrating state violence. One concept missing from these early, unstructured discussions was that of 'healing'. This was surprising given the dominance of popular psychology and the language of healing both implied and explicit in the literature on narrating violence. Godwin Phelps (2004: 56) argues that 'psychological studies have shown that victims of loss and violence are helped in their recovery by telling a story about

Introduction   11

what happened to them, and that in doing so, engenders a transformation from victim to survivor'. Contemporary cultural discourses too, often present the revealing and public discussion of personal traumas as deeply beneficial. Popular phrases such as 'a problem shared is a problem halved' and warnings about the 'bottling up' of powerful emotions all depict the sharing of painful experiences as a positive and valuable endeavour. Equally, the existence of a 'confessional' culture of chat shows, 'reality' television and so-called 'misery literature' (O'Neill 2007) evidences that there is a vast public interest in the narratives of those who have suffered abuses across a wide range of contexts and settings.

This desire for knowledge about violence and the sharing of experiences is also witnessed within a more formal political context. For Neier (1994: 5), there is 'perhaps universal agreement that the truth about abuses of the past must be known'. This may be partially because of the 'psychological benefit that it is believed the process of "truth sharing" has for the victims and their families' and it is this which has in part led to the development of a number of Truth Commissions (Sangster 1999: 12). Such Commissions act as a partial conduit for the narration of personal experiences of violence fuelled by an understanding of the therapeutic value of 'going public', and are often underpinned by the influential 'testimony method' used in Latin America with Chilean survivors of state violence (Okawa and Hauss 2007). This theory that 'revealing is healing' is supported with studies by Duvenage (1999) and Herman (2001: 175), who argues that telling painful stories 'transforms the traumatic memory, so that it can be integrated into the survivor's life story'. In an analysis grounded around 'transcend[ing] atrocities', Herman argues that the 'survivor mission' usually begins with the recognition of:

> a political or religious dimension in their misfortune and the discovery that they can transform the meaning of their personal tragedy by making it the basis for social action ... giving to others is the essence of the survivor mission.
>
> (Herman 2001: 207–209)

In acknowledging the importance of audience in the narration of violent experiences, Herman (2001: 209) also suggests that 'survivors undertake to speak about the unspeakable in the belief that it will help others ... in taking care of others, survivors feel recognised, loved and cared for'. Across disciplines, other authors have used clinical testing to attempt to show that narrating previous experiences of violence is beneficial, often as a form of 'exposure therapy' or 'testimony therapy' (see e.g. Cienfuegos and Monelli 1983; Agger and Jensen 1990, 1996). These arguments form the basis of a number of approaches towards 'truth sharing' and it is therefore important to directly analyse what survivors themselves feel is helpful or not (Danieli 1992). In his memoir *If This is a Man*, Levi (1987: 15) describes his feelings about 'making public' his experience of the Holocaust as being akin to 'an interior liberation'. This perception is very similar to that of Mario Villani, a torture survivor of Argentina's 'Dirty War' who recalls:

12   *Introduction*

> the first time I [spoke] out publicly ... I realized that there were no torturers at my side threatening to blow me up. Rather the torturers were in my head. Inside I was still a prisoner. And realising that set me free.
>
> (Feitlowitz 1998: 87)

Similarly, Graybill (2002: 83) describes how Lukas Baba Sikiwepere – who survived being blinded by a police shooting – told the South African Truth and Reconciliation Commission (SATRC) that 'I feel that what has been making me sick all the time is the fact that I couldn't tell my story. But now it feels like I got my sight back by coming here and telling you the story.' Graybill's (2002: 83) research also includes the statements of another survivor of South African state violence, who alleged that 'when the officer tortured me at that time in John Vorster Square, he laughed at me, "you can scream your head off, nobody will ever hear you". He was wrong, today people hear me.'

Chapter 4 therefore seeks to address the extent to which former detainees in Northern Ireland were motivated to make public their experiences by a desire for 'healing through revealing'. Their original narratives offer only a fragmented outline of the patterns of causation which led to the publication of their narratives of the conflict. This book therefore emerged out of a desire to find out more about the motivations behind 'going public'. Part of this was a desire to understand why the public narration of violence is often portrayed as 'healing' and granted such a mythological status through the supposed 'universality of testimony as a ritual' (Herman 2001: 181), particularly when some who have lived through violence suggest that revealing their experiences remains a painful and harmful process (Hamber *et al.* 2000). The popular portrayal of catharsis emerging from the narration of violence can be found across many disciplines. Chapter 4 finds that, for many former detainees, healing was not understood to be the main motivation for making public their accounts. This contrast between the centrality of healing in the literature and its absence in both early discussions with former detainees and in the literature of Republican prisoners was thought worthy of further exploration, in order to add to knowledge about the diverse motivations, significance and consequences of making private memories part of a contested public history.

Former detainees' casual asides in the pre-interview stage about 'maybe it is a "man-thing" not to talk about this [victimhood]' contributed to the development of Chapter 5 of this book. This unique chapter examines the significance of hegemonic masculinity for those male detainees who chose (or were pressured into) narrating their experiences of state violence, with its associated vulnerability and pain. Although certainly not the 'inept' approach argued by Messerschmidt (1993: 2) there is still a tendency for men's 'gendered' experiences of victimhood to be somewhat sidelined within much of Criminology, despite excellent work by e.g. Stanko and Hobdell (1993); Newburn and Stanko (1994); Sim (1994) and Goodey (1997, 2005). The lacuna is particularly pronounced in relation to the recently emerging sub-field of transitional justice within Criminology. Here the dominant focus is undeniably on men as both victim and perpetrator, but the 'gendered'

Introduction 13

aspect of men's experiences of making public state violence is a less common feature (Hamber 2007). This book contributes to a refocusing of the study of male victimhood, by offering an early critical insight into men's experiences of victimisation and how these understandings of gender contribute (or not) towards making private memories a part of a contested public history.

The sidelining of men's gendered victimhood is all the more surprising given the violence against them. In the British Crime Survey 2007/08, young men aged between 16 and 24 were reported as being at risk of violent victimisation, with 13.4 per cent acknowledging that they had experienced a violent crime in the twelve months prior to the survey, compared with 6.4 per cent of female respondents (Kershaw *et al.* 2008). Despite the significant problems of representativeness, reliability and validity which are inherent in all measures of statistical analysis, such annual figures repeatedly suggest that large numbers of men are experiencing violence, usually with other men as the perpetrators. However, despite the extent of male victimhood, it is more often the perpetrator 'as male' who finds himself the focus of analysis (see Messerschmidt 1993; Collier 1998). As Collier (1998: 6) argues, 'Post War Criminology in Britain has also been concerned with violence against women and some kind of correlation was being made between the power of men, their masculinity and their crime'. Thus inquiries into victimhood often focused on female experiences of male power and violence. The female is positioned as the victim of crime, subjugated and at risk from male power, male violence and male sexuality (see e.g. Dworkin 1981; Hanmer *et al.* 1989). Although this important literature on gender and violence has led to an increased awareness of the harmful, commonplace and very real potentials of male power and violence, it has also re-inscribed and perpetuated the depiction of women as victims. This depiction of women as victims can be critiqued as being disempowering, deterministic and inherently pessimistic about the multiple opportunities for agency and resistance which exist within a system of patriarchal power which is always incomplete. Discussions labelled as being about 'gender and crime' are, in fact, often better understood as discussions about 'women and victimhood', given the comparative paucity of research into male experiences of victimisation. As Heidensohn (1987: 23) accurately suggests 'gender is no longer ignored' yet the dominant depiction remains that gender issues involve or affect only women.

Criminological literature about lived experiences of imprisonment also reflects a similar understanding. There have been a number of excellent and influential studies of women in prison (e.g. Carlen 1983, 1988; Carlen and Worrall 2004). Gender is inscribed overtly in discussions of women's experiences in prison and often cited as both a cause and effect of women's experiences in the criminal justice and detention apparatus. These academic studies are deeply beneficial in raising awareness of male power and female victimisation, and their worth and importance to Criminology remains undiminished. However, an explicitly 'gendered' analysis of violence and victimhood *need not* be limited *just* to the experiences of women. The violence experienced by women socially, politically and culturally is not negated or lessened, nor is the violence of men ignored, by the study of male victimhood, especially as male victimisation

14   *Introduction*

frequently occurs through the actions of other men. This is not to suggest that men's experiences have thus far 'fallen outside' academic analysis, but oddly that work on men and masculinities tends to take place elsewhere within the social sciences and not within a discipline concerned with harm and crime. Connell (1987, 2002, 2005) writes extensively on the construction of diverse masculinities and the way in which particular forms of masculinity become hegemonic under particular circumstances. Seidler (1994, 2007) includes in his discussions about masculinities an analysis of future ways in which social and cultural understandings about gender may become subjected to change. The study of masculinity and masculinities remains important, in order to better understand the lived experiences of this 'increasingly visible category that has contextually specific meanings attached to it' (Mac An Ghaill and Haywood 2007: 2).

Within the Criminological sub-field of prison studies, 'experiences of mortification and brutality in male prisons have been acknowledged since the classic study by Sykes in 1957' (Davies 2007: 191). Yet these American explorations of male prison violence have largely not been mirrored by British or Irish based studies involving male prisoners – with some important exceptions (see Scraton, Sim and Skidmore 1991; Jewkes 2005; Evans and Wallace 2007; Crewe 2009). Over a decade and a half ago, Carrabine and Longhurst (1998: 161) argued that the incorporation of gender into discussions of imprisonment was 'an important development' yet it is one still in its infancy. Despite the presence of 81,572 men in the prison system compared to 3,941 women (as of 14 March 2014), it would appear that 'although known about, [the subject of male prisoners as victims] has been little cared about, and victimologically men have not constituted real victims behind the closed doors of the prison' (Davies 2007: 191). Chapter 5 contributes to this discussion by adding a gendered dimension to the analysis of 'going public' about violence experienced in detention in Northern Ireland.

In regards to that localised context of conflict, the issues of sectarianism and political ideology have dominated (Bairner 1999a, 1999b). The contemporary field of research about the conflict would therefore benefit from a broadening of its analysis to ensure that the experiences of men, not just as perpetrators, but also as victims and survivors can be fully acknowledged. Though the wider study of masculinities continues to grow, most studies of the conflict:

> ignore the irrefutable facts that during almost thirty years of violence, men have done the bulk of the killing (as well as a large proportion of the dying); the security forces charged with confronting the civil unrest have been predominantly male; and the politicians who have sought (or in most cases failed to seek) ways out of the political impasse have been men.... However, the men in question are studied not first and foremost as men but as ministers, priests, industrialists, terrorists, and so forth. Seldom if ever, has masculinity per se been a matter for discussion.
>
> (Bairner 1999a: 285)

Despite the notable work of Bairner (1997, 1999a, 1999b, 2001), gendered examinations of detention during the conflict are usually concerned with women (Aretxaga 1997; Corcoran 2006a, 2006b), or as members of male prisoners' families (McEvoy *et al.* 1999; Shirlow and Dowler 2010). The experiences of men 'whose masculinities become mobilised and often highly militarised when the conflict escalates have been largely neglected' (McKeown and Sharoni 2002 n.p.). The recognition that 90 per cent of those killed in the conflict were men (Fay *et al.* 1999; Morrissey and Smyth 2002) makes this relative dearth of research into male victimhood even more surprising.

As a result of former detainees' early 'asides' about masculinity witnessed in early, informal, rapport-building pre-interviews, and as a consequence of the limited literature on this topic, gender thus forms a central part of Chapter 5 of this book. It explores former detainees' understanding of the meaning of 'masculinities' and their possible impact on experiences of narrating state violence. The chapter adds to discussions of gender, agency and political violence in work by the author published elsewhere (White 2012). It analyses the relationship between popular understandings of the 'invulnerable male' and former detainees' own depictions of victimhood, with particular reference to the Republican prisoners' 'struggle' which took place in and around the H-Blocks at Long Kesh. The material in Chapter 5 illustrates how former detainees utilised a range of devices to ensure that their narration of pain was concomitant with hegemonic masculinity. This included recasting their narratives not as personal pain but as communal resistance.

In addition to gendering experiences of truth sharing, former detainees also provided insights into the language of propaganda. Within Northern Ireland, allegations of state violence were often dismissed by representatives of the Government and labelled as being 'propaganda'. Chapter 6 examines the significance of these dismissals for those whose private narrative of state violence form(ed) part of a contested narrative of the conflict. It represents the detailed examination of the extent to which those who narrate state violence do so because of a 'propagandist intention'. More often than not, the label of propaganda is something applied by others. It now typically denotes the spreading of lies or falsehood. Yet the term has not always been used as censure. In the seventeenth century, the language of propaganda was used to refer to the dispersal of religious doctrines. It was not until the early twentieth century that the dominant popular meaning of propaganda shifted under the ideological pressures of two world wars and an increasingly communicative relationship between different nations, groups and communities (led in part by globalisation and by extensive developments in technology). By the mid twentieth century, the meaning of propaganda had thus become replete with negative connotations and was used to signify the production of 'imbalanced argumentation, dishonesty, disinformation, exaggerations, or *whatever* is necessary to manoeuvre the broad audience toward desired points of view' (MacDonald 1989: 23, emphasis added). Rather than being used as a neutral term, the language of propaganda became stigmatised by these negative associations and now is commonly understood *only* as a pejorative

16   *Introduction*

term, one utilised only against ideas or interpretations which are perceived to threaten one's own interests or understandings. Those who use the label propaganda intend it to signify that the content of allegations, narratives and the like are not only politically biased but also fictitious (Smith 1989).

Thus the language of propaganda has become used as a tool through which to disempower the 'other', as a label which hopes to destroy any of their claims to truth or veracity. However, other readings of the meaning of propaganda frame it only as purposive communication. Seeking to disempower the stigma around propaganda, Pratkanis and Aronson (1991) and Jackall (1995) focus on the role of persuasion. As the book illustrates, it would be naive to believe that the narratives of former detainees could not be used to persuade an audience of the legitimacy of Republicanism and of Republican violence. However, the extent to which former detainees who had 'gone public' with accounts of state violence felt that their own narrative *was* significant in this regard is unexplored within the literature, both on the conflict and on propaganda more broadly. Chapter 6 therefore analyses how the label of propaganda was actually experienced by former detainees and whether or not they felt their narratives were significant to the Republican movement, given their own understanding of the meaning of propaganda.

Like gender and propaganda, the existence of official accounts which contrasted with the detainees' allegations of state violence were also commented upon in early informal discussions with former detainees. These conversations directed the research produced in Chapter 7. Here, existing literature on official discourse, supported by a framework found in Cohen (2001) – itself adapted from Sykes and Matza's (1957) 'techniques of neutralisation' thesis – is used to provide examples of the literal, interpretive and implicatory denials of official discourse observable during the conflict in Northern Ireland, and importantly, to explore the consequences of such discourses on the lived experiences of former detainees themselves. As Feldman (1991: 13) argues in his ethnography of history as cultural currency in Northern Ireland 'the narrator writes himself [*sic*] into an oral history because the narrator has already been subjugated to powerful inscriptions'. Narratives by former detainees have been critiqued through a range of semantic devices which seek to deny or discredit their stories of state violence. This often takes the shape of framing allegations as 'black propaganda', prisoners' injuries as self-inflicted (see Curtis 1998) or, alternatively, by depicting prisoners as dehumanised 'outsiders' whose perceived criminality necessitates a strong response from agents of the state.

Research by Morgan (2000), Cohen (2001) and Crelinsten (2003) illustrate the power of the state to re-conceptualise both state violence and its victims. These representations aim to enable the UK to portray itself as a stable, liberal democracy in which human rights, equality and freedoms are protected (White and White 1995). The rewards of such a portrayal can be seen through membership of international human rights bodies, the regional mechanisms of the European system and in the resulting economic and political benefits of European Union membership, for example. Respect for human rights brings status from an

Introduction 17

external audience, and theoretically contributes to greater internal stability within the state. Furthermore, respect for rights also signals to other members of the international community about the domestic practice of a state (Risse and Sikkink 1999). It adds weight to criticisms made against other states and allows greater pressure to be brought to bear on states which violate the norms of international human rights law. Motivated through principle and/or instrumentalism, the need to maintain this image of respect for rights, particularly within liberal democracies, requires the careful political management of state violence and the avoidance of shaming as sanction.

Though deeply repressive, and with what Rolston and Scraton (2005: 548) rightly label 'a partial, weakened and suspended' democratic process, the State in Northern Ireland still contained space for some dissenting voices. Such spaces were used by civil society organisations and advocacy groups to bring pressure onto the British State. Official discourse was therefore not monolithic. Narratives of state violence could be used to challenge the image of the State as legitimate and this potential was something which was clearly recognised by Republicans. As the work of Blain (1994: 805) illustrates, these 'movement actors must mobilise a discursive arsenal to organise, educate and activate – to engage opponents in the public theatre'. The State's power to define legitimate/ illegitimate violence remained incomplete, as despite various attempts at containment, criminalisation, normalisation and management, the violence of the paramilitaries was still perceived as legitimate (even if illegal) by those involved (Alonso 2001). Narratives of state violence experienced during detention represent the 'breaking through' of subjugated knowledges that liberal democratic states must respond to in order to maintain their image of neutrality and openness.

In Northern Ireland, the narratives of state violence were carried in a relatively 'free press' (see Curtis 1998) and attracted the attention of well-known international human rights organisations, including Amnesty International. The coverage brought pressure onto the State to respond, particularly in relation to allegations emerging from the Holding Centres of Castlereagh. Yet these opportunities to challenge the British State also consolidated other forms of state power, as *being seen to respond* through investigations, inquiries and court cases gave (and gives) the State a veneer of accountability for their actions in the conflict. As evidenced by Rolston and Scraton's (2005: 558) study into public inquiries in Northern Ireland,

> the law was used for political ends. [The British Government] narrowed the field of inquiry, avoided obvious and objective conclusions that might show state forces in a bad light, delayed reporting to mute the impact of negative criticism of the report and ensured that security force personnel would not be prosecuted or reprimanded for their actions.

In exploring the personal impact of these observations, Chapter 7 is also influenced by Smyth's (2007: 2) assertion of a 'move beyond perceiving even

18 *Introduction*

victimhood and responsibility as matters not merely of elite agreement and negotiation, but of popular contestation and interest'. By applying Cohen's (2001) tripartite framework of denial to the narratives of state violence which emerged during the conflict, and by deconstructing the politics of official discourse, Chapter 7 explores the patterns of dialogue, both implicit and explicit, between the State and former detainees. It examines the extent to which official discourse could define the experiences of former detainees and the impact of such definitions on former detainees themselves. As a chapter on the sociology of denial, it constructs official discourse as a form of state power akin to governmentality and argues that counter-hegemonic accounts of state violence can both challenge and consolidate the power of the state to act as primary definer.

Chapter 8 builds on the previous chapters to explore the suitability of current mechanisms for holding the British State to account for its violence. It examines in detail the role of inquiries, inquests and court cases in responding to the legacy of state violence, not only against detainees but against the wider population in Northern Ireland. It shows how and why the criminal justice system was largely unable or unwilling to hold members of the security community to account for their role in the killing of one in ten of the conflict's dead. In addition to this examination of the role of the justice system during the conflict, Chapter 8 also analyses some of the more recent legal attempts to manage the legacy of state violence. It unpicks the work of the Historical Enquiries Team (HET) and the Office of the Police Ombudsman for Northern Ireland (OPONI). Both of these organisations have faced criticism from survivors of state violence, who feel that greater attention is paid to crimes committed by non-state agents whilst cases involving the British State are subjected to only the most rudimentary investigation (if investigated at all). Lastly, the chapter comments on the recent work of the Consultative Group on the Past (Eames and Bradley 2009) in seeking potential ways for Northern Ireland to respond to the legacy of conflict.

These chapters are explored in depth using a thematic format in which original qualitative data is analysed alongside theory and a multidisciplinary range of secondary literature. This method is preferred as it enables the closer inspection and comparison of trends in the literature with the expressed words (and 'worlds') of those former detainees who had previously 'gone public' with narratives of state violence. It adds an extra layer of analysis by exploring *why* many former detainees published detailed accounts of their experiences, and the significance and consequences which emerge from those testimonies. These themes – defining experiences of state violence, of healing, gender, propaganda and denial – emerged out of very early unstructured discussions with former detainees about their public narratives, and as such, illustrate their centrality to the research project.

What emerges from this book is that there is a lacuna of detailed analysis about the motivation, significance and consequences of narrating state violence. The reasons behind the public narration of accounts have been unexplored, and the significance and consequences of making private memories part of a contested public discourse left without consideration. The book therefore hopes to address this absence. Chapter 2 introduces the reader to the history of state violence in Northern Ireland. Chapter 3 examines how former detainees *define* their experiences of a violent state. Chapter 4 analyses the impact of popular discourses around 'healing' upon the motivation of former detainees to make public their experiences, whilst Chapter 5 discusses former detainees' perceptions of gendered concepts of hegemonic masculinity and the impact such perceptions may or may not have had on their decision to 'go public'. Chapter 6 explores the extent to which former detainees' perceived their narratives to be significant as political propaganda for the Republican movement in Northern Ireland. In Chapter 7, the consequences of official discourse are explored from the perspective of those whose accounts challenged the imagery of a benevolent state. Chapter 8 examines the current 'state of play' regarding accountability for state violence, both in relation to abuses within the detention system and outside it. Lastly, the final chapter brings together these arguments into an illustration of the motivation, significance and consequences of narrating state violence in Northern Ireland.

Notes

1 The term 'detainees' is used to refer to those whose freedom has been curtailed by the security community (see note 3). It includes those being interrogated, placed under arrest, interned and/or imprisoned.
2 The title 'Northern Ireland' is itself contentious. Those who wish to see a united Ireland tend to refer to it as the 'Six Counties', the 'Occupied Six Counties', 'The North' or 'North of Ireland'. Terms such as 'Ulster' (though geographically misleading) and 'The Province' are often used by those who wish for Northern Ireland to remain in the United Kingdom. The term 'Northern Ireland' is preferred here as it is sometimes used by both communities and is internationally recognised.
3 'Security Community' is used throughout the text to refer to the British Army; the Special Air Services (SAS); the Ulster Defence Regiment (UDR); the Royal Ulster Constabulary (RUC); the Prison Service and the British Police.
4 Northern Ireland's predominately Protestant police force, which included the Ulster Special Constabulary 'B-Specials'. The 'B-Specials' had a particular reputation for violence and were viewed by many Catholics as a sectarian organisation (Farrell 1976, 1983).
5 A group set up in 1971 to monitor the workings of the justice system. It included Catholic Priest Monsignor Raymond Murray in its founding members. Along with Monsignor Denis Faul, Murray published a steady stream of pamphlets detailing state violence, including that against detainees (e.g. Faul and Murray 1971, 1972, 1973, 1974, 1975a, 1975b, 1978, 1979, 1981).
6 The group works with Republican former prisoners to help find ways to address the social, economic and psychological impact of imprisonment.
7 Despite acts of violence throughout the conflict, the UDA remained legal until 1992 and carried out most of its actions under the label of the UFF.
8 The terms 'victim' and 'survivor' are used interchangeably throughout this book, reflecting the extent to which people's own understanding of their experiences may shift between these two statuses.

20 *Introduction*

References

Agger, I. and Jensen, S. (1990). 'Testimony as Ritual and Evidence in Psychotherapy for Political Refugees', *Journal of Traumatic Stress*, 3(1), 115–130.

Agger, I. and Jensen, S. (1996) *Trauma and Recovery Under State Terrorism*. London: Zed.

Aiken, N.T. (2010) 'Learning to Live Together: Transitional Justice and Intergroup Reconciliation in Northern Ireland', *International Journal of Transitional Justice*, 4(2), 166–188.

Alonso, R. (2001) *The IRA and Armed Struggle*. London: Routledge.

Ardoyne Commemorative Project (2002) *Ardoyne: The Untold Truth*. Belfast: Beyond the Pale.

Aretxaga, B. (1997) *Shattering Silence: Women, Nationalism, and Political Subjectivity in Northern Ireland*. Princeton: Princeton University Press.

Bairner, A. (1997) '"Up to Their Knees?" Football, Sectarianism, Masculinity and Protestant Working-Class Identity', in Shirlow, P. and McGovern, M. (eds) *Who are 'The People'? Unionism, Protestantism and Loyalism in Northern Ireland*. London: Pluto Press.

Bairner, A. (1999a) 'Soccer, Masculinity and Violence in Northern Ireland – Between Hooliganism and Terrorism', *Men and Masculinities*, 1(3), 284–301.

Bairner, A. (1999b) 'Violence, Masculinity and the Irish Peace Process', *Capital and Class*, 69(3), 125–144.

Bairner, A. (2001) 'Gender, Class and Nation', *Peace Review*, 13(1), 21–26.

Barrett, J. (2001) 'The Prohibition of Torture Under International Law: Part 1 The Institutional Organsiation', *The International Journal of Human Rights*, 5(1), 1–36

Bell, C. (2009) 'Transitional Justice, Interdisciplinarity and the State of the "Field" or "Non-field"', *International Journal of Transitional Justice*, 3(1), 5–27.

Blain, M. (1994) 'Power, War and Melodrama in the Discourses of Political Movements', *Theory and Society*, 23(6), 805–837.

Campbell, B., McKeown, L. and O'Hagan, F. (1994) *Nor Meekly Serve My Time: The H Block Struggle*. Belfast: Beyond the Pale.

Campbell, B., McKeown, L. and O'Hagan, F. (2006) *Nor Meekly Serve My Time: The H Block Struggle*. Belfast: Beyond the Pale.

Carlen, P. (1983) *Women's Imprisonment: A Study in Social Control*. London: Routledge.

Carlen, P. (1988) *Women, Crime and Poverty*. Buckingham: Open University Press.

Carlen, P. and Worrall, A. (2004) *Analysing Women's Imprisonment*. Devon: Willan.

Carrabine, E. and Longhurst, B. (1998) 'Gender and Prison Organisation: Some Comments on Masculinities and Prison Management', *Howard Journal of Criminal Justice*, 37(2), 161–176.

Cienfuegos, A.J. and Monelli, C. (1983) 'The Testimony of Political Repression as a Therapeutic Instrument', *The American Journal of Orthopsychiatry*, 53(1A), 43–51.

Cohen, S. (2001) *States of Denial: Knowing About Atrocities and Suffering*. London: Polity Press.

Coleman, R., Whyte, D. and Tombs, S. (eds) (2009) *State, Power, Crime*. London: Sage.

Collier, R. (1998) *Masculinities, Crime and Criminology: Men, Heterosexuality and the Criminal(ised) Other*. London: Sage.

Connell, R.W. (1987) *Gender and Power: Society, the Person and Sexual Politics*. Cambridge: Polity Press.

Connell, R.W. (2002) *Gender*. Cambridge: Polity Press.

Connell, R.W. (2005) *Masculinities*. California: California University Press.

Corcoran, M.S. (2006a) *Out of Order: The Political Imprisonment of Women in Northern Ireland, 1972–1998*. Collumpton: Willan.

Corcoran, M.S. (2006b) 'Talking About Resistance: Women Political Prisoners and the Dynamics of Prison Conflict, Northern Ireland', in Barton, A., Corteen, K., Scott, D. and Whyte, D. (eds) *Expanding the Criminological Imagination: Critical Readings in Criminology*. Devon: Willan.

Council of Europe (1950) European Convention for the Protection of Human Rights and Fundamental Freedoms. Available at: http://conventions.coe.int/treaty/en/treaties/html/005.htm (accessed 13 May 2013).

Council of Europe (1987) European Convention for the Prevention of Torture and Inhuman or Degrading Treatment or Punishment. Available at: http://conventions.coe.int/Treaty/en/Treaties/Html/126.htm (accessed 13 May 2013).

Crawford, C. (1999) *Defenders or Criminals? Loyalist Prisoners and Criminalisation*. Belfast: Blackstaff Press.

Crelinsten, R.D. (2003) 'The World of Torture: A Constructed Reality', *Theoretical Criminology*, 7(3), 293–318.

Crewe, B. (2009) *The Prisoner Society*. Oxford: Oxford University Press.

Curtis, L. (1998) *Ireland: The Propaganda War*. Belfast: Sásta.

Danieli, Y. (1992) 'Preliminary Reflections from a Psychological Perspective'. *Seminar on the Right to Restitution, Compensation and Rehabilitation for Victims of Gross Violations of Human Rights and Fundamental Freedoms*. Maastricht, 11–15 March.

Darby, J.P. (1997) *Scorpions in a Bottle: Conflicting Cultures in Northern Ireland*. London: Minority Rights Publications.

Davies, P. (2007) 'Lessons from the Gender Agenda', in Walklate, S. (ed.) *Handbook of Victims and Victimology*. Devon: Willan.

Duvenage, P. (1999) 'The Politics of Memory and Forgetting After Auschwitz and Apartheid', *Journal of Philosophy and Social Criticism*, 25(3), 1–28.

Dworkin, A. (1981) *Pornography: Men Possessing Women*. London: Women's Press Ltd.

Eames, R. and Bradley, D. (2009) *Report of the Consultative Group on the Past.* (HC171) London: HMSO. Available at: www.cgpni.org/fs/doc/Consultative%20Group%20on%20the%20Past%20Full%20Report.pdf (accessed 7 January 2013).

English, R. (2003) *Armed Struggle: A History of the IRA*. London: Pan Macmillan.

Evans, T. and Wallace, P. (2007) 'A Prison within a Prison? The Masculinity Narratives of Male Prisoners', *Men and Masculinities*, 10(4), 484–507.

Farrell, M. (1976) *Northern Ireland: The Orange State.* London: Pluto.

Farrell, M. (1983) *Arming the Protestants: The Formation of the Ulster Special Constabulary and the Royal Ulster Constabulary*. London: Pluto.

Faul, D. and Murray, R. (1971) *The Hooded Men: British Torture in Ireland*. Dungannon: The Authors.

Faul, D. and Murray, R. (1972) *British Army and Special Branch RUC Brutalities, December 1971–February 1972.* Dungannon: The Authors.

Faul, D. and Murray, R. (1973) *Whitelaw's Tribunals, Long Kesh Internment Camp, Nov.1972–Jan. 1973*. Dungannon: The Authors.

Faul, D. and Murray, R. (1974) *Long Kesh - The Iniquity of Internment, August 9th 1971–August 9th 1974.* Dungannon: The Authors.

Faul, D. and Murray, R. (1975a) *The RUC: The Black and Blue Book.* Dungannon: The Authors.

Faul, D. and Murray, R. (1975b) *The Shame of Merlyn Rees: 4th Year of Internment in Ireland, Long Kesh 1974–1975.* Dungannon: The Authors.

22   Introduction

Faul, D. and Murray, R. (1978) *The Castlereagh File: Allegations of Police Brutality 1976-77.* Dungannon: The Authors.

Faul, D. and Murray, R. (1979) *H-Blocks: British Jail for Irish Political Prisoners.* Dungannon: The Authors.

Faul, D. and Murray, R. (1981) *The British Dimension - Brutality, Murder and Legal Duplicity in Northern Ireland.* Dungannon: The Authors.

Fay, M., Morrissey, M. and Smyth, M. (1999) *Northern Ireland's Troubles: The Human Costs.* London: Pluto Press.

Feitlowitz, M. (1998*) A Lexicon of Terror: Argentina and the Legacies of Torture.* Oxford: Oxford University Press.

Feldman, A. (1991) *Formations of Violence: The Narrative of the Body and Political Terror in Northern Ireland.* Chicago: University of Chicago Press.

Godwin Phelps, T. (2004) *Shattered Voices: Language, Violence and the Work of Truth Commissions.* Philadelphia: University of Pennsylvania Press.

Goodey, J. (1997) 'Boys Don't Cry: Masculinities, Fear of Crime and Fearlessness', *British Journal of Criminology*, 37(3), 401–441.

Goodey, J. (2005) *Victims and Victimology: Research, Policy and Practice.* Harlow: Pearson Education.

Gormally, B. and McEvoy, K. (2009) *Dealing with the Past in Northern Ireland From Below: An Evaluation.* Belfast: Community Foundation for Northern Ireland.

Graybill, L.S. (2002) *Truth and Reconciliation in South Africa: Miracle or Model?* London: Lynne Rienner Publishers.

Green, P. and Ward, T. (2004) *State Crime: Governments, Violence and Corruption.* London: Pluto.

Hamber, B. (2002) ' "Ere their Story Die": Truth, Justice and Reconciliation in South Africa', *Race and Class*, 44(1), 61–79.

Hamber, B. (2007) 'Masculinity and Transitional Justice: An Exploratory Essay', *International Journal of Transitional Justice,* 1(1), 375–390.

Hamber, B., Nageng, D. and O'Malley, G. (2000) 'Telling It Like It Is: Understanding the Truth and Reconciliation Commission from the Perspective of Survivors', *Journal of Psychology in Society*, 20, 18–42.

Hanmer, J., Radford, J. and Stanko, E. (eds) (1989) *Women, Policing and Male Violence.* London: Routledge.

Hayner, P.B. (2002) *Unspeakable Truths: Facing the Challenge of the Truth Commissions.* London: Routledge.

Heidensohn, F. (1987) 'Women and Crime: Questions for Criminology' in Carlen, P. and Worrall, A. (eds) *Gender, Crime and Justice.* Milton Keynes: Open University Press.

Herman, J. (2001) *Trauma and Recovery: From Domestic Abuse to Political Terror.* London: Rivers Oram Press.

Hughes, G. (2000) 'Understanding the Politics of Criminological Research' in Jupp, V., Davies, P. and Francis, P. (eds) *Doing Criminological Research.* London: Sage.

Jackall, R. (ed.) (1995) *Propaganda.* London: Macmillan.

Jamieson, R. and Grounds, A. (2002) *No Sense of an Ending: The Effects of Long Term Imprisonment amongst Republican Prisoners and Their Families.* Monaghan: SEESYU Press.

Jewkes, Y. (2005) 'Men Behind Bars: "Doing" Masculinity as an Adaption to Imprisonment', *Men and Masculinities*, 8(1), 44–63.

Kelly, G. (2005) *Storytelling Audit: An Audit of Personal Story, Narrative and Testimony*

Initiatives Related to the Conflict in and about Northern Ireland. Belfast: Healing Through Remembering.

Kelly, G. (2007) *Storytelling Audit: An Audit of Personal Story, Narrative and Testimony Initiatives Related to the Conflict in and about Northern Ireland.* (Updated Edition) Belfast: Healing Through Remembering.

Kershaw, C., Nicholas, S. and Walker, A. (eds) (2008) *Crime in England and Wales 2007/08. Findings from the British Crime Survey and Police Recorded Crime.* London: The Home Office Research, Development and Statistics Directorate.

Kretzmer, D. (2007) 'The Torture Debate: Israel and Beyond', in Downes, D., Rock, P., Chinkin, C. and Gearty, C. (eds) *Crime, Social Control and Human Rights: From Moral Panics to the Sociology of Denial.* Devon: Willan.

Levi, P. (1987) *If This is a Man/The Truce.* London: Abacus.

Lundy, P. and McGovern, M. (2001) 'The Politics of Memory in Post-conflict Northern Ireland', *Peace Review*, 13(1), 27–33.

Lundy, P. and McGovern, M. (2005) 'Community Based Approaches to Post Conflict "Truth-telling": Strengths and Limitations', *Shared Space: A Research Journal on Peace, Conflict and Community Relations in Northern Ireland*, 1, 35–52.

Lundy, P. and McGovern, M. (2006) 'Participation, Truth and Partiality Participatory Action Research: Community-based Truth-telling and Post-conflict Transition in Northern Ireland', *Sociology*, 40(1), 71–88.

Lundy, P. and McGovern, M. (2008) 'Whose Justice? Rethinking Transitional Justice from the Bottom Up', *Journal of Law and Society*, 35(2), 265–292.

Mac An Ghaill, M. and Haywood, C. (2007) *Gender, Culture and Society.* London: Palgrave Macmillan.

MacDonald, F.J. (1989) 'Propaganda and Order in Modern Society', in Smith III, T.J. (ed.) *Propaganda: A Pluralistic Perspective.* London: Praeger.

Mahoney, J. (2007) *The Challenge of Human Rights: Origin, Development, and Significance.* Oxford: Blackwell Publishing.

McEvoy, K. (2013) *Dealing with the Past in Northern Ireland: An Overview of Legal and Political Approaches.* Belfast: Healing Through Remembering.

McEvoy, K., O'Mahony, D., Horner, C. and Lyner, O. (1999) 'The Home Front: The Families of Paramilitary Prisoners in Northern Ireland', *British Journal of Criminology*, 39(2), 175–197.

McKeown, L. (2001) *Out of Time: Irish Republican Prisoners and Long Kesh 1972–2000.* Belfast: Beyond the Pale.

McKeown, L. and Sharoni, S. (2002) *Formations and Transformations of Masculinity in the North of Ireland and in Israel-Palestine.* Available at: www.simonasharoni.com/Docs/GenderingConflict.pdf (accessed 31 August 2012).

McKittrick, D. and McVea, D. (2001) *Making Sense of the Troubles.* Belfast: Blackstaff.

Messerschmidt, J.W. (1993) *Masculinities and Crime: Critique and Reconceptualization of Theory.* Lanham: Rowan and Littlefield Publishers.

Morgan, R. (2000) 'The Utilitarian Justification of Torture: Denial, Desert and Disinformation', *Journal of Punishment and Society*, 2(2), 181–196.

Morrissey, M. and Smyth, M. (2002). *Northern Ireland after the Good Friday Agreement: Victims, Grievance and Blame.* London: Pluto Press.

Murray, R. (1998) *State Violence: Northern Ireland.* Dublin: Mercier Press.

Neier, A. (1994) 'Keynote Speech: Dealing with the Past', in Boraine, L., Levy, J. and Scheffer, R. (eds) *Dealing With the Past: Truth and Reconciliation in South Africa.* Cape Town: Institute for Democracy.

24 *Introduction*

Newburn, T. and Stanko, E. (1994) 'When Men Are Victims', in Newburn, T. and Stanko, E. (eds) *Just Boys Doing Business? Men, Masculinities and Crime*. London: Routledge.

Ní Aoláin, F. (2009) 'Women, Security, and the Patriarchy of Internationalized Transitional Justice', *Human Rights Quarterly*, 31(4), 1055–1085.

Nickel, J.W. (2007) *Making Sense of Human Rights* (2nd Edition). Oxford: Blackwell Publishing.

O'Neill, B. (2007) 'Misery Lit ... Read On', BBC News, 17 April. Available at: http://news.bbc.co.uk/1/hi/magazine/6563529.stm (accessed 30 August 2012).

O'Rawe, R. (2005) *Blanketmen: The Untold Story*. Dublin: New Island Books.

Okawa, J.B. and Hauss, R.B. (2007) 'The Trauma of Politically Motivated Torture', in Carll, E.K. (ed.) *Trauma Psychology: Issues in Violence, Disaster, Health and Illness*. California: Greenwood Publishing.

Organization of American States (1985) Inter-American Convention to Prevent and Punish Torture. Available at: www.refworld.org/docid/3ae6b3620.html (accessed 13 May 2013).

Pratkanis, A. and Aronson, E. (1991) *Age of Propaganda: The Everyday Use and Abuse of Persuasion*. New York: WH Freeman and Company.

Punch, M. (2012) *State Violence, Collusion and the Troubles*. London: Pluto.

Risse, T. and Sikkink, K. (1999) 'The Socialization of International Human Rights Norms into Domestic Practices: Introduction', in Risse, T., Ropp, S.C. and Sikkink, K. (eds) *The Power of Human Rights: International Norms and Domestic Change*. New York: Cambridge University Press.

Rolston, B. (2005) '"An Effective Mask for Terror": Democracy, Death Squads and Northern Ireland', *Crime, Law and Social Change*, 44(2), 181–203.

Rolston, B. and Scraton, P. (2005) 'In the Full Glare of English Politics: Ireland, Inquiries and the British State', *British Journal of Criminology*, 45(4), 547–564.

Sangster, K. (1999) 'Truth Commissions: The Usefulness of Truth Telling', *Australian Journal of Human Rights*. 5(1), n.p. Available at: www.austlii.edu.au/au/journals/AJHR/1999/5.html (accessed 31 August 2012).

Scraton, P., Sim, J. and Skidmore, P. (1991) *Prisons Under Protest*. Buckingham: Open University Press.

Seidler, V.J. (1994) *Unreasonable Men: Masculinity and Social Theory*. London: Routledge.

Seidler, V.J. (2007) 'Masculinities, Bodies and Emotional Life', *Men and Masculinities*, 10(1), 9–21.

Shirlow, P. and Dowler, L. (2010) '"Wee Women No More": Female Partners of Republican Political Prisoners in Belfast', *Environment and Planning*, 42(2), 384–399.

Shirlow, P. and McEvoy, K. (2008) *Beyond the Wire: Former Prisoners and Conflict Transformation in Northern Ireland*. London: Pluto.

Shirlow, P. and Murtagh, B.J. (2006) *Belfast: Segregation, Violence and the City*. London: Pluto.

Silverman, D. (2005) *Doing Qualitative Research*. London: Sage.

Sim, J. (1994) 'Tougher than the Rest? Men in Prison', in Newburn, T. and Stanko, E. (eds) *Just Boys Doing Business? Men, Masculinities and Crime*. London: Routledge.

Sluka, J. (ed.) (1999) *Death Squads: An Anthropology of State Terror*. Pennsylvania: Pennsylvania University Press.

Smith III, T.J. (ed.) (1989) *Propaganda: A Pluralistic Perspective*. London: Praeger.

Smyth, M. and Fay, M. (2000) *Personal Accounts from Northern Ireland's Troubles: Public Conflict, Private Loss*. Pluto: London.

Smyth, M.B. (2007) *Truth Recovery and Justice after Conflict*. London: Routledge.

Stanko, E.A. and Hobdell, K. (1993) 'Assault on Men: Masculinity and Male Victimization', *British Journal of Criminology*, 33(3), 400–415.

Stanley, E. (2002) 'What Next? The Aftermath of Organised Truth Telling', *Race and Class*, 44(1), 1–16.

Stanley, E. (2005) 'Truth Commissions and the Recognition of State Crime', *British Journal of Criminology*, 45(4), 582–597.

Stanley, E. (2009) *Torture, Truth and Justice: The Case of Timor Leste*. London: Routledge.

Sykes, G. and Matza, D. (1957) 'Techniques of Neutralisation: A Theory of Delinquency', *American Sociological Review*, 22(6), 664–670.

Taylor, P. (1980) *Beating the Terrorists: Interrogation in Omagh, Gough and Castlereagh.* London: Penguin.

Taylor, P. (1998) *Provos: The IRA and Sinn Féin.* London: Bloomsbury.

Taylor, P. (2002) *Brits: The War against the IRA.* London: Bloomsbury.

United Nations (1948) Universal Declaration of Human Rights. Available at: www.un.org/en/documents/udhr/ (accessed 13 May 2013).

United Nations (1966) International Covenant on Civil and Political Rights. Available at: www.ohchr.org/en/professionalinterest/pages/ccpr.aspx (accessed 13 May 2013).

United Nations (1984) UN Convention Against Torture and Other Cruel, Inhuman or Degrading Treatment or Punishment. Available at: www.ohchr.org/EN/ProfessionalInterest/Pages/CAT.aspx (accessed 13 May 2013).

White, L. (2012) 'Masculinities, Pain and Power: "Gendering" Experiences of "Truth Sharing"' in Shepherd, L.J. and Åhäll, L. (eds) *Gender, Agency and Political Violence*. Basingstoke: Palgrave.

White, R. and White, T.F. (1995) 'Repression and the Liberal State: The Case of Northern Ireland 1969–1972', *The Journal of Conflict Resolution*, 39(2), 330–352.

2 The history of state violence in Northern Ireland

Some contextual knowledge of events in Northern Ireland is required in order to better understand the motivation, significance and consequences of 'making public' experiences of state violence regarding detention. The actions of the British State in Northern Ireland since 1969 have resulted in the publication of many narratives of personal trauma, including those of internees and prisoners – some of whom were the perpetrators of violence themselves. The following chapter outlines the political, public and penal contexts in which these private experiences have become part of a contested public history of the conflict. It examines the existence of state violence in Northern Ireland in a range of contexts, but is not intended to be a detailed, conclusive account of the conflict, as such accounts exist elsewhere (e.g. Conflict Archive on the Internet 'CAIN' n.d.) and can be observed most poignantly in the detailed biographies of those killed (McKittrick *et al.* 2007).

The context of state violence

The following section is limited only to describing the context in which narrative testimonies about state violence have emerged. Based on the figures recorded by McKittrick *et al.* (2007), between 1966 and 2006, 367 people were killed by what Punch (2012) describes as the 'security community'. This relates to around 10 per cent of all recorded deaths. This 'community' included the British Army, the Special Air Services (SAS), the Ulster Defence Regiment (UDR) and the Royal Ulster Constabulary (RUC), as well as the British Police, An Garda Síochána and the Irish Army (the Irish State forces being responsible for five of the 367 deaths). Of the 301 killed by the British Army, approximately 160 were civilians, with 138 having a Catholic community background. The RUC was responsible for some fifty deaths, including the deaths of twenty seven Catholic civilians and five civilians from a Protestant background (McKittrick *et al.* 2007). There is also evidence of collusion between sections of the security community with paramilitary groups that led to death and injury (Dillon 1991; Punch 2012).

State violence in Northern Ireland took many forms, including intentional lethal force, torture, ill-treatment, brutality, harassment, threat, and the violent

The history of state violence   27

suppression of disorder using CS gas, water cannons and plastic or rubber bullets (Murray 1998). The use of violence by the state is intimately related to its power to act and to offer dominant definitions for its actions. As Weber (1948 [1919]) has suggested, this power not only emerges in part from the state's monopoly on the use of force, but also from its ability to define that force as 'legitimate'. At 'the core of the institutional identity of the state, *qua* political entity, lies organised violence. The state furthermore monopolises this means to the domination of people over people' (Poggi 2006: 110). The state provides legitimacy for particular forms of violence by selected groups, such as the army or the police and is considered 'the sole source of the "right" to use violence' (Weber 1948: 78 [1919]). This 'right' is communicated through law and enforced through the workings of the legal system. This 'legalised' violence can include the full remit from street level harassment, stop and search procedures, corporal punishments and the 'violence of incarceration' found in states' use of imprisonment for a range of 'offences' (both criminal and administrative) and also in the use and maintenance of the death penalty in 100 states currently thought to be retentionist (see Amnesty International 2013).

However, law is not the only means through which the state retains its monopoly on the use of 'legitimate' force. For Gramsci (1971), the interrelationship between coercion and consent is crucial if the state itself is to be seen as legitimate. Coercion is manifested through the 'political society ... of the armed forces, police and prisons' (Simon 1982) as well as in the law courts and administrative centres. Coercion intersects with the consent brought about through other forms of persuasion, as power is diffused through 'civil society' (Gramsci 1971). Thus the legitimation of the 'integral' state operates in a hegemonic sense, flowing back and forth from coercion to the instilling of consent through discourse and ideology. As a result, legitimacy for state violence is always in a constant process of restructuring and redefinition, as the 'continuous process of formulation and superseding of unequal equilibria' (Gramsci 1971: 31). As Foucault (1980) suggests, power in all of these forms operates as a system of domination, but only in a reconstituted and reconstituting system which is always incomplete and within which exists occasional opportunities for resistance – such as through the publication of narratives of state violence. This means that there are rare occasions where the violence of the state *is* framed as illegitimate, both by some forces within what Gramsci (1971) labelled as a (perhaps exaggeratedly homogeneous) 'civil society' and occasionally, by the state's own discursive systems.

Within the rhetoric of liberal democracy, the law is presented as autonomous and apolitical under the separation of powers. This represents an idealised imagery of an impartial executive, an independent legislative and a detached judiciary, each with minimal ideological influence over the other. These 'powers embodied in the state have been legitimated by the democratic process [yet it is one in which] law provides a veneer of equality, a mask of impartiality and so contrives to hide the reality of structural inequality' (Scraton 1985: 260). Such a formulation can be seen in Northern Ireland and not only in the basic demographics of state agencies but also in the formal political and legal processes

28   *The history of state violence*

which have emerged as both a cause and consequence of the conflict. As Hill-yard (1987: 279) states:

> The central element of the Unionist repressive state apparatus was the *Civil Authorities (Special Powers) Act 1922* [which] allowed the Minister of Home Affairs the power to 'take all steps ... as may be necessary for preserving peace and maintaining order'. It granted the police wide powers of arrest, questioning, search, detention and internment ... Northern Ireland from the outset was therefore a state with extraordinary powers.

Paragraph 23 of the Act allowed for indefinite internment in a clear negation of the doctrine of due process. Presented as 'emergency' legislation, the Act lasted until 1972, when direct rule from Westminster was returned under the equally expansive Northern Ireland (Temporary Provisions) Act 1972. Prior to direct rule, Northern Ireland had been under the control of a Unionist-controlled regional government which had largely ignored pressure from the Civil Rights movement. This contributed to increasing levels of violence and in August 1969 the British Army was sent in under the supposed guise of preserving order. However, partly because of a failure to protect Catholic areas from Loyalist violence, the Army was soon seen by the Catholic population as another repressive arm of an illegitimate State. Significantly, many of the so-called 'Special Powers' of this period were consolidated under the Northern Ireland (Emergency Provisions) Act 1974, which also enabled the use of juryless 'Diplock' courts. For Ní Aoláin (2000: 14), such powers signify that 'ordinary law has been bent out of shape and beyond all recognition' in Northern Ireland. Not only do such laws represent an abrogation of due process principles, they also illustrate the British State's tendency to push through draconian legislation and suspend civil liberties (Punch 2012). The majority of those whose rights were abused belonged to the Catholic population (Donohue 1998) and this can be seen most clearly during internment.

Internment

Internment was re-introduced to Northern Ireland on 9 August 1971 under Section 12 of the Civil Authorities (Special Powers) Act (1922). This broad instrument meant that a person could be arrested and detained on the suspicion that they had acted, or were thought to be going to act, in a way which was 'prejudicial to preservation of the peace or maintenance of order'. Over 345 suspected Irish Republicans were 'lifted'[1] in the initial operation in August 1971. It was invoked in a discriminatory and disproportionate manner, targeting mostly those living in nationalist areas and was seemingly used as a political measure rather than solely for reasons of security (McKittrick and McVea 2001). Rather than reduce the levels of conflict and unrest, it instead contributed to a steep increase in violence (Tonge 2006). Internment represented the strengthening of the authoritarian state, legitimated through its own laws and procedures, underpinned by a narrative of the conflict in which those living in Catholic and nationalist communities were 'the enemy within'. The British Army arrested hundreds of people in their homes under this 'Operation Demetrius' and brought them to special internment camps in a poorly planned and badly executed intervention (Tonge 2006). Many of those detained had been 'lifted' on the basis of old and out of date intelligence held by the RUC Special Branch and 116 of the 342 initial detainees were released within two days. It 'proved to be a political and military disaster', bringing together most Catholics, contributing to further civil unrest and violence, and encouraging support for armed Republicanism (O'Leary and McGarry 1993).

The resulting internment narratives (Kennally and Preston 1971; O Tuathail 1972) are broadly indicative of the state violence which took place during that period. Bobby Devlin was one of an estimated 1,981 people interned during the period from 9 August 1971 to 5 December 1975. Devlin (1982) would later publish a short booklet about his experiences. In this, Devlin (1982: 1) only partially illuminates the motivations behind his 'going public' by arguing that his 'reasons for writing this book are many-fold, but a primary one was to capture the memory of the antics and behaviour of those men who were in the Cages of Long Kesh[2] from 1972–1974'. Although not describing in minute detail the violence he experienced, Devlin (1982: 2) asserts that 'Long Kesh was a concentration camp and still is! I shall never forget the barbed wire, the rats, and the degrading treatment of internees'. He recalls how:

> The Brits really enjoyed humiliating the internees by destroying personal items and throwing food on the floor to be trampled on, or urinated on. Outside we had to run the gauntlet of steel helmeted figures as they smacked the backs of our legs with their batons.
>
> (Devlin 1982: 14)

Some of those who were detained were sent to secret interrogation centres[3] to be interrogated by British Army intelligence officers, with the support and knowledge of the RUC Special Branch (Fields 1980). Those singled out for further interrogation had canvas hoods put over their heads and were made to stand spreadeagled against a wall for long periods (Faul and Murray 1971). They would later be known as 'The Hooded Men' as a result of this treatment. The men were also blasted with continuous high pitched noise, deprived of sleep and fed on a basic diet of bread and water during a process which came to be labelled as the 'Five Techniques' (Coogan 2002). Some of the men were also hooded and pushed out of helicopters they believed were hundreds of metres up, when in reality they were hovering just a few feet from the ground (Coogan 2000). Despite attempts by the British State and its agents to keep public knowledge of the 'Five Techniques' to a minimum, many internees would soon 'go public' with accounts of what they experienced. PJ McClean, Liam Shannon and Jim Auld were three former detainees who agreed to take part in the research for this book and edited extracts from their original published narratives are reproduced here:

30 *The history of state violence*

A hood was pulled over my head and I was handcuffed and subjected to verbal and personal abuse, which included the threat of being dropped from a helicopter which was in the air, being kicked and struck about the body with batons on the way.... During all this time I could hear a low droning noise ... I stood there, arms against the wall, feet wide apart. My arms, legs, back and head began to ache.... They struck me several times on the hands, ribs, kidneys and my knee-caps were kicked. My hood-covered head was banged against the wall ... I collapsed several times, only to be beaten and pulled to my feet again and once more pushed, spread-eagled against the wall.

(Extracts from PJ McClean's narrative of interrogations during internment in McGuffin 1973 n.p.)

Liam Shannon's narrative of interrogation also tells a story of abuses experienced during detention. Part of his original narratives are repeated here as an illustration of the various forms of state violence which took place in Northern Ireland during the internment phase:

At one stage I was put into a room with my face against the wall. A shot was fired. It sizzled past me.... There were several police outside and they all had a good laugh at this ... I was beaten three or four times by a police officer in uniform who had some sort of a plastic hose.... On quite a few times a gun was put at the back of my head and the trigger pulled ... I had nothing to eat for, I reckon, four days, except a cup of water and one round of dry bread each time. I got asleep after three days.

(Extracts from Liam Shannon's narrative of interrogation during internment in McGuffin 1973 n.p.)

Lastly, former detainee Jim Auld's narrative describes in detail the physical violence he had experienced during detention and the desperation he had personally felt:

Some fairly serious physical damage was done to me.... They beat me with batons, they kicked me all around the place. They were aiming towards my privates and my head and they were making me keep my hands at my sides. I went unconscious a couple of times ... I was trailed along, with the hood on, couldn't see where we were going at all, and they just ran me straight into a post. Straight into my head, flying full force into it, and I just went down.... Every time I dropped they kicked me all around the place and forced me back up onto the wall ... I remember crying at that stage and saying, 'I just can't take this, mister, I am sorry, I just don't know what to do'. I couldn't do anything, I just felt so helpless and so isolated that I would have told anybody anything. I was saying to myself 'there is no way I can take this any longer [maybe] if I threw myself down the on ground, I could maybe crack my head or break my neck on this pipe'. And I hit my head off the pipe okay, but all I did was hurt my head. I ended up crying because I didn't die.

(Extracts from Jim Auld's narrative about interrogation during internment in Conroy 2000: 4–8)[4]

These experiences are representative of a wider pattern of discriminatory violence by State agents against those from the Catholic and/or nationalist communities.[5] This violence was carried out by members of the RUC and also the British Army. The Parachute Regiment had a particular reputation for brutality. Richard O'Rawe described how members of the Parachute 'Para' Regiment had taken him to Black Mountain Barracks in 1972:

I was placed in a cubicle and a Para – one of the biggest bastards I have ever seen – entered the room and hit me the most tremendous slap on the side of my face.... He then proceeded to punch me, making sure not to mark my face ... Another Para was sweeping the corridor outside the room, and the big guy took the brush off him and told him to get lost ... [T]hey once again turned me to the wall. The little guy opened my trousers and pulled them and my underpants to my ankles.... While the big guy held up my hands, his compatriot pushed the brush into my anus. I screamed in agony as it was pushed further into me. While the pain was excruciating, the humiliation was excruciating, the humiliation was even worse.

(Extracts from Richard O'Rawe's narrative in O'Rawe 2005: 60–62)

These narratives illustrate the range of violence experienced by some detainees whilst they were in detention. They show how violence was not simply limited to lethal force, on-street harassment and verbal abuse. They are vivid, literal representations of what Crelinsten (2003: 293) calls the 'closed world of torture'. Yet the boundaries of this closed world are neither omnipotent nor omnipresent. As more detainees were released, opportunities to 'go public' became greater and the number of testimonies began to increase. On 12 August 1971, the *Irish News*[6] featured several, separate descriptions of people being forcefully batoned by groups of soldiers whilst suffering sectarian verbal abuse. These articles described brutal beatings and kickings taking place as detainees were being forced to run obstacle courses of wood and water tanks. An RUC spokesman was quoted as 'having no comments to make about the allegations', before dismissively adding 'these fellows are likely to allege absolutely anything. We don't believe these reports' (*Irish News* 12 August 1971). Organisations such as the Association for Legal Justice continued to collect testimonies. Civil society groups also published detailed pamphlets featuring the treatment of detainees at this time. The Campaign for Social Justice in Northern Ireland (1971) reported that detainees at Girdwood Park army camp had been made to run barefoot on broken glass whilst being attacked by the camp's Alsatian dogs.

Despite this coverage, a process of censorship was being observed by other outlets. On 31 December 1971, the *New Statesman*[7] magazine reported that radio

32   *The history of state violence*

and television reporters working for the publicly funded British Broadcasting Corporation (BBC) were forbidden to broadcast interviews with released internees who had alleged brutality by the RUC and British Army (in Curtis 1998). In many regimes, state violence against detainees is an 'open secret', designed to maintain an appearance of respectability whilst at the same time perpetuate a climate of fear which seeks to deter potential dissent. However, in Northern Ireland, considerable pressure was put on media outlets not to cover the story and this manifested itself through internal censorship, particularly after Defence Secretary Lord Carrington demanded that the BBC should avoid publishing reports that 'are unfairly loaded to suggest improper behaviour by British troops' (in Coogan 2002: 353). This was designed to try and ensure that public knowledge of the 'Five Techniques' was kept to a minimum, not least because the Government was keen to keep Army morale high, preserve the imagery of liberal democracy and maintain the respect of British and international audiences.

However, rather than being discouraged by this climate of political censorship, many former internees continued to 'go public' with their experiences. According to Curtis (1998), most of the British public had heard nothing of the detail of the allegations of violence against detainees until 17 October 1971, when an article in the *Sunday Times*[8] featured the testimony of one of the internees, Patrick Shivers. There had previously been short articles about internment in smaller circulation current affairs magazines such as the *New Statesman* and *The Economist*,[9] but it was the coverage in the *Sunday Times* (17 October 1971) under the headline 'How Ulster Internees Are Made to Talk' which brought the allegations surrounding internment to a wider audience in the UK. Representatives of the security community responded by claiming the allegations were IRA propaganda and this assertion was repeated throughout the conflict and often in the most imaginative of circumstances (Curtis 1998). The British Army and RUC also countered allegations of violence by attributing the injuries and bruises of detainees to other members of the IRA, or by claiming that they had been self-inflicted during detention.

Despite such dismissals, the publication of detainees' narratives of torture and brutality still provoked something of a domestic and international outcry which persuaded the Government to launch two Committees of Inquiry into the application and legality of the 'Five Techniques' (Taylor 1978). On 31 August 1971, just three weeks after the initial internment operation, Sir Edmund Compton was appointed to report on allegations against the security forces of physical brutality. The remit of the report (Compton 1971) was deeply restricted and concerned only with arrests made on the first day of 'Operation Demetrius' (9 August 1971). According to Taylor (1980: 21), this limited remit meant that 'no complainant gave evidence [in person], as they felt that the terms of reference were too narrow, [nor was] any evidence given under oath; and there was no cross-examination of witnesses'. The loose findings of Compton (1971) stand in sharp contrast to the detailed narrative testimonies alleging violence collected by journalists and civil society groups. It reported that:

As regards the initial arrests it is clear that ... complaints ... carried very little substance. The record of events reflects great credit on the security forces who carried out a difficult and dangerous operation in adverse conditions with commendable restraint and discipline ... [We have found] no evidence of physical brutality, still less of torture or brain-washing.

(Compton 1971: v para. 14)

However, Compton (1971) *did* suggest that there had been 'measures of ill-treatment' against a small number of detainees. The definitional difficulties observable in Compton (1971) are common to discussions of torture, brutality, and inhuman and degrading treatment. Compton defined brutality as 'an inhuman or savage form of cruelty, and that cruelty implies a disposition to inflict suffering coupled with an indifference to, or pleasure in, the victim's pain' (cited in Taylor 1980: 23). Such a definition of brutality saw the Inquiry conclude that none of the 40 complainants it investigated 'had suffered physical brutality as we understand the term' (Compton 1971: 71). These findings had seemingly ignored the details of many of the allegations made by former detainees and had been 'hamstrung by its own definition of what constituted physical brutality' (Taylor 1980: 22).

In November 1971 – prior to the Parker Report (1972) into the legality of the 'Five Techniques'– the Irish Government had referred detainees' allegations of ill-treatment to the European Human Rights Commission for possible breaches of the European Convention on Human Rights and Fundamental Freedoms (1950, hereafter ECHR), including for the possible breach of Article 3. This was (and is) a non-derogable right which states: 'No one shall be subjected to torture, or to inhuman or degrading treatment or punishment.' In a 16-month period, over 100 witnesses gave oral evidence as the European Commission of Human Rights sought to establish whether ill-treatment had been an instrument of policy during internment. Representatives of the British Government went to great lengths to stall the Commission, including moving proceedings to an isolated Sola Airbase in Stavanger, Norway. The British Government was so keen to limit public knowledge of the techniques (and the inevitable embarrassment caused by a critical judgment) that ways to pressure the Irish into 'a friendly withdrawal' were discussed in secret meetings, as evidenced by confidential documents now released (see Author Unknown n.d., Document 'E40' *The Irish Case at Strasbourg*). There were suggestions that sanctions could be invoked against the Irish State or that it could be challenged under international law for 'allowing ... territory to be used as a base and a place of refuge for terrorists', or under the ECHR (1950) 'in respect of their prohibition of divorce and birth control' (Author Unknown n.d., Document 'E40' *The Irish Case at Strasbourg*: 5 para. 17–22). The Irish Government, however, pressed forward with the case and the Commission eventually reached the view that the use of the 'Five Techniques' *had* cumulatively constituted a practice of torture and inhuman treatment, and furthermore, that a practice of inhuman treatment which violated Article 3 had evidently been in place at Palace Barracks.[10] In March 1976,

34 *The history of state violence*

against the wishes of the British Government, the case was then referred to the European Court of Human Rights (ECtHR). Yet in January of 1978 the Court released a judgment which contrasted with the findings of the Commission, and alternatively stated that the interrogation methods used in 1971 *did not* in fact constitute torture under Article 3, but were still to be deemed inhuman and degrading treatment.

The limited reference of the Compton (1971) and Parker (1972) Inquiries combined with attitudes towards the ECtHR illustrate the extent to which the British State valued favourable coverage, and the lengths to which it could go to deny, dismiss and/or dehumanise those who made allegations of violence against its agents. As Boyle *et al.* (1975: 3) argue, '[when] the state is threatened the legal system will be used by those in power in whatever way seems to them most likely to restore stability'.

Special Category Status

In September 1971, the remaining internees were moved from Crumlin Road prison and HMS Maidstone to compounds at Long Kesh. They were then detained in conditions reminiscent of a Prisoner of War camp, with Nissen huts bordered by barbed wire, watched over by helicopters and guarded by armed troops. In June 1972, those who had been convicted of 'scheduled offences' were given 'Special Category Status' with the agreement of the paramilitary groups involved. Special Category prisoners now had a right to unlimited mail, could wear their own personal clothing and freely associate with other prisoners. The Special Category system operated as political status in all but name and contributed to a level of prisoner autonomy within the confines of an otherwise penal setting (Crawford 1999).

However, the existence of Special Category Status did not mean that the detention system operating in Northern Ireland was a benevolent place for those detained. It remained a contained penal institution and in March 1974, following one of many partly successful escape attempts by Republican detainees, all visits were stopped and changes were made to the visiting area which meant the loss of privacy for detainees. In September 1974, following another escape attempt, allegations about violence in Long Kesh increased, with many IRA prisoners claiming that they had been physically assaulted by prison officers (McKeown 2001). In a description of events otherwise sympathetic to the prison establishment in Long Kesh/HMP Maze, Ryder (2000) acknowledges the violence against prisoners, particularly during searches in the winter of 1974. Around this time, Republican prisoners released a public statement threatening to burn down the prisons if the violence against them did not cease. The following week, Special Category IRA prisoners began to destroy their huts and set them alight, and according to Ryder (2000) were joined when possible by internees and Official IRA[11] prisoners. Loyalist prisoners also broke out of their compounds, raided medical supplies and amassed to 'observe the battle' (Crawford 1999: 42). Armed with rubber bullets and riot gas, British troops were sent in to regain control and eventually an agreement was reached whereby prisoners would return to their compounds on the assurance that there would be no reprisals. However, communications which emerged from prisoners afterwards suggest that there *were* reprisals and that many of the men were made to stand for five hours against the prison fences, ill from the effects of CS gas and whilst being beaten by prison officials and bitten by guard dogs (McKeown 2001). The BBC (2008 [1974]) reported that over 130 prisoners had been injured. The Northern Ireland Office later put that figure at 29 (in Coogan 2000: 404) and did not explain in any depth what had happened. Within days there were further disturbances followed by further allegations of state violence. Accounts also emerged which suggested that after disturbances within the prison on 15–16 October 1974, the British Army used CR gas on prisoners, many of whom Republican groups report 'have since developed cancers at an unusually young age' (Ceartais n.d.).[12]

The politics of criminalisation

Internment was formally brought to an end in 1975, along with an approach categorised as reaction, containment and negotiation (McEvoy 2001; Shirlow and McEvoy 2008). The roots of the resulting criminalisation policy can be seen in the Diplock Report of December 1972. This Commission was established to 'consider legal procedures to deal with terrorist activities in Northern Ireland' amidst a context of frequent public unrest and periods of paramilitary activity. Diplock (1972) argued for an amended criminal justice response and suggested a shift towards non-jury courts for those accused of 'terrorist' scheduled offences. The shootings and violence by police and British soldiers passed without further comment. Diplock (1972) claimed that the likelihood of witness intimidation by 'terrorist' groups was so great as to justify the use of non-jury courts. His report also recommended changes to the burden of proof in order to put the emphasis on the suspect to prove they had no knowledge or 'suspicion' of e.g. arms dumps or the locations of explosives. The presumption of innocence so central to the due process model was broken down. In a further negation, Diplock (1972) centralised confessions as suitable and sufficient evidence for convictions. The bulk of the recommendations were enacted in the Northern Ireland (Emergency Provisions) Act in 1973, and included the lowering of thresholds around the admissibility of confessions, with the continued availability of internment as a 'law enforcement "safety net"' (Greer *et al.* 1985: 4).

The use of non-jury courts, changes around the burden of proof and the centrality of confession evidence furthered the development of a parallel system of criminal justice. Rather than representing a clear shift from reactive containment to criminalisation as Gormally *et al.* (1993) imply, Diplock's (1972) recommendations emerged in parallel to the continued use of internment and alongside a criminal justice system which was so adapted it appeared to contradict the British Government's own rhetoric that events in Northern Ireland were little more than a 'law and order' problem. It was not until December 1975 that the

36   The history of state violence

last remnants of containment began to be phased out and internment was brought to an end. In this sense, the early to mid 1970s represented not simply containment, but instead was a short period of fluidity and flux between two approaches. The ending of internment in 1975 brought a modicum of coherence to British policy, although the parallel criminal justice system remained and would be further consolidated by the Gardiner Report (1975).

Gardiner (1975) recommended that internment and Special Category Status for those convicted of scheduled offences should be phased out. For Greer *et al.* (1985), Gardiner (1975) consolidated the Government's portrayal of events in Northern Ireland. Instead of the implicit recognition of the political nature of their violence, the actions of groups including the IRA was hereafter explicitly framed as criminal. Gardiner (1975: 5 para. 8) claimed that 'because they are attempting to destroy Northern Ireland as a political society, terrorists who break the law ... are not heroes but criminals; not the pioneers of political change but its direst enemies'. The report further argued that the existence of Special Category Status had been a 'serious mistake' (Gardiner 1975: 34 para. 107). These changes in policy evidence the need of the British State to represent its actions as being those of a normal, liberal democratic state operating within the law (Rolston 2005). Within the official discourse, the implicit acceptance of the political nature of the conflict was replaced with an explicit framework of criminalisation, even if the criminal justice system had to be reshaped to fit around it. It sought to undermine support for proscribed paramilitary groups and their actions and was directed at activists, their present and future supporters and wider communities, as well as domestic and international audiences (Gearty and Kimbell 1995).

Alongside criminalisation came an attempt to grant primacy to the RUC, married with what McEvoy (2001: 231) describes as 'fairly harsh interrogation techniques designed to secure confessions'. According to Bishop and Mallie (1987), 3,000 people were charged with terrorist offences in the period 1976–1979, mostly on the basis of confessions. The policy of criminalisation contributed to the creation of a criminal justice system for non-state actors that now resembled a 'conveyor belt' of intense interrogations and non-jury 'Diplock' Courts, yet failed to hold the British State to account for violence and abuse. It had a significant impact upon Republican discourses and on the narratives of state violence which emerged during this period. Whilst the State's discourse was one of crime control and 'normalisation', rather than war and insurrection, in reality a parallel legal system had been created which sought to deny any political motivation for (suspected) actors in the conflict, and to delegitimise Republican violence and any underlying discourses which sought to justify the actions of Republican groups.

This 'conveyor belt' approach to 'justice' continued with greater intensity following the opening of RUC East Belfast Castlereagh Holding Centre as a full time Interrogation Centre in 1976. Many detainees would also go public with allegations of violence experienced during interrogations at Omagh, Springfield Road Belfast, Palace Barracks and Girdwood Park Barracks and elsewhere, but it is from

The history of state violence 37

Castlereagh that the most violent and detailed testimonies emerged in the latter years of the 1970s (Taylor 1980). The narratives of former detainees illustrate the extent to which violence spread throughout the time and space of the State security apparatus, and was therefore not limited only to the internment period. Adams (1990: 10) recalls being 'black and blue after being used as a punchbag in Springfield Road British Army barracks and spending a few days in Castlereagh interrogation centre'. The narratives of former detainees interviewed for this book tell a similar story. Tommy McKearney's original narrative of state violence during interrogation features in Taylor (1980: 218) where he details how he

> had been held by the elbow whilst his wrist was bent ... punched in the stomach, slapped around the face and grabbed around the throat until he nearly passed out, and that his fingers were also bent ... he was made to stand for long periods ... and his head and trunk were covered with a black plastic bag.

Tommy would also 'go public' with his story through the local newspaper the *Tyrone Democrat*. Other former detainees had their stories of interrogations carried by organisations such as Amnesty International. Amnesty's Report (1982) makes public Michael Culbert's experiences in the late 1970s of being 'completely disorientated as a result of continuous interrogation, lack of sleep and being made to stand for long periods during interrogation' (Amnesty International 1982: 306). Both men were interviewed for this book.

Other detainees told their story to police doctors or visiting priests. Such testimonies were published frequently by Father Raymond Murray and Father Denis Faul (see Faul and Murray 1972, 1975a, 1975b, 1978, 1981). Former detainees' testimonies also gained some influential audiences. The *Report of Amnesty International* (1978: 70) concluded that 'maltreatment had taken place with sufficient frequency to warrant a public enquiry to investigate it'. Another Inquiry was established to investigate police procedures. Amidst heated media discussions about the apparent integrity of Dr Robert Irwin[13] in a debate which at times resembled a 'smear campaign' (Curtis 1998: 63), the conclusions of Bennett (1979) were eventually made public in February 1979. Although generally favourable towards the RUC, the Report concluded that there had been cases where 'there can, however, whatever their precise explanation, be no doubt that [some of] the injuries ... were not self-inflicted but were sustained during the period of detention' (Bennett 1979: 55 para. 163). The significance of this official discourse is explored later in this book.

Criminalisation in the prisons

The criminalisation policy also impacted upon the prisons. Following Gardiner's (1975) recommendations, the relative freedoms which had been contained within Special Category Status were removed. All those newly convicted in 1976 were required to wear prison uniforms, carry out prison work

38 *The history of state violence*

and have only limited association with other prisoners. They were to be housed in the newly constructed 'H-Block' cells, a place which became a frequent feature in many former prisoners' accounts of state violence (for example, McKeown 2001). The policy of treating paramilitary prisoners as 'ordinary criminals' was intended to isolate and demotivate them whilst weakening their belief systems (Tomlinson 1995, 1998). It sought to depoliticise both the image and the self of Republican (and Loyalist) detainees and their supporters. Yet in practice the policy fuelled a long running prison protest, increased public knowledge of the way in which the prison system operated, and placed the Republican prison struggle at the centre of the conflict in the late 1970s and early 1980s (in particular).

Amidst continuing violence outside the prisons, Republican Kieran Nugent was sentenced to three years imprisonment, but due to the timing of his offences was ineligible for Special Category Status and was instead sent to the H-Blocks at Long Kesh. In an episode now central to the public history of the Republican movement, Nugent refused to wear the prison uniform and was given a blanket instead, thus beginning a protest that led to yet more violence both inside and outside the prison system. More prisoners joined the 'blanket protest' and by 1977, up to three thousand (mostly Republican) prisoners refused to wear the prison uniform or carry out prison work. By the end of the year, protesting prisoners refused to leave their cells, alleging that prison staff were carrying out a campaign of humiliation, violence and harassment designed to break the protest. The protest escalated within weeks, as prisoners' cells became covered with excrement and food waste smeared onto the walls with bits of foam mattress. A statement from Archbishop (later Cardinal) Thomas Ó Fiaich criticising the conditions as resembling the 'slums of Calcutta' (in Coogan 2002: 265–266) embarrassed the prison authorities and gave the protest increased coverage.

Republican prisoners therefore forcefully rejected the change in status, as well as the language and symbolism of the criminalisation regime. The desire to remove political motivation from discourses around armed action actually further politicised the prison struggle and strengthened the prisoners' desire to reject criminalisation (Corcoran 2006a, 2006b). They resisted prison rules on the basis that they had not been convicted by the normal processes of the criminal justice system (Walker 2005). Yet their opposition to criminalisation was not simply to protest against the justice process, but was also designed to emphasise the political nature of the conflict and to mark paramilitary prisoners out as different from the 'criminals' they were being portrayed as. An unintended and unforeseen consequence of the policy was that it allowed

> political prisoners [to draw] on a variety of ideological and sociological resources for rendering their imprisonment intelligible as part of a legitimate political struggle [and] translated the deprivations of confinement into a wider historical and collective event.
>
> (Corcoran 2006a: 139)

The history of state violence 39

Criminalisation failed to sever the ties between the community and armed Republicanism (Bairner 1999b), and to delegitimise the actions and underlying ideology of Republicanism itself. Rather than successfully casting the conflict as a law and order problem, the criminalisation policy and resulting protests mobilised further resistance to the State and its agents.

The criminalisation strategy impacted upon detainees and their narratives of state violence in a number of ways. First, the parallel system of justice fuelled the crime control approach operating in the interrogation centres such as those at Castlereagh. Between 1976 and 1979, Northern Ireland's non-jury courts were achieving an incredible 94 per cent conviction rate, with the vast majority of these convictions rested wholly or mainly on confessions signed under police interrogation (Taylor 1980). Thus the criminalisation strategy enabled detainees to locate their experiences of state violence within a wider meta-narrative of human rights abuses, one in which the British State could seemingly act with impunity. As convictions could be secured by confession evidence in a greater number of cases, detainees were under pressure to prove that any confessions they may have made had been obtained under torture, or inhuman or degrading treatment. Although narratives alone would not be enough for a defence and would be dismissed by the prosecution, any additional evidence could in theory challenge the admissibility of any supposed confession.

A further sense in which criminalisation impacted upon detainees and their narratives of state violence relates to the prison struggle and the wider battle for legitimacy. By portraying those in the detention system (and the H-Blocks in particular) as 'criminals', the State tapped into the pre-existing lack of public sympathy for 'hardened criminals'. When narratives of violence emerged from prisons, the Northern Ireland Office responded by unequivocally stating that:

> it is [the prisoners] alone who are creating bad conditions out of very good conditions.... Those found guilty, after the due process of law, if they are sent to prison by the courts, serve their sentence for what they are, convicted criminals.
>
> (NIO Statement is cited in Beresford 1987: 185–186)

The adaptions made to the criminal justice system were ignored within such discourses, and further critiques only 'appeared to add impetus to the sense of isolation and beleaguerement [felt by prison staff and management], and reinforced their belief in the criminalisation project' (McEvoy: 2001: 243). The label of 'criminal' was intended to dehumanise and delegitimise detainees, and isolate them from actual and possible audiences who might be more sympathetic to prisoners whose motives were political. The sense of collective struggle and community support was downplayed within the official discourse, and the violent actions of individuals were emphasised. It was an operation in 'othering' and dehumanisation, with the foreseeable consequences of further state violence inside the detention system. Criminalisation therefore created further violence against detainees and prisoners which actually consolidated support for the

40 *The history of state violence*

detainees and their attempts to resist. The protests which emerged as a result of criminalisation later led to increased support for Republican prisoners, culminating in the 'broadening of the battlefield' described by Clarke (1987). Narrative testimony was one of the central ways through which the prison system could be shown to be violent and abusive. The increased power of prison staff was matched not only with violence inside and outside the detention system, but with another form of power in which the dehumanising aspects of criminalisation were being replaced with or undermined by prisoners' stories, in which the male[14] prisoners of the H-Blocks could present themselves not as 'convicted criminals' but as fathers, brothers and sons who were being brutalised by the State. The duality with which Republican prisoners could simultaneously present themselves both as vulnerable victims and as men determined to resist and strike back against the violence of incarceration undermined the attempts at isolation represented by the criminalisation policy. It enabled Republican communities to draw strength from the Republican prison struggle and allowed others to sympathise with the human beings being victimised by the British State.

It is from the H-Blocks that these forms of narratives about state violence mostly originate (Faul and Murray 1979; Murray 1998). Narratives about this period describe the violence carried out against Republican prisoners on the protest and how protesting prisoners were 'forcibly washed ... [as] another opportunity for the screws to brutalise us' (McKeown 2001: 60). One participant in the research for this book, Laurence McKeown recalled how:

> At the latter end of 1978 ... several men had been badly beaten after they had been taken out, forcibly washed and shaved.... The men had been removed to an outside hospital for examination of their injuries.... Brutality had been taken to a new level ... I was sent to H4 with about nine others and a 'reception committee' of screws welcomed us. All of us were put through a fairly rough time in cell 26.... This encounter was more frightening as the impression was immediately formed that this was the norm for the Block.
>
> (McKeown 2001: 61–66)

An application to the European Human Rights Commission claiming a breach of Article 3 had been made surrounding the prison protests in 1979, yet was largely unsuccessful as the Commission found that the prison conditions were 'self-inflicted and designed to create maximum sympathy and to enlist public support for ... aims which involved self-inflicted debasement and humiliation to an almost sub-human degree' (in Taylor 1998: 229–234). Following this announcement and the apparent failure of the legal system to bring about adequate redress, Republican prisoners announced that a hunger strike to secure 'Five Demands' would begin. These included the right to wear their own clothes; the right not to do prison work; the right to freedom of association; the right to organise their own leisure activities; and the right to restoration of lost remission (reduction of sentence). These demands equated essentially to political status and the strike to

The history of state violence   41

bring them about would begin in October 1980. There had been many hunger strikes in the past, some of which may have contributed to the introduction of Special Category Status in 1972. Seven men went on the hunger strike in 1980, six from the Provisional Irish Republican Army (IRA)[15] and another, John Nixon, from the Irish National Liberation Army (INLA). In December, three women[16] in Armagh prison also joined the strike.

As another 30 prisoners were preparing to join the strike, striker Sean McKenna became critically ill. Hurried negotiations took place between the authorities, church leaders and prisoner representatives. The strike was then called off with the prisoners believing that their demands had been met. Yet, within two months it became clear that little of substance had changed. Through communications smuggled to the outside world, Republican prisoners went public with an announcement that a second hunger strike was to begin in March 1981, therefore increasing public knowledge of the situation which existed in the H-Blocks. This time, it was to be a staggered strike, which ended in the deaths of ten prisoners.[17]

Throughout the strike, the prisoners – Bobby Sands in particular – would often 'go public' with their experiences through communications smuggled outside the prison and carried by a range of media outlets. Sands was the first of the ten to die, but not before successfully contesting an election and winning a seat in the Westminster Parliament with just over 52 per cent of the ballot and a total of 30,492 votes. Other hunger strikers also contested elections. In the Republic of Ireland, Kieran Doherty would be voted into the Dáil Éireann (Republic of Ireland Parliament) prior to his death, alongside another Republican prisoner (Paddy Agnew, who did not participate in the hunger strike).

Other prisoners joined the strike to replace those who had died, whilst a tense and hidden dialogue continued between the authorities and prisoners' representatives. However, gradually public interest in the strikes diminished, and the authorities showed no (public) signs of conceding to the demands of the prisoners (English 2003, 2006). With increasing regularity, those on the strike drifted in and out of consciousness and were unable to prevent their families from taking medical action to save their lives. In the autumn of 1981, a communication smuggled out of the prison brought the strike to an end. Minor concessions had been made in relation to association and visits, but nothing that amounted to political status at that time. However, the impact of the prisoners' private experiences in terms of levels of public knowledge was highly important and support for Sands in particular contributed to increasing levels of sympathy for and interest in the prisoners.

The centrality of the hunger strikes to Republican prison experiences is reflected in the considerable literature which surrounds it and the extent to which that event still resonates today in cultural activities and commemorations. Numerous commentaries exist, each with their own claims to the truth of those experiences (see Morrison 2006; McIntyre 2005; O'Rawe 2005, 2010). The public memory of the hunger strikes and the debates[18] about whether they were necessary, whether they were intentionally drawn out by the Republican leadership

42   *The history of state violence*

and/or whether they really achieved anything at all, illustrates how ownership of these personal experiences is still highly valuable to those involved and also to the communities from which they came (Chrisafis 2005). The question of what is remembered and what is forgotten is therefore of crucial importance in any debate about the legacy of state violence.

It would be a mistake, however, to categorise former detainees' narratives of state violence in the early 1980s as 'only' being linked to the formal politics around the hunger strikes. In 1983, 38 Republican prisoners escaped from the H-Blocks. Although nineteen men were recaptured within three days, the prison escape embarrassed the British government and led to the Hennessy Inquiry (1984). Within Republican discourse, the escape has become legendary and details of that event are regularly celebrated in Republican clubs (*Iris*, 19 June 2008). Yet not all Republican recollections of the escape are so celebratory. The published narrative of one of the participants in the present study describes the violence of state agents following the escape. In his original testimony, Harry Murray described how he had initially managed to scale a fence during the escape:

> I felt a dull thump in my thigh ... I knew then I'd been shot ... pretty soon the screws were on top of me. They punched [and] kicked me ... some were screaming 'Turncoat bastard!' (I was raised a Protestant in Loyalist Tigers Bay).
>
> (Excerpt from Harry's narrative of post-escape violence in '*Iris*' *Irish Republican Magazine* 1993: 28)

This chapter has therefore outlined the background to the conflict and has traced the political and penal conditions out of which detainees' narratives emerged. It has highlighted the British State's frequent recourse to violence and the ways in which it often worked to cast that violence as legitimate and to deny victimhood to those designated as enemies of the State. Such a context evidences the complex conditions in which the narratives of former detainees are located. This understanding of the history of the conflict in Northern Ireland is necessary in order to show how violence against detainees was not an isolated occurrence, but was broadly representative of a wider mix of policy and practice which failed to mask the authoritarianism of the British State. Knowledge of the history of the conflict also facilitates greater understanding of the significance of state denials and the role of Republican propaganda both during and after the conflict in Northern Ireland. The chapter has illustrated the violence of those years and shown how men were both the main victims and perpetrators of a range of harms. It has hinted at some of the experiences that former detainees and the wider population may need to heal from. As such, the chapter has provided an introduction to the background context which has shaped former detainees' experiences of narrating state violence and the motivation, significance and con-sequences of making these private memories part of a contested public history.

Notes

1 Detained by state forces.
2 Former Royal Air Force base used from 1971 as a detention centre to house internees in Nissen huts. The site later became HMP Maze (nicknamed the 'H-Blocks' due to the architecture of the prison). The centre was patrolled by the British Army's Prison Guard Force and staffed by prison officers, many of whom were on secondment from prisons in England, Scotland and Wales.
3 Recently uncovered documents suggest that this secret camp was located in Ballykelly (Allan 2013).
4 Jim's account of these events is also contained in Faul and Murray (1971), published in the months following the first internment swoops of August 1971.
5 Such terms are often used interchangeably in both the literature and the words of the interviewees themselves. They reflect the oversimplification of the conflict in which religious, 'ethnic' and political labels are often used to create falsely homogeneous communities. Though most Nationalists and Republicans are Catholics, and most Unionists and Loyalists Protestant, these groupings have never been absolute and have been subjected to greater degrees of movement over the last few years (see e.g. Northern Ireland Life and Times Survey 2013).
6 Northern Ireland based newspaper with a generally Nationalist audience.
7 Centre-left-leaning British weekly magazine with an emphasis on political and cultural reporting.
8 Conservative 'British Establishment' broadsheet newspaper.
9 Right-leaning British weekly news magazine.
10 A British Military base in County Down.
11 The Republican movement split into the Provisional IRA and Official IRA (OIRA) in December 1969. The OIRA favoured greater political participation and would begin a ceasefire in 1972, contributing to a further split and the creation of the Irish National Liberation Army (INLA) in 1974. During the 'Peace Process', other Republican groups have also emerged, including the Real IRA, the Continuity IRA, and Óglaigh na hÉireann. Despite differences in political ideologies, often regarding the strength of Marxist influences, all of these groups claim a relationship with the Easter Rising of 1916 and share a desire to unite the island of Ireland (Bowyer Bell 1979; Hanley and Millar 2010).
12 Ceartais are a lobby group of Republican former prisoners and their families who are calling for greater state openness about the role of the Army in responding to a riot in Long Kesh in 1974 during which gas canisters were used against prisoners. They argue that these canisters contained Dibenzoxazepine (CR gas) and that this gas is responsible for the growth of cancers in the former prisoner population (see Ceartais n.d.).
13 Dr Irwin was a police doctor who had been involved in 'going public' with detainees' experiences. Following his appearance on the *Weekend World* television programme, stories began to appear in the *Daily Telegraph* and *Daily Mail* (both right-leaning British newspapers) which implied that Irwin's wife had been raped by a British soldier, and that Irwin's anger at the RUC's failure to arrest the perpetrator underpinned his allegations of state violence against detainees. See Taylor (1980) and Curtis (1998).
14 Women's experiences do not feature in the literature about Northern Ireland's prisons to the same extent as their male counterparts. Yet they were also affected by the criminalisation policy and a number took part in acts of protest and resistance. The experiences of Republican women prisoners are explored in e.g. McCafferty (1981), Loughran (1986), Aretxaga (1997), Corcoran (2006a, 2006b, 2007) and in Brady *et al.* (2011). They also feature in Moore and Scraton (2014). The published stories of Loyalist women prisoners are rarer still, reflecting the lower numbers of Loyalist

44 *The history of state violence*

women prisoners, but also the relative absence of Loyalist prison testimonies more broadly (see Crawford 1999).

15 Brendan Hughes, Thomas McFeeley, Sean McKenna, Leo Green, Tommy McKearney and Raymond McCartney.

16 Mairead Farrell, Mairead Nugent and Mary Doyle.

17 IRA prisoners were Francis 'Frankie' Hughes, Raymond McCreesh, Kieran Doherty, Thomas McElwee and Martin Hurson. IRA prisoners Bobby Sands and Joe McDonnell and INLA prisoners Patsy O'Hara, Kevin Lynch and Michael 'Mickey' Devine also died during the strike.

18 In the books *Blanketmen: The Untold Story of the Hungerstrike* (2005) and *Afterlives: The Hunger Strike and the Secret Offer that Changed Irish History* (2010), O'Rawe argues that the IRA leadership outside of the prison extended the hunger strike against the wishes of the prison leadership who wished to accept a deal made in July 1981 that appeared to concede to the prisoners' demands. O'Rawe (2005, 2010) suggests that the leadership outside the prison pushed for the rejection and six more hunger strikers died as a result. This recollection of events has contributed to a continuing (and increasingly personalised) dispute amongst Republican former detainees. Former Sinn Féin Publicity Officer Danny Morrison has strongly criticised O'Rawe's (2005) writings, and refutes O'Rawe's claims in a blog post entitled 'Thatcher's Defender' (Morrison 12 January 2012). O'Rawe's (2005) interpretation is, however, supported by some other Republican groups, including the Irish Republican Socialist Party, and some other former prisoners including Anthony McIntyre, author of *Good Friday: The Death of Irish Republicanism* (2008). For an outline of the debates around differing recollections of the 1981 hunger strike, see Chrisafis (2005).

References

Adams, G. (1990) *Cage Eleven*. Dingle: Brandon Books.

Allan, C. (2013) 'Hooded Men Were Held in Ballykelly'. *Derry Journal*. 6 August. Available at www.derryjournal.com/news/hooded-men-were-held-in-ballykelly-1-535 8385 (accessed 6 August 2013).

Amnesty International (1978) *Report of an Amnesty International Mission to Northern Ireland 28 November–6 December 1977* [AI Index:Eur 45/01/78/].

Amnesty International (1982) *Annual Report*. [Online] Available at: www.amnesty.org/ar/library/asset/POL10/004/1982/en/cc4aa2e6-ba5b-43b7-8245-4a63a7bb91b3/POL100041982eng.pdf (accessed 5 August 2010).

Amnesty International (2013) *Death Sentences and Executions in 2013*. Available at: http://issuu.com/amnestypublishing/docs/death_sentences_and_executions_2013 (accessed 5 August 2014).

Aretxaga, B. (1997) *Shattering Silence: Women, Nationalism, and Political Subjectivity in Northern Ireland*. Princeton: Princeton University Press.

Author Unknown (n.d.) *The Irish Case at Strasbourg*. Outline of HMG Policy and Commission Procedure Document 'E40'.

BBC (2008 [1974]) *On This Day: Maze Prison Goes Up in Flames*. Available at: http://news.bbc.co.uk/onthisday/hi/dates/stories/october/16/newsid_2531000/2531083.stm (accessed 31 August 2011).

Bennett Report (1979) *Report of the Committee of Inquiry into Police Interrogation Procedures in Northern Ireland* [Cmnd 7497] London: HMSO.

Beresford, D. (1987) *Ten Men Dead: The Story of the 1981 Hunger Strike*. London: Harper Collins.

Bishop, P. and Mallie, E. (1987) *The Provisional IRA*. London: Heinemann Ltd.

Bowyer Bell, J. (1979) *Assassin: Theory and Practice of Political Violence*. New York: St. Martin's Press.

Boyle, K., Hadden, T. and Hillyard, P. (1975) *Law and the State: The Case of Northern Ireland*. London: Martin Robertson.

Brady, E., Patterson, E., McKinney, K., Hamill, R., Jackson, M. and Jackson, P. (eds) (2011) *In the Footsteps of Anne: Stories of Republican Women Ex-Prisoners*. Belfast: Shanaway Press.

CAIN (Conflict Archive on the Internet) (n.d.) *Conflict Archive on the Internet*. Available at: http://cain.ulst.ac.uk (accessed 14 January 2011).

CAIN (n.d.) *Internment: A Chronology of the Main Events*. Available at: http://cain.ulst. ac.uk/events/intern/chron.htm (accessed 31 August 2011).

Campaign for Social Justice in Northern Ireland (1971) *Northern Ireland - The Mailed Fist: A Record of Army and Police Brutality from August 9–November 9, 1971*. Dungannon: The Authors.

Ceartais (n.d.) 'Revealing the Truth Behind the CR Gas Exposure'. [Online] Available at ceartais.blogspot.co.uk (accessed 14 May 2013).

Chrisafis, A. (2005) 'Hunger Strike Claims Rile H-Block Veterans' *Guardian*. 4 March. Available at www.guardian.co.uk/politics/2005/mar/04/northernireland.northernireland1 (accessed 31 August 2013).

Compton Report (1971) *Report of Inquiry into Allegations Against the Security Forces of Physical Brutality in Northern Ireland Arising out of Events on the 9th August 1971* [Cmnd 4823]. London: HMSO.

Conroy, J. (2000) *Unspeakable Acts, Ordinary People: The Dynamics of Torture*. London: University of California Press.

Coogan, T.P. (2000) *The IRA*. London: Palgrave Macmillan.

Coogan, T.P. (2002) *The Troubles: Ireland's Ordeal 1966–1996 and the Search For Peace*. New York: Palgrave.

Corcoran, M.S. (2006a) *Out of Order: The Political Imprisonment of Women in Northern Ireland, 1972–1998*. Collumpton: Willan.

Corcoran, M.S. (2006b) 'Talking About Resistance: Women Political Prisoners and the Dynamics of Prison Conflict, Northern Ireland', in Barton, A., Corteen, K., Scott, D. and Whyte, D. (eds) *Expanding the Criminological Imagination: Critical Readings in Criminology*. Devon: Willan.

Corcoran, M. (2007) 'Normalization and its Discontents: Constructing the "Irreconcilable" Female Political Prisoner in Northern Ireland', *British Journal of Criminology*, 47(3), 405–422.

Council of Europe (1950) European Convention for the Protection of Human Rights and Fundamental Freedoms, as amended by Protocols Nos 11 and 14, 4 November.

Crawford, C. (1999) *Defenders or Criminals? Loyalist Prisoners and Criminalisation*. Belfast: Blackstaff Press.

Crelinsten, R.D. (2003) 'The World of Torture: A Constructed Reality', *Theoretical Criminology*, 7(3), 293–318.

Curtis, L. (1998) *Ireland: The Propaganda War*. Belfast: Sásta.

Devlin, B. (1982) *An Interlude with Seagulls: Memoirs of a Long Kesh Internee*. Belfast: The Author.

Dillon, M. (1991) *The Dirty War*. London: Arrow Press.

Diplock Report (1972) *Report of the Commission to Consider Legal Procedures to Deal with Terrorist Activities in Northern Ireland* [Cmnd 5185]. London: HMSO.

46 *The history of state violence*

Donohue, L.K. (1998) 'Regulating Northern Ireland: The Special Powers Acts 1922–1972', *The Historical Journal*, 41(4), 1089–1120.

English, R. (2003) *Armed Struggle: A History of the IRA*. London: Pan Macmillan.

English, R. (2006) *Irish Freedom: The History of Nationalism in Ireland*. London: Pan Macmillan.

Faul, D. and Murray, R. (1971) *The Hooded Men: British Torture in Ireland*. Dungannon: The Authors.

Faul, D. and Murray, R. (1972) *British Army and Special Branch RUC Brutalities, December 1971–February 1972*. Dungannon: The Authors.

Faul, D. and Murray, R. (1975a) *The RUC: The Black and Blue Book*. Dungannon: The Authors.

Faul, D. and Murray, R. (1975b) *The Shame of Merlyn Rees: 4th Year of Internment in Ireland, Long Kesh 1974–1975*. Dungannon: The Authors.

Faul, D. and Murray, R. (1978) *The Castlereagh File: Allegations of Police Brutality 1976-77*. Dungannon: The Authors.

Faul, D. and Murray, R. (1979) *H-Blocks: British Jail for Irish Political Prisoners*, Dungannon: The Authors.

Faul, D. and Murray, R. (1981) *The British Dimension–Brutality, Murder and Legal Duplicity in Northern Ireland*. Dungannon: The Authors.

Fields, R.M. (1980) *Northern Ireland: Society under Siege*. New Brunswick: Transaction Press.

Foucault, M. (1980) *Power/Knowledge: Selected Interviews and Other Writings 1972–1977*. London: Harvester Press.

Gardiner Report (1975) *Report of a Committee to Consider, in the Context of Civil Liberties and Human Rights, Measures to Deal with Terrorism in Northern Ireland* [Cmnd 5847]. London: HMSO.

Gearty, C. and Kimbell, J. (1995) 'Legislating for Change', *Fortnight*, 337, 14–15.

Gormally, B., McEvoy, K. and Wall, D. (1993) 'Criminal Justice in a Divided Society: Northern Ireland Prisons', *Crime and Justice: A Review of Research*, 17, 51–135.

Gramsci, A. (1971) *Selections from the Political Notebooks*. Edited and Translated by G.N. Smith and Q. Hoare. New York: International Publishers.

Greer, S., Hadden, T. and Hagan, M. (1985) 'Civil Liberties in Northern Ireland: From Special Powers to Supergrasses', *Fortnight*, 4–17.

Hanley, B. and Millar, S. (2010) *The Lost Revolution: The Story of the Official IRA and the Workers' Party*. London: Penguin Books Ltd.

Hennessy Report (1984) *Report of an Inquiry by HM Chief Inspector of Prisons in the Security Arrangements at HMP Maze* [H.C. 203]. London: HMSO.

Hillyard, P. (1987) 'The Normalisation of Special Powers: From Northern Ireland to Britain', in Scraton, P. (eds) *Law, Order and the Authoritarian State*. Milton Keynes: Open University Press.

Irish News (1971) 'Brutally Treated by Soldiers, Say Released Men'. 12 August.

'Iris' Irish Republican Magazine/An Phoblacht (1993 Re-Issue) 'The Greatest Escape'. 14 October.

Kennally, D. and Preston, E. (1971) 'A Case to be Answered'. London: Independent Labour Party. [Online] Available at: http://cain.ulst.ac.uk/events/intern/docs/kennally 71.htm#contents (accessed 31 August 2011).

Loughran, C. (1986) 'Armagh and Feminist Strategy: Campaigns Around Republican Women Prisoners in Armagh Jail', *Feminist Review*, 23, 59–79.

McCafferty, N. (1981) *The Armagh Women*. Dublin: Co-Op Press.

The history of state violence   47

McEvoy, K. (2001) *Paramilitary Imprisonment in Northern Ireland: Resistance, Management and Releas*e. Oxford: Oxford University Press:

McGuffin, J. (1973) *The Guinea Pigs*. London: Penguin Books Ltd. [Online] Available at: www.irishresistancebooks.com/guineapigs/guineapigs.htm (accessed 14 February 2012).

McIntyre, A. (2005) 'A Blanketman Still Fighting to Be Heard'. *The Blanket*. 4 March.

McIntyre, A. (2008) *Good Friday: The Death of Irish Republicanism*. New York: Ausubo.

McKeown, L. (2001) *Out of Time: Irish Republican Prisoners and Long Kesh 1972–2000*. Belfast: Beyond the Pale.

McKittrick, D. and McVea, D. (2001) *Making Sense of the Troubles*. Belfast: Blackstaff.

McKittrick, D., Kelters, D., Feeney, B., Thornton, C. and McVea, D. (2007) *Lost Lives: The Stories of the Men, Women and Children Who Died as a Result of the Northern Ireland Troubles*. London: Mainstream Publishing.

Moore, L. and Scraton, P. (2014) *The Incarceration of Women: Punishing Bodies, Breaking Spirits.* London: Palgrave Macmillan.

Morrison, D. (2012) 'Thatcher's Defender', Blog Post, 12 January. Available at*:* www.dannymorrison.com/?p=2172 (accessed 12 October 2012).

Morrison, D. (ed.) (2006) *Hunger Strike: Reflections on the 1981 Hunger Strike.* Dingle: Brandon.

Murray, R. (1998) *State Violence: Northern Ireland*. Dublin: Mercier Press.

Ní Aoláin, F. (2000) *The Politics of Force: Conflict Management and State Violence in Northern Ireland.* Belfast: Blackstaff.

Northern Ireland (Emergency Provisions) Act 1973. London: HMSO.

Northern Ireland (Emergency Provisions) Act 1974. London: HMSO.

Northern Ireland (Temporary Provisions) Act 1972. London: HMSO.

Northern Ireland Life and Times (2013) *Northern Ireland Life and Times Surveys.* Available at www.ark.ac.uk/nilt/ (accessed 12 February 2014).

O Tuathail, S. (1972), *They Came in the Morning: Internment, Monday August 09, 1971: Torture and Brutality in the North*. Dublin: Sinn Féin (Official). Available at: http://cain.ulst.ac.uk/events/intern/pdfs/otuathail.pdf (accessed 31 August 2011).

O'Leary, B. and McGarry, J. (1993) *The Politics of Antagonism.* London: Athlone Press.

O'Rawe, R. (2005) *Blanketmen: The Untold Story of the Hungerstrike*. Dublin: New Island Books.

O'Rawe, R. (2010) *Afterlives: The Hunger Strike and the Secret Offer that Changed Irish History.* Dublin: The Lilliput Press.

Parker Report (1972) *Report of the Committee of Privy Counsellors Appointed to Consider Authorised Procedures for the Interrogation of Persons Suspected of Terrorism* [Cmnd 4901]. London: HMSO.

Poggi, G. (2006) *Weber: A Short Introduction*. Cambridge: Polity Press.

Punch, M. (2012) *State Violence, Collusion and the Troubles*. London: Pluto.

Rolston, B. (2005) '"An Effective Mask for Terror": Democracy, Death Squads and Northern Ireland', *Crime, Law and Social Change*, 44(2), 181–203.

Ryder, C. (2000) *Inside The Maze: The Untold Story of the Northern Ireland Prison Service.* London: Methuen Publishing.

Scraton, P. (1985) *The State of the Police*. London: Pluto Press.

Shirlow, P. and McEvoy, K. (2008) *Beyond the Wire: Former Prisoners and Conflict Transformation in Northern Ireland.* London: Pluto.

Simon, R. (1982) *Gramsci's Political Thought*. London: Lawrence and Wishart.

48 *The history of state violence*

Taylor, P. (1978) 'Reporting Northern Ireland', *Index on Censorship*, 7(6), 3–11.

Taylor, P. (1980) *Beating the Terrorists: Interrogation in Omagh, Gough and Castlereagh.* London: Penguin.

Taylor, P. (1998) *Provos: The IRA and Sinn Féin.* London: Bloomsbury.

Tomlinson, M. (1995) 'Imprisoned Ireland', in Ruggiero, V., Ryan, M. and Sim, J. (eds) *European Prisons Systems: A Critical Anatomy.* London: Sage.

Tomlinson, M. (1998) 'Walking Backwards into the Sunset: British Policy and the Insecurity of Northern Ireland', in Miller, D. (ed.) *Rethinking Northern Ireland: Culture, Ideology and Colonialism.* Harlow: Longman.

Tonge, J. (2006) 'Sinn Féin and "New Republicanism" in Belfast', *Space and Polity*, 10(2), 135–147.

Walker, R.K. (2005) *The Hunger Strikes.* Belfast: Langan Books.

Weber, M. (1948) *From Max Weber: Essays in Sociology.* Edited and Translated by C.W. Mills and H.H. Gerthe. Oxford: Oxford University Press.

3 Defining experiences of state violence in detention

An examination of the possible motivation for and significance of narrating detention experiences is central to understanding the legacy of state violence in Northern Ireland. Yet, before all of this, it is first useful to explore the definitional problems and possibilities that surround the language used by former detainees to describe their own experiences, in order to understand how those individuals come to name what has happened to them. The following chapter examines how and why experiences of state violence become defined as 'torture' or 'brutality', and the significance of those definitions for former detainees who have previously made their narratives of state violence part of a contested public history. It argues that for some former detainees, the semantics of torture, brutality and ill-treatment contain a multiplicity of subjective meanings with different levels of personal significance, all of which become lost in the distant definitions employed by law.

The semantics of 'brutality'

In 1971, the British Government acted quickly to establish a Committee of Inquiry into allegations against the security forces of 'physical brutality arising out of events on the 9th August 1971' (Compton 1971). The subsequent report, published in November 1971, found that elements of the treatment of 40 persons detained during internment had constituted 'ill-treatment' but not 'physical brutality' (Compton 1971). Central to this understanding were the interpretations of Sir Edmund Compton, Judge Edgar Fay, QC and Dr Ronald Gibson, who all argued that 'brutality' properly so-called required the perpetrators to take pleasure in the acts committed against detainees, in essence, that their 'use of brutality must be motivated by a cruel disposition' (Spjut 1979: 270). Compton (1971: 23 para. 23) argued that no evidence of this had been presented during their investigations, and thus claimed that 'we do not think that [it] happened here'.

This definition of 'brutality' offered by Compton (1971) focused solely on an understanding of the perpetrator's intentions and not upon the (equally subjective) experiences and lived understanding of the detainees. Yet, despite Compton's (1971) rejection of the term 'brutality', it repeatedly features in detainees' narratives surrounding state violence, both in regards to internment

50 *Defining experiences of state violence*

(1971–1975) interrogations in Holding Centres (*c.*1976–1978) and again in relation to violence within the formal prison system (particularly *c.*1978–1985). All of those interviewed as part of the present study had in the past 'made public' their experiences of state violence and many of these original testimonies feature in the previous chapter. Though the research was primarily concerned with the experience of 'going public' (rather than the details of their experience itself), many of those interviewed chose to again recall the details of the violence they had suffered, and often located those experiences within the semantic space offered by the language of 'brutality':

> I faced the usual forty eight hours of brutality.
>
> (Liam)

> The weight of evidence was changed, the length of detention was extended and there was quite obviously, a blind eye turned to what was clearly brutality.
>
> (Tommy)

> Castlereagh that I was taken to ... became particularly notorious in terms of torture and brutality and such like.
>
> (Laurence)

> It was very difficult to get out the degree of brutality, particularly from the screws.
>
> (Richard)

> At that time, it was happening morning, afternoon and night every day for almost a fortnight but culminated in a week of non-stop brutality and barbarity against us. It was brutality, the sort of brutality that all of us on the protest would have been the victim of ... I can still picture the brutality, horror and impact of it on us all at the time. It is important that you know of these examples of brutality.
>
> (Interviewee 'P')

These five testimonies are broadly symbolic of interviewees' perceptions of the three interrelated phases of state violence described above. They show similarities in their depiction of state violence as 'brutality' throughout the detention system. Yet this concept of 'brutality' deployed by the former detainees about their experiences is largely without reference to the perpetrator-focused restrictions employed by Compton's (1971) definition. For these detainees, Compton's (1971) distinction was of little significance. Jim (whose allegations were amongst those that initially led to the Inquiry) argued that:

> Them saying that the difference was that the people who were inflicting it didn't get any enjoyment from it?! [rolls eyes].... As one of those who was

Defining experiences of state violence 51

having all that inflicted on them, it really didn't mean anything to me if the guy that was doing it was enjoying it or not.

For Jim, the motivations of the perpetrators were an irrelevance with little impact on his experience or its legacy. It did not appear to matter to him whether or not the violence against him was carried out for the purposes of pleasure or for any other reason, as it simply did not change his feelings about what he had suffered during internment. The remaining former detainees were similarly unconcerned about the motivations of those who had carried out violence towards them, suggesting that the distinctions made by Compton (1971) held little significance for former detainees and their narratives.

Locating 'torture' in Northern Ireland

The following section provides a brief discussion of the semantics of 'torture, inhuman and degrading treatment', with the aim of exploring the significance of these distant legalisms in relation to former detainees' lived experience. After the publicity surrounding allegations of brutality against detainees following internment in 1971, the Government of Ireland launched a prosecution of the UK through the mechanisms provided by the ECtHR. It argued that the treatment of internees had violated Article 3 of the ECHR (1950), which states that 'no one shall be subjected to torture or to inhuman or degrading treatment or punishment'. The primary focus of the case against the UK was a particular form of so-called 'interrogation in depth', which consisted of forced 'wall-standing'[1], the use of hooding, subjection to 'white' noise, sleep deprivation and deprivation of food and drink. The Irish Government argued that used in combination, these 'Five Techniques' violated Article 3 of the ECHR on the grounds that they amounted to torture. During the case, the European Commission of Human Rights agreed that there had indeed been a violation of Article 3, and that this had reached the threshold of torture. However, significantly, the European Court of Human Rights then differed from the view of the Commission, asserting that 'although they were used systematically, [the "Five Techniques"] did not occasion suffering of the particular *intensity and cruelty* implied by the word torture as so understood' (*Republic of Ireland* v. *United Kingdom* ECtHR 1978 para. 167, my emphasis). Instead, the Court argued that the techniques:

> accordingly fell into the category of inhuman treatment within the meaning of Article 3. The techniques were also degrading since they were such as to arouse in their victims feelings of fear, anguish and inferiority capable of humiliating and debasing them and possibly breaking their physical or moral resistance.
>
> (*Republic of Ireland* v. *United Kingdom* 1978: para. 167)

The Court argued that the treatment of detainees had not reached the level of severity required to differentiate it from inhuman or degrading treatment, and

52 *Defining experiences of state violence*

therefore suggested that torture was distinguishable by the intensity of the suffering inflicted and the cruelty with which it was carried out. In its decision making, it referred to General Assembly Resolution 3452 (9 December 1975) to support its findings, which states that 'torture constitutes an aggravated and deliberate form of cruel, inhuman or degrading treatment or punishment' (in Spjut 1979: 269). The Court 'also made reference to the *1975 Declaration Against Torture*, which declares "Torture constitutes an aggravated and deliberate form of cruel, inhuman or degrading treatment or punishment"' (in Barrett 2001: 8).

In this way, the judgment and discussions of the ECtHR in the *Ireland* v. *UK* (1978) case sought to draw distinctions between experiences of torture and those of cruel, inhuman or degrading treatment. The sliding scale that the European Commission of Human Rights had earlier hinted at, in what became known as, *The Greek Case* (1969) had been rendered explicit by the Court in the case of *Ireland* v. *UK* (1978). Here, for an act to be legally defined as torture it must first be deemed to be degrading treatment. Severe mental or physical suffering is required to move the act (or omission) into inhuman treatment and such things must be 'aggravated' if this treatment is to be considered torture (Barrett 2001). With the final judgment of the ECtHR clearly in mind, some of those former detainees directly involved in the case discussed the power and significance of the sliding scale implied by the judgment's semantics:

> Torture is the word, there is no other word for it. The European Court at Strasbourg called it 'inhuman and degrading treatment'. Well, what can we call that? When you take people away, out of their district, you hood them, you blindfold them, you put into them intense noise, you dress them in Army boiler suits and you put them through all forms of abuse – there is no other word for that but *torture*.
>
> (Interviewee PJ, emphasis in interview)

Other detainees, such as Liam, had mixed feelings about the Court's judgment:

> The case was successful – well, partly successful. The British Government was found guilty in the European Court of Human Rights of degrading and inhuman treatment towards us thirteen detainees, but not of torture. And if you look it up in the dictionary, the dictionary meaning of torture is degrading and inhuman treatment (sighs).

For Liam, the distinction between torture and degrading and inhuman treatment has little personal value. Through his own interpretation, he argued that he and the other detainees had been victims of state torture:

> But we were all a bit sickened when it came back that they weren't found guilty of torture and it was a crying shame to be honest with you that they weren't! But they were playing with words and that is basically all it was.
>
> (Liam)

Defining experiences of state violence 53

He recognised the pejorative power of the language of 'torture' and the dilution of his experiences seemingly inherent in the semantics of 'ill-treatment'. Assisted by the Court's narrow interpretation, the concept of 'torture' still resonates with greater pejorative power and this is reflected in its status as a non-derogable human right and norm of customary international law. Furthermore, it has an additional symbolic power in that torture has been 'most commonly used against people who are not full members of a society, such as slaves, foreigners, prisoners of war and members of racial, ethnic and religious outsider groups' (Einolf 2007: 1010). However, for some detainees detained in Castlereagh during the criminalisation period, torture was further understood as having a particular purpose, which went beyond discrimination, the symbolic dehumanisation of suspected 'enemies of the state' and the sadism implied by Compton's (1971) interpretation of 'brutality'. Like Cullen (2008), two former detainees suggested that it was the apparently functional and purposeful role of torture which they thought was a key part of its definition:

> I'd say I was tortured, because I think torture involves a prolonged, deliberate, physical assault on another human being for a particular end. It is functional torture, isn't it? I don't think torture is sadism, you are doing it for other reasons. But this was functional, it was to an end. The end was to get me to say that I had done this [shooting].
>
> (Michael)

> It wasn't done for fun. They used it to get information.
>
> (Tommy)

Many of those interviewed (whose original narratives often concerned later experiences of state violence within the formal prison system of the H-Blocks) chose to depict events as part of a wider attempt to 'break' prisoners' resistance, yet did not describe their experiences as being those of torture. This third stage of state violence can be observed in the narratives of those imprisoned in the H-Blocks in the period 1976–1985. Interviewees Richard and 'P' vividly described:

> the brutality of the H-Blocks.... For four years whilst we were in jail, we were beaten up. Most visits you got a beating, there was one waiting for you when you came back because you wouldn't bend over a mirror.[2] So if you didn't bend, they beat you. During wing shifts you invariably got a beating.... This was the sort of thing that was going on regularly. Some of our men would have been very spirited and would have tried to hit them back, but they would've got their balls squeezed until they fainted.
>
> (Richard)

> Over the mirror they held his legs apart, spread him wide open. Four 'screws'[3] [grabbed] two arms and two legs and then this other big, heavy

54 *Defining experiences of state violence*

'screw' – he was fat but he was muscular – he hit the fella such a merciful boot in the balls. [The prisoner's] two legs went out akimbo. [The prison officer] took his time and just slammed the boot into his groin with the obvious intention of severely damaging him.

(Interviewee 'P')

According to the narratives of participants in this book, this stage of state violence was not clearly motivated by a desire for information, but was instead part of a wider attempt to brutalise and 'break' those who took part in (or offered support for) protesting prisoners. Similar narratives by Republican prisoners featured in Campbell *et al.* (2006) and repeatedly define state violence experienced during the protests as 'brutality'. Other prisoners describe the violence as 'frenzied savagery' and 'barbarous treatment', 'degradation and humiliation' (Campbell *et al.* 2006: 84–107). Despite perceiving the violence as functional, they did not apply the label of torture to what they had experienced.

Some of those interviewed defined violence motivated *by hatred* as most harmful. They presented many of the prison staff of the H-Blocks as particularly malicious, vindictive and unmerciful, implying that violence against detainees was committed (in part) for pleasure:

Your man just got a hold of me … my head was twisted and they just trailed me up the wing. It took about four minutes to get out of the block and into the van for a five minute drive. Well, it took twenty minutes, deliberately, because they had me down into the floor, one had his foot on my head pressing down on it. Another had my arm bent at the wrist trying to break it. I said to him 'What?! Are you trying to break my arm?!' He said 'you're right, you fucking bastard, get down in the dirt where you belong'.

(Harry)

Not all the screws were animals but some of them were. Some of them absolutely detested us, because a) we were Provos and b) we were on this 'Dirty Protest' and it was horrendous working conditions for them, although they were being paid for it. They hated us, and some of them used to just open the door and punch you.

(Richard)

It was a combination of trying to break you but also absolute hatred. The screws used to walk up and down the wing calling us vermin and scum … They [had many] opportunities to humiliate, treat us like animals and beat the crap out of us. They would never let an opportunity go by them. There were several of them in particular who were vicious.

(Interviewee 'P')

Interestingly, the language of torture becomes replaced within most of the prison narratives by a narrative of brutality. Many of those interviewed chose to

Defining experiences of state violence 55

emphasise that the violence against prisoners was not *only* functional (i.e. for a purpose) but, in their view, was also motivated by hatred. Although here they are concerned with experiences within the prison setting of the H-Blocks, such understanding of the meaning and significance of the language of brutality clearly echoes with the earlier definition employed by Compton (1971) concerning allegations emerging from the period of internment. Therefore, when recalling prison experiences, the language of torture is to an extent replaced by a narrative of brutality by those who had experienced state violence during the time of the prison protests. For Liam, who had previously defined his interment experiences as torture, the violence in the H-Blocks was perceived as far worse and its legacy much more problematic:

> What I suffered was nothing compared to what those people suffered. The degradation and the brutality suffered against the people who refused to wear prison uniforms was absolutely incredible ... I was out of prison before that took place and when I speak to a number of my friends ... what they went through is scary. It is absolutely scary. What I went through, I don't think it was anything like what they went through – the brutality, particularly the brutality. Mine was mind games, okay, but theirs was straightforward brutality, of beatings because they refused to be criminalised. That is basically it.

Problems and possibilities

In conclusion, since the *Ireland* v. *UK* (1978) case, the ECtHR has remained unpredictable in its judgments about torture, particularly in relation to the treatment of prisoners and detainees (see Livingstone 2000; Nagan and Atkins 2001). The *Ireland* v. *UK* (1978) case is symbolic of the Court's wariness – perhaps one not shared to the same extent by the Commission – to reach a finding of torture in regards to the treatment of detainees, although it has begun to issue judgments of 'inhuman and degrading treatment' against detainees with greater frequency, famously in cases such as *Tomasi* v. *France* (1992) and *Ribitsch* v. *Austria* (1995). In *Selmouni* v. *France* (1999), the Court suggested that if the 'Five Techniques' used against detainees during internment in Northern Ireland were to be re-evaluated under present conditions, then they would indeed constitute torture in the contemporary legal climate of Europe in the late twentieth/ early twenty-first century. Yet, despite these pronouncements concerning Article 3, the supposed lowering of the threshold in relation to ill-treatment and repeated referrals to the Convention as a 'living instrument', judgments of torture reached by the Court in relation to detainees and prisoners still appear to be rare, thus illustrating the destructive primacy the concept is perceived to hold within the hierarchy of human rights violations. The successful cases are most often against the post-Soviet states of Russia and Ukraine, or against Turkey (see e.g. *Vladimir Romanov* v. *Russia* (2009), *Novoselov* v. *Russia* (2013), *Tarasov* v. *Ukraine* (2013), *Aksoy* v. *Turkey* (1996) and *Mesut Deniz* v. *Turkey* (2013)) and suggest

56 *Defining experiences of state violence*

that torture retains its narrowly defined high threshold of severe pain and suffering. Furthermore, as Livingstone (2000: 321) argues:

> Strasbourg has done little more than legitimate the existing practice of most states … [its] decisions give the impression that, except in the most egregious of cases, such matters are seen as too detailed and too threatening to the authority of prison staff for a court to tamper with.

In essence, international legal mechanisms are presently in a state of confusion around the meaning of torture which enables them to be perceived as both a useful tool and a problematic obstacle. According to Roth (2008) any collapsing of distinctions between torture and cruel, inhuman and degrading treatment could, for example, lead to extra-territorial prosecutions of foreign state agents in national courts. However, even with the risk of politically motivated prosecutions, it must be argued that such legal actions are desirable, particularly if they contribute to a process of accountability and prevention for instances of state violence and violations of human rights. A further critique of collapsing the distinction between torture and cruel, inhuman and degrading treatment concerns the special status of the language of torture. Torture is presented as the pinnacle of state harm in a hierarchy of treatment (Smith 2003) and that to collapse any distinctions between harms risks removing the special ignominy allegedly attached to the term 'torture'. The existence of such stigma was clear in the *Ireland* v. *United Kingdom* (1978) case. The Court's distinction between torture and inhuman or degrading treatment reflected a deliberate and intentional 'weighting' (Spjut 1979). A 'global approach' which collapses these distinctions may lead to greater attempts by states to avoid treating detainees in ways which may be seen as 'degrading', if these 'lesser' violations are to be regarded in the same manner as 'torture' in years to come.

Yet it may also be that international mechanisms may become *less* likely to find states guilty of violations if all aspects of degrading treatment are to be granted the same powerful status as torture. Thus, even within international human rights discourses, there remains great uncertainty about the meaning and interpretation of freedom from torture, inhuman and degrading treatment or the value of those distinctions, despite their continued depiction as fundamental human rights. This confusion was reflected on by former detainees:

> What is torture? I remember someone saying to me – it was a Republican publicist – saying 'You are talking about ill-treatment and beatings, you should be using the word torture, because it is torture'. I was reluctant to use the word torture because what is torture? Torture has so many different definitions of what it is. The British Government always denied torture, but then accepted there might have been ill-treatment. The 'Guinea Pigs' people[4] – what is 'degrading and inhuman treatment'? Human beings are capable of all sorts of things that animals aren't. I think it is obscene to the animal

Defining experiences of state violence   57

world to call some of the things we do 'inhuman'. We do the worst things in the world. So what does 'inhuman' mean? All those definitions I have difficulty with – actually, I think everyone has difficulty with.

(Interviewee 'F')

For those who have claimed to experience state violence, the semantics of brutality and torture remain entirely subjective, and are unchanged by the texts of public inquiries, legal pronouncements, customs and case law. The apparent simplicity of a concept based upon severity, intent, purpose and official character (Cullen 2008) breaks down when applied to lived experiences. In contrast to the exaggerated depictions of homogeneity both within and around the 'Republican movement' (particularly in relation to the prison struggle experience), former detainees attached a wide range of meanings to their experiences. For some of those interviewed, to hear prison officers 'talk about letters from your family without letting you read them was torture' (Interviewee 'P'). For others, torture was 'being left unconscious on the floor several times through using … "flexi-wrists"' (Tommy). This diversity of experiences, in combination with the frequency with which floating signifiers such as torture and brutality were employed by interviewees, reflects back a personal understanding which is distant and in many ways distinct from the legal categories of 'torture, cruel, inhuman or degrading treatment':

All I can do is describe it and let people decide for themselves whether they regard it as torture or not. For me, if torture is about systematic use of psychological or physical abuse in order to break someone down and get information from you – then it was torture.

(Interviewee 'F')

In conclusion, state violence in the detention system of Northern Ireland has taken many different forms. The fluid terminology employed to describe the experiences of detainees reflects this uncertain and subjective nature of violence and raises interesting questions about how best to respond to the private and public legacy of these experiences. As Hillyard *et al.* (2004) suggest, harm itself remains difficult to quantify in such abstract terms. State violence against detainees in Northern Ireland, therefore, can often be presented interchangeably as brutality, ill-treatment and/or torture in order to frame it as a personal experience. This is not to suggest uniformity between different experiences, but rather to emphasise the different interpretations participants give to their own experiences of violence and the language used to describe it in their narrative testimonies. In labelling their experiences as torture and/or brutality (sometimes interchangeably) former detainees reflect on the personal and subjective nature of those events and the significance which they themselves have given to those experiences of harm, its narration and its legacy.

58   Defining experiences of state violence

Notes

1 'Wall-standing' refers to detainees being "spread-eagled against the wall, with their fingers put high above their head against the wall, the legs spread apart and the feet back, causing them to stand on their toes with the weight of the body mainly on the fingers' (*Ireland* v. *UK* (1978) para. 96).
2 A reference to the post-visit, mandatory mirror searches in which 'prisoners habitually refused to adopt a squatting position, giving rise, they said, to blows and kicks, sometimes with a warder sitting on a prisoner's back. A metal detector was used to inspect the anal area and according to the prisoners this came in handy for beating them on the testicles as well. Other sorts of harassment were alleged, such as using the same finger to explore a prisoner's mouth as had just been used to investigate his rectum' (Coogan 2002: 22).
3 Slang for Prison Officer.
4 Another popular term for the 'Hooded Men'.

References

Aksoy v. *Turkey* (1996) Application no. 21987/93 ECHR 68.
Campbell, B., McKeown, L. and O'Hagan, F. (2006) *Nor Meekly Serve My Time: The H Block Struggle*. Belfast: Beyond the Pale.
Compton Report (1971) *Report of Inquiry into Allegations Against the Security Forces of Physical Brutality in Northern Ireland Arising out of Events on the 9th August 1971* [Cmnd 4823]. London: HMSO.
Coogan, T.P. (2002) *The Troubles: Ireland's Ordeal 1966–1996 and the Search for Peace*. New York: Palgrave.
Cullen, A. (2008) 'Defining Torture in International Law: A Critique of the Concept Employed by The European Court of Human Rights', *California Western International Law Journal*, 34(1), 29–47.
Einolf, C. (2007) 'The Fall and Rise of Torture: A Comparative and Historical Analysis', *Sociological Theory*, 25(2), 101–121.
The Greek Case (1969) Application no. 00003321–3/67. 11 Yearbook of the ECHR 501.
Hillyard, P., Pantazis, C., Tombs, S. and Gordon, D. (eds) (2004) *Beyond Criminology: Taking Harm Seriously*. London: Pluto Press.
Ireland v. *UK* (1978) Application no. 5310/71 ECHR 1.
Livingstone, S. (2000) 'Prisoners' Rights in the Context of the European Convention on Human Rights', *Punishment and Society*, 2(3), 309–324.
Mesut Deniz v. *Turkey* (2013) Application no. 36716/07 ECHR 313.
Nagan, W.P. and Atkins, L. (2001) 'The International Law of Torture: From Universal Proscription to Effective Application and Law Enforcement', *Harvard Human Rights Journal*, 14(2), 87–121.
Novoselov v. *Russia* (2013) Application no. 33954/05 ECHR.
Republic of Ireland v. *United Kingdom* (1978) 2 EHRR 25.
Ribitsch v. *Austria* (1995) Application no. 18896/91 ECHR 55.
Roth, B. (2008) 'Just Short of Torture: Abusive Treatment and the Limits of International Criminal Justice', *Journal of International Criminal Justice*, 6(1), 215–239.
Selmouni v. *France* (1999) Application no. 00025803/94 ECHR.
Smith, R.K.M. (2003) *International Human Rights*. Oxford: Oxford University Press.
Spjut, R.J. (1979) 'Torture Under the European Convention on Human Rights', *The American Journal of International Law*, 73(2), 267–272.

Tarasov v.*Ukraine* (2013) Application no. 17416/03 ECHR.
Tomasi v. *France* (1992) Application no. 12850/87 ECHR.
UN General Assembly (1984) Convention Against Torture and Other Cruel, Inhuman or
Degrading Treatment or Punishment. 10 December.
Vladimir Romanov v. *Russia* (2009) Application no. 41461/02 ECHR.

4 Revealing as healing?

The language of 'torture' now explored, the following chapter analyses the extent to which former detainees' publication of their experiences of state violence in detention was motivated by a perceived need for personal healing. The chapter comments upon the popularised depiction of 'truth sharing' and its possible role in restoring a sense of self to those who may feel harmed through an experience of violence. It explores the attitudes of some former detainees in Northern Ireland to the legacy of their detention and to the language of catharsis and healing, and suggests that for many, a multitude of diverse, highly personal and contextual motivations may interact in making private memories part of a contested public history.

Within the context of the Northern Ireland conflict, the existence of documentary materials of books, newspaper clippings and pamphlets shows that there has been a constant dissemination of narratives *throughout* what might have appeared at times to be an intractable violent conflict, rather than simply after its apparent cessation. Elements of 'truth sharing' about violence are thus not restricted purely to post-conflict or transitional contexts, but can take place during times of war and/or unrest. These painful testimonies may be a divisive part of a cultural history which perpetuates conflict, rather than brings peace and transition. However, they may also contribute to 'moving on', and become part of the fragments of knowledge and shared experiences which may assist in bringing about an end to conflict. Thus the many complexities inherent in 'going public' are to be explored, rather than underestimated, and the dominant perceptions of 'truth sharing' must be deconstructed in order to better understand that the narration of violence is not something with clear beginnings and endings, which must only occur at particular historical moments or in societies labelled 'transitional'. There are a range of means and mechanisms available to those who wish to 'tell their story', and such mechanisms are not exclusive to post-conflict Truth Commissions, courtrooms, trauma centres or television studios. Nor can universal motivations and consequences be applied to those using these mechanisms to make their experiences public. This chapter explores the extent to which a perceived need for healing motivated former detainees to 'go public' about the state violence they had experienced in detention.

'Revealing as healing' in Northern Ireland

In order to understand what Cohen (2001) critiques as the deep veneration given to 'truth sharing' across many disciplines, it is important to study the lived experiences of narrating violence. Although the conflict in Northern Ireland contains (like all other conflicts) its own meanings, motivations, contexts, scales and significance, 'going public' about state violence has at its core the giving of testimony and the act of making private experiences public. This is not to collapse the vast differences between and/or within different Truth Commissions, memoirs and newspaper accounts, but rather to illustrate that each comes into being in much the same way, i.e. through the 'making public' of one's personal experiences of violence. The literature around 'truth sharing' across different instruments and contexts is full of abstract concepts, including 'healing'. These are often left undefined, particularly in discourses around transitional justice (Kerr and Mobekk 2007; Saunders 2011). Within much of the transitional justice literature, the individual is 'restored' through sharing their experiences, and the individual is themselves central to that process. Parmentier (2003) and Lambourne (2008) imply that this restoration is linked to healing. Yet, within official transitional justice mechanisms, such as those of the South African Truth and Reconciliation Commission (SATRC), individual healing risks becoming subsumed under a wider discourse of national healing. This illustrates some of the complexity of concepts like healing, when such language is tied into not only individual restoration, but the restoration of a shattered community, with all of the resultant political, social, economic and cultural nuances which further problematise attempts at definition (Minow 1998).

The former detainees who took part in the present study each constructed the meaning of healing in personal terms. It was seen as something which needed to take place at the level of the individual. Kerr and Mobekk's (2007: 136) claim that healing 'indicates restoring mental health to individuals who have suffered and been traumatised perhaps for a period of several years', was one which seemed to reflect the understanding shown by most former detainees. All of those interviewed for this book had previously 'gone public' with narratives of state violence which detailed regular beatings, scaldings and other forms of brutality and humiliation by state agents. They were asked to comment on the significance of healing in their own 'truth-sharing' experiences. In discussing the extent to which healing was a motivation behind publicising their own experiences, two interviewees recalled:

> I do not think I could have kept it to myself. I do not think I could. I think if I had kept it to myself I would have went mad. I think that there was a therapeutic reasoning for needing to tell the story. I do not think that any human being could *not* have told the story and still remained sane. To bottle up all those different emotions would have driven anybody round the twist.
>
> (Jim, emphasis in interview)

62 *Revealing as healing?*

The alternative for me would have been saying nothing, and looking back on it now, that would have been more detrimental to my mental well-being[1] than 'going public' and saying 'Right, it is out there now, now I'll deal with it!' I would always say 'go public'.

(Richard)

For Jim and Richard, revealing what had happened to them in detention was not directly perceived as psychologically beneficial in itself, but rather was a way of avoiding the greater harm they felt would result from keeping their experiences of state violence private. 'Going public' was related to a perceived need to prevent the worse trauma of silence. Despite otherwise describing himself as 'a very private type of person', Jim also claimed that 'talking about it to other prisoners at the beginning ... was therapeutic'. There are strong parallels here with the analysis offered by Stover (2005: 29), who argues that 'the notion that storytelling is healing is based on ... psychological studies demonstrating that individuals who repress intense emotional pain can suffer from physical and psychological problems'. Additionally, some otherwise critical voices, such as Wessely and Deahl (2003: 12), still acknowledge that ideas around 'talking about trauma must be better than "repressing" or "bottling up" accords with a long and distinguished tradition in psychological treatment ... and has face validity'. Although it is not the intention here to consider in any depth the strengths and weaknesses of psychoanalytical perspectives and debates,[2] several of those interviewed alluded to the apparent repression of memories of victimhood in the present, despite having 'gone public' with these experiences in the past:

It is not that I have forgotten about it, but it does not sit at the front of my mind or consciousness. I do not know if you have detected it or not but I have to sort of jog my memory to bring things back. I suppose – I mean, I always think it is risky to try and one, self-medicate, and two, to be an armchair psychologist – but perhaps there is a certain amount of deliberately ignoring it, but I am not in a good position to say that. Others might decide that that is what I am doing, that I have buried it away there because it was unpleasant and have left it parked there so I can get on with my life. Over the years we all have to cope with our ups and downs, I have had to cope with ups and downs. What I try to do is just put them out of sight and get on with the other parts that I can cope with.

(Tommy)

Tommy thus reflected upon the popular understanding of concepts like 'repression', the demarcation of expert knowledges and the possible perceptions of his own 'deliberate ignorance' (Tommy). Other interviewees shared in this view that repression could be a conscious decision and one which could be broken down if desired:

I suppose on one level I have compartmentalized it, that allows me to pluck out when I need to the different strands or different pieces or the whole lot

Revealing as healing? 63

of it without it emotionally affecting me, and I can put it back into the box whenever I am finished and then just get on with my life.

(Jim)

Rather than the accidental and unwelcome 'slipping' of unpleasant memories into full awareness, Jim asserted complete control over his story of state violence, arguing that he could choose when to consider his experience. He chose to further emphasise his own freedom and agency in doing so by suggesting that: 'I would speak about it now and again, but it is not something I would let intrude into my life. It is not major. It is not a major thing for me.' For both Jim and Tommy, agency was a central aspect of their narrative experiences. They were able to control their experiences in a way which framed them as no longer harmful.

The consequences of revealing

However, in contrast to Jim and Richard, a number of former detainees did not frame their motivation for 'going public' in terms of a need to avoid the harm of silence. They chose instead to comment on healing as a possible unintended consequence (rather than cause) of their public narrative about experiences of detention. Although the ability of individuals to 'armchair self-diagnose' had been critiqued by Tommy, some of those interviewed suggest that revealing their experiences had contributed towards a sense of personal healing, even though they did not recall it as a significant and/or motivating factor for 'going public'. Most of those interviewed recalled that 'going public' had been a positive experience and one that they would often seek to repeat. Laurence indicated that 'it felt good to get it all out. I don't have any problems in talking about it'. Similarly, Interviewee PJ, who was not involved in the IRA's armed struggle, asserted:

Anytime that I speak to people about these experiences I feel good, because I know that it is going to reach somebody's ear. I spoke out quite a lot, all my life and still do.

The existence of an audience to bear witness to their narratives of state violence was linked into 'feeling better' by Interviewee PJ and was also deemed important by Liam, who stated that:

I would have to admit I do get satisfaction from letting people know what these people did to us. I do ... I think it is a healing – maybe it is a silly way I have of dealing with it, but to me it worked and it works. I think I am a better person for it and I feel better for it.

'Going public' therefore was experienced as beneficial for these two former detainees at the personal level. The related language of catharsis conveys a range of complex meanings. For Hayes (1998, 2002), it forms part of a popular journalistic

64 *Revealing as healing?*

shorthand for the release which might be felt as people tell their story, as a purging or cleansing of harmful elements. It in part reflects the possibility of empowerment through testimony and storytelling (Braithwaite 2006). In contrast to Jim, Liam and PJ (in particular), other interviewees had less positive recollections about their experiences of narrating state violence, which suggests that attitudes to 'truth sharing' are diverse and heterogeneous, even within a community of former detainees that contains many elements of shared or similar experiences. Tommy, Harry and Michael (especially) attached little significance to their experience of narrating state violence. Michael stated that 'it has never been difficult to speak about it ... I've no regrets about going public. But I don't think it was a catharsis. Not that I am aware of.' He argued that 'going public' was not healing, as his memories of state violence were not experienced (or at least not remembered) as so harmful that they could be damaging to his sense of self. Tommy also analysed the potential for his own testimony to result in catharsis:

> I certainly never felt that that was what I was doing or that it was of any great benefit because I had a whole lot of problems to cope with. [That time when your story was recorded – can you describe to me how you felt afterwards?] I don't really think there was any great sense of relief, catharsis or anything ... I can't recall feeling any great sense of relief. It wasn't like that ... I don't think telling the story was any great catharsis and it certainly didn't lift the pain. I don't want to be facetious, but it didn't cure my wrists[3] or anything like that.
>
> (Tommy)

Tommy did not experience 'revealing as healing', but nor was his 'going public' with a personal narrative of violence felt to be harmful. It may have failed to heal the long-lasting injuries he sustained as a result of his violent interrogation, but 'going public' about his experiences of violent interrogation was 'not damaging to [his] equilibrium' (Tommy). Other interviewees also shared this neutral or indifferent perception of the potential for personal healing through the public narration of experiences of violence:

> There was no sense of relief, or [the feeling] 'Glad we got that out' ... I didn't feel anything the first time [my story was recorded]. It was just a story of what happened. To me there was no trauma about it, no elation about telling it or no relief. To me it was just something that had happened and I came though it and that was it ... I've no problems in telling it, but it won't make me feel any better in telling it.
>
> (Harry)

Such examples reflect former detainees' feelings about the limited therapeutic value of 'going public'. They suggest that the dominant popular imagery of 'revealing as healing' is oversimplified, and is, as Hayes (1998) suggests, a convenient soundbite which obfuscates a complex and unpredictable process. Yet it

Revealing as healing? 65

remains a powerful and popular mantra, and one which maintains the dominance of a 'common and collective wisdom that it is better to "cough it out" ... than to keep pain festering inside' (Hamber 2003b: 7).

This is not to say that former detainees reject the notion of 'revealing as healing' outright. Despite their own perceptions, some of those interviewed who had previously dismissed the healing potential of revealing their own experiences still recognised the apparently cathartic power of testimonies for others:

> My wife is a counsellor and people come to her. Some have been ex-prisoners and they have told her stories. She says to me that they do need to tell it, and get it out because it still affects them.
>
> (Harry)

> For some people the catharsis of telling the story may be beneficial.
>
> (Michael)

Therefore the potential for healing through revealing was still recognised by those former detainees who recalled (or were still) feeling relatively neutral or even dismissive about the healing value of making their own experiences of state violence part of a contested public history. As witnessed in the words of former detainees, revealing *may* be healing for some people, but should not be perceived as a universal 'easy' panacea for all who experience violence and its legacy (Hayner 2002). The apparent indifference of some former detainees towards the 'healing' potential of public testimony may be the result of several factors which are not mutually exclusive. First, the initial trauma and the memories of those experiences may not have been recalled as so personally destructive that they required 'healing' from. Some of those interviewed were now partly dismissive of the violence they had experienced so powerfully in the past. Here the language of 'catharsis' feels misplaced. Second, there may have been other additional factors which meant that individual 'healing' was problematic, such as the scars and physical sequelae of violent experiences. Third, a personal indifference to the dominant therapeutic paradigm of healing may be related to motivations for going public which were never linked or intended to bring about personal healing, but were instead motivated by other socio-political factors, such as the need to address state denials, assert legitimacy, raise awareness or promote particular conceptions of the conflict. These motivations are addressed throughout this book.

Revealing and risks

Cohen (2001) warns against any oversimplification or exaggeration of the 'healing power' of 'truth sharing', and offers a convincing critique of the theory behind such popular discourses. His work is equally dismissive of the 'assumption that mental health requires the excavation, explanation and even reliving of painful experiences' and argues 'the value[s] of telling the truth ... are not

66   *Revealing as healing?*

universal brain mechanisms, but highly contextualised linguistic devices and cultural practices that vary across time and social space' (Cohen 2001: 50). Ross (2003: 45) also warns against the 'simplistic assumptions about violence and voice, testimony, truth and healing' which lie at the heart of many official 'truth-sharing' exercises, particularly in relation to the SATRC.

Hayner (2002: 6) too, notes that 'it is often asserted that digging into the truth and giving victims a chance to speak offers a healing or cathartic "experience" [and yet] little scientific evidence is yet available on this question'. Hamber *et al.* (2000: 19) uses data collected following the South African Truth and Reconciliation Commission (SATRC) to critique the dominance of discourses which profess revealing as healing, and asserts that the uncomfortable reality that sharing harmful experiences will not suddenly result in healing can be evidenced by the critical recollections held by some survivors and their families about the work of the SATRC. Similar studies of the SATRC by Graybill (2002) also concluded that 'perhaps the cathartic value of testifying ... [was] overemphasised ... [and that] many victims, after their initial relief, found themselves months later re-experiencing the trauma and despondency'.

Thus those who 'go public' might be vulnerable to emotional distress and physical pain when reliving experiences of violence (Mollica 2006). Socio-cultural factors might contribute to a stigma against survivors (Hamber *et al.* 2000; Oravecz *et al.* 2004). In their work on the SATRC, Ross (2003: 45) illustrates how socio-cultural pressures impacted upon the experiences of female truth-sharers in South Africa 'who spoke about secrecy and the multiple levels at which activism and violence created silences, [even] within family life'. Only half of the interviewees in Hamber *et al.*'s (2000) SATRC research expressed relief about participating in the public narration of their experiences, which would suggest that the therapeutic value of 'truth sharing' has been somewhat exaggerated: 'although the telling of the truth may have been cathartic for some; it does not seem to have helped many of the victims cope with their tragedies in a convincing manner' (Hamber *at al.* 2000: 33: see also Hamber 2002).

The sense in which state violence is experienced may be different both between and within combatant and non-combatant groups at the SATRC, and the experiences of that Commission should certainly not be seen as universalised norms or easily transferred mechanisms that can be applied to all situations of conflict and/or transition, including Northern Ireland. Yet, the frequent use of truth sharing to achieve 'healing' raises questions that traverse cross socio-political, psychological and cultural boundaries (Sangster 1999). Sangster (1999) describes two perspectives on the purpose of 'truth sharing'; first, truth as a means to achieve justice, and second as 'the act of giving voice to truth as useful in itself' (Sangster 1999: 2). It is this latter formulation which Sangster (1999) finds most problematic, and argues that something else is needed to turn truth sharing into something beneficial. It is not revealing which is healing, but the possible socio-political and legal consequences which might result from the narration of state violence which are of greater benefit to survivors (Sangster 1999). In support, Field (1999:7) asserts that:

Revealing as healing? 67

the act of 'truth sharing' itself is insufficient for complete healing and falls far short of what is necessary for these survivors to rebuild their lives; the 'healing' possibilities of ... testimony should not be exaggerated to mythical curative levels.

Whilst the works of e.g. Sangster (1999), Field (1999) and Cohen (2001) rightly caution against the simplistic assumption that revealing results in healing, the potentially harmful relationship between experiences of violence and their narration remains relatively ambiguous and unexplored. Although generally supportive of the healing power of testimony, Laub (1992: 67) recognises that for some people, making public their experiences can be painful. This appears to be reflected in the present study by Interviewee 'F', a former detainee who *had* 'gone public' about the state violence he had experienced whilst in detention, but argued that 'I never bought into the idea that revealing is healing. I don't think revealing what happened to me is healing.... It hasn't got any easier to talk about.' Other former detainees recalled similar *negative* feelings about their experiences of 'going public'. Interviewee 'P' observed that 'sometimes after I've spoken out about the brutality, I just want to blank it out. I think it gets harder to speak about it'.

Popular depictions of the catharsis achieved through revealing personal experiences of violence are therefore strongly contrasted by the feelings of some former detainees, some years after they first made their private experiences of violence part of a public narrative of the conflict in Northern Ireland. For Interviewees 'F' and 'P', there were no therapeutic consequences which they felt had resulted through revealing what had happened to them. Interviewee 'F' in particular, recalled that 'going public' had been difficult and unpleasant, and had remained so despite all the years which had passed since he first told his story. He stated 'I remember having a bad feeling about an interview and I still have a bad feeling ... I did not want to do those interviews, basically because I am quite a private person – believe it or not!' (Interviewee 'F').

In this instance 'going public' was perceived not as healing, but as harmful to the individual. Some interviewees – including Interviewee 'F' recalled feeling mildly pressured by family, friends and other external influences into telling their stories about the violence they had experienced (and this is explored in greater depth in the following chapters). The dominant discourses that depict revealing as personally desirable thus begin to fracture, in spite of populist assertions that 'mental health requires the excavation, explanation and even reliving of painful experiences', which are similarly critiqued by Cohen (2001: 124). The revealing seen in the testimony of Interviewee 'F' had not been healing but instead had been difficult and painful and still remained so years later:

Talking about that period would – for me – be traumatising. It would not and did not benefit me at all.... The only reason I am talking to you now is because of ... pressures towards change. I strongly believe that knowledge and ideas need to be the right knowledge and the right ideas and they all

68 *Revealing as healing?*

need to be thrown into the middle along with all the other ideas … [It is problematic] if the information is not there from all perspectives.

(Interviewee 'F')

During the data collection process, Interviewee 'F' asserted that although 'talking about the period is traumatic', he felt a strong motivation to take part in the discussion of his reasons for 'going public' and to elaborate on the ways in which the experience had not been beneficial for him on a personal level. 'Going public' had not led to the powerful imagery of 'catharsis … healing through purging ourselves of the offending emotions, freeing ourselves from the shackles of a traumatic past and ridding ourselves of bad memories' (Hayes 1998: 44). Yet, like most of the former detainees interviewed for this book, a deeply personal healing had never been his motivation for 'going public'. Instead, the potentially educative function of speaking out was a motivating factor in making his private memories part of a wider public narrative, though he still felt that his narrative had not healed the personal and highly individualised harm of the state violence he had experienced during detention.

Remaining silent

Within the context of the conflict in Northern Ireland, most of those featured in the study had 'gone public' during the 1970s at a time when violence was at its most prevalent (according to figures by Smyth and Fay 2000; McKittrick *et al.* 2007). Fears of further violence can be seen in the recollection by Interviewee 'F' of his feelings of uncertainty around an early discussion with media outlets about what he and others had experienced in detention:

I think what happened was the paper came up to us and said 'We heard you were beaten around. We want that information. Are you prepared to do it?' All of us said 'No'. We did not want our names in the paper, we did not want to be targeted, and we did not want all the rest of it. We wanted to be able to go about our lives as reasonably easily as possible. But eventually they convinced us, 'Let us put your stories in, without mentioning your names'.

(Interviewee 'F')

Although Interviewee 'F' did later 'go public' about the violence he experienced against him using his own name, his initial reticence further illustrates the complicated nature of 'revealing as healing'. The IRA was targeted by state forces as an illegal organisation and members, suspected members, so-called sympathisers and their families were regularly subjected to harassment by the security forces (Boyle *et al.* 1975). As a result of the synthesis of a 'crime control' model with the theories and counter-terrorism strategies described by Kitson (1971), those living in areas labelled as 'nationalist' were particularly subjected to high levels of state surveillance and regularly had their day-to-day lives disrupted by harassment, house

Revealing as healing? 69

searches and raids. Furthermore, to be publicly identified as somebody suspected of being in the IRA regardless of the accuracy of that claim, may have had harmful consequences for those alleging an experience of state violence, and by association, their families and friends.

In addition to further harassment by the security community, some interviewees also suggested that their testimonies had the potential to make them targets for assassination by other paramilitary originations:

> In the North in those days, people would have been afraid to come out and say things because of the impact it might have had on their lives. They would have been afraid to come out and say 'I was brutalised' because they would be identified firstly as a suspect, and as one that was making these allegations against the state. Secondly, they would then be identifiable in the community. There are different reasons why people would be reluctant to go public, it is the same with anything. You want to protect your own person.
>
> (Interviewee 'F')

Interviewee 'F' later discussed how the security forces had taken him from detention into a staunchly Loyalist area where he had felt unsafe and vulnerable. This experience had further contributed to his feelings of discomfort in relation to 'going public'. Within this context of the conflict, there are thus significant pressures upon former detainees to refrain from going public with individual accounts of state violence. They may have remained silent about what harms may have occurred in detention and have decided to keep their own experiences of state violence private for a variety of reasons. There may be a real fear of reprisals, like those suggested by Interviewee 'F'.

The research has shown that 'going public' is a powerful process which attempts to reveal something of the multiplicity of 'truths' inherent in an experience of violence, but that this should not automatically be equated with healing. Furthermore, few studies describe the socio-cultural phenomena which may impact upon the silence of those who have experienced state violence in Northern Ireland and any discussion about the healing potential of testimony remains incomplete without such a consideration. Brutality against detainees was commonplace, particularly in the period 1971–1985, yet the number of personal narratives which have been publicised is quantitatively less than the number of complaints received. According to the Bennett Report (1979) between 1975 and 1978, there were approximately 7,538 recorded complaints made against the RUC alone. Of these recorded complaints, 21 per cent (1,562) concerned alleged assaults during interview (Bennett 1979). This suggests that there may be a very high number of former detainees who have personally experienced state brutality, but remained silent and have instead witnessed others 'go public' with similar stories. Former detainees who feature in this book suggested that, for those others, the desire to 'let sleeping dogs lie' and avoid the recalling and 'putting into words' of painful memories may have contributed to their silence.

70   *Revealing as healing?*

Harry, for example, vividly contrasted his own lack of discomfort in narrating his experiences with the silence of a close friend:

> It was never hard for me. I have mates who the same thing happened to and they will say 'I don't want to talk about this'. See [identifies another former detainee]? He does not like to talk about these things, they give him nightmares. I slag him a few times about jail, and he will say 'Shut up, I will not sleep at night!'. But it does not annoy me at all.
>
> (Harry)

The existence of former detainees' narratives of pain is in contrast to the silence of many others who share those experiences of violence, but whose only wish may be to forget or 'cope' in silence (Mollica 2006). Thus there may be many multifaceted explanations as to why some survivors of violence are silent about their experiences. Those who do not wish to 'go public' may be aided by 'official' silences regarding the subject of state violence and by strict controls on what forms of knowledge are deemed acceptable. Experiences of violence may remain locked in a deeply personal dimension, too difficult or too painful to be discussed, as a secret to be kept private. Such feelings may be temporary, or last indefinitely. Any knowledge of the violence experienced may be passed quietly from generation to generation only as rumour, hearsay or family secret. For others, their silence may not be driven by that difficult desire to forget, but by a fear of not being believed, or because of wider social, cultural or political processes that pressure both male and female survivors of state violence (and many other forms of violence and humiliation) into remaining silent (see Stanley 2002). These pressures might include personal experiences of powerful social control mechanisms, such as dominant depictions of masculinity or the powerful imagery of the 'Rough Tough Provo' (explored in Chapter 5). Like the friend referred to by Harry, some former detainees may not wish to 'go public' because their memories of state violence were and are experienced as too destructive, and they remain apparently unconvinced by the language of 'catharsis'. Several interviewees also referred to their practical 'opportunities to go public' that many other former detainees simply did not have. One anonymous former detainee (who chose not to be interviewed as part of the study) suggested that former IRA members who wished to go public in the present time about the violence they experienced in detention during the period 1971–1985 may now find their opportunities limited, in part due to the increasingly closer relationship between some elements of Republicanism and the British State and its agents, including the RUC's successor, the Police Service of Northern Ireland (PSNI).

There are thus no universally applicable reasons for the silence of some former detainees, just as there are no uniform explanations for the earlier reticence of those (such as Interviewee 'F') who *would later* 'move through' their initial silence in order to make their private memories part of a contested public narrative. Those who do not 'go public' about state violence may hope to act as gatekeepers to their own lived experiences and their lack of public testimony

Revealing as healing? 71

means that what happened to them (and how they felt about it) remains largely outside any historical narrative. The question 'why did you not tell your story?' cannot be asked of 'silent' former detainees if there is no public knowledge of their individual, personal experiences. As suggested throughout this book, the frequency, depth and commonalities inherent in many of the publicised narratives about experiences of state violence in the detention system of Northern Ireland suggests that there are many former detainees who *have* indeed remained silent and do not wish to discuss their experiences in a public way. They appear only in the shadows of the narratives of others and in the stories about what happened to 'other comrades' in 'other cells' at 'other times'.

Additionally, 'going public' about state violence experienced during detention may not readdress a connection to wider society which can break down during conflict and render survivors silent (Ross 2003; Yawar 2004). One former detainee commented:

> I took [name] up to the Kesh and I said to [them] before 'You will not get anything out of this'. [They] said 'How do you know?' and I said 'Unless you have been there and went through it, you cannot experience what it was like, the whole feeling, the mental things, the whole lot about going on the blanket' and all of that.
>
> (Harry)

For Harry, simply communicating his experiences had limited meaning and he further suspected that those who would later visit the spaces in which he had experienced state violence would be unable to understand what he had felt. For him, his personal narrative held power and meaning only within the community of former prisoners who may have had similar experiences. Feldman's (1991) work into the cultural construction of the 'body', memory and violence in Northern Ireland also suggests that a number of former detainees feel this sense of enclosed ownership over their narratives and that this has helped to strengthen relationships within the former detainee community. This, however, came at the cost of excluding others, who were thought by detainees such as Harry to be unable to 'relate' to former detainees' experiences of detention and imprisonment.

To 'bear witness'

'Going public' therefore remains a deeply personal decision and one which results from a wide range of motivations, as explored throughout this book. It is both a public and a private process, the experiences of which remain unpredictable and highly individualised. Liam commented upon the diversity of narrative experiences within communities of former detainees:

> Everybody is different. People are comfortable going public with things that other people are not. Maybe they are more reserved. They are not as forward

72 *Revealing as healing?*

as other people might be. I respect that and I think other people should respect that.

The process of making private memories part of a public discourse is also an inherently social process that can risk locating survivors in harmful narratives of victimisation (Minow 1998; Paris 2001) in which they remain symbols of state violence, rather than human beings with agency and dignity. Survivors of state violence and their stories should not be reduced to a legacy of dehumanised, sensationalised pornographies of violence and victimhood, or to the 'spectacles of suffering' described by Linfield (2000). When such an unbalancing occurs, the personal and individualised pain of survivors may be overlooked (Quiroga and Jaranson 2005). All involved in research with survivors of state violence must recognise that 'the appropriation of people's stories of pain, for whatever well intentioned reasons, is a morally and ethically problematic act' (Godwin Phelps 2004: 9). As Minow (1998), Hamber *et al.* (2000), Hamber (2003a), Paris (2001) and Ross (2003) all suggest, when survivors of state violence become little more than political symbols, processes of 'truth sharing' may be experienced as equally dehumanising as the initial abuse itself and deeply harmful to a person's sense of self.

However, not all those interviewed experienced the consequences of 'truth sharing' as reductionist, harmful or dehumanising. Although not explicitly framed in the language of healing, some former detainees wished to discuss the positive reactions from Republican communities to their testimonies:

> I think people would have a respect for me because I came forward and told my side of it, and I think people would have a sort of admiration there ... There is a certain respect there from Republicans and from Nationalist people.
>
> (Liam)

> People who know me in the social aspect would say I was a reasonably pleasant sort of guy, but people who would know me and know that I had been a political activist, former prisoner and blanket man – someone as quite strong in my unbendingness – then I think they would have a particular regard for me and my character.
>
> (Michael)

> I suppose that if you were to go away somewhere, you could go out into town and into Nationalist and Republican circles there would be comments. Someone would introduce you as one of the 'Hooded Men' or something, or buy you a pint.
>
> (Jim)

'Going public' with detailed experiences of state violence may lead to an increased sense of respect and status within sections of Republican communities.

Revealing as healing? 73

The role of audience is thus a crucial part of 'truth sharing' and it may be the response of an audience which transforms a difficult experience into a positive one. Liam, Michael and Jim argued that their narrative testimonies led to a greater awareness of their experiences within their own communities and contributed to a sense of valour and kudos in relation to their 'unbendingness' (Michael).[4]

It would therefore be an oversimplification to construct a binary argument which is clearly for or against the 'making public' of personal experiences of state violence. The recognition of narrative as an intersection between two dynamics and not a complete transformation from the private pain into public knowledge is particularly powerful. Stories of state violence are a place where both of these aspects intersect (Feitlowitz 1998), thus publicising experiences of state violence can be both an intrinsically private and deeply public act simultaneously.

Looking back but 'moving on'

The former detainees interviewed as part of the present study had already taken part in a form of 'truth sharing', as they all made their private experiences of pain part of a public narrative through a range of different mechanisms, including local and national media, the publications of civil society and non-governmental organisations, and/or in detailed memoirs. Many of those interviewed had done so contemporaneously or as soon as possible after their experiences of state violence, often through smuggled 'comms' and notes from prisons, yet there were others who had 'gone public' twenty years after their experiences (e.g. Laurence and 'P'). Their perception of the potential of new testimony to 'heal' detention experiences of the 1970s and 1980s contrasted with much of the discourse on 'truth sharing' and might be worth bearing in mind as Northern Ireland seeks to 'make peace with the past'. There was a sense of pessimism about the potential of 'new' testimonies to facilitate positive change of any kind:

> It is still my story but [pauses]. I think you need to move on with your life. Life is too short. You will not forget about it. You do not forget about it. But I think you need to move on. That is why my big mate thinks the world owes him everything – he is not moving on.
>
> (Interviewee 'P')

Several former detainees who had not described feeling traumatised in 'going public' also made reference to similar semantics of 'moving on,' yet they located these within other people, rather than themselves. This reflects the extent to which communities of former detainees are, like all communities, internally fractured and fragmented, rather than a homogeneous whole in which all knowledge, understanding and experiences are universal:

> A lot of people have been saying to themselves 'It is over. I am out of jail. I am away from it.' Or even maybe something like 'I am not in the movement

74   *Revealing as healing?*

anymore'. I am living my life now. I am not saying they will forget about it, what happened to them, but they will not talk about it. They just want to get on with their lives.

(Harry)

It has happened, and it has been compartmentalised and put away in the archives of their memory never to come out again. A lot of them would say 'How relevant [for today] are the "Hooded Men" of 1971?' How relevant is that now? They would say 'Well, it has happened now and that is it, I have no need to go over that again.' That would be the attitude of quite a lot of people.

(Richard)

Yet not all former detainees were so dismissive of the value of 'going public' with accounts of previous state violence. This finding further emphasises the diversity and heterogeneity of former detainees' experiences. Interviewees 'F', Michael and Tommy argued that there was some *limited* value in 'going public', but that this was entirely subjective and 'depend[ant] on the reasons why you are doing it' (Interviewee 'F'). They argued that:

I probably would not see any reason for doing it now. There is no big push for it, there are no big reasons why. If, as individuals, their stories are told and put into some sort of record then that might help them, but not other than that. I just cannot see a process for it.

(Michael)

I think it is *over.* But I would still see it as a useful thing to be carried out in controlled circumstances by academics with the objective of teaching the world.

(Tommy, emphasis in interview)

I do not think there is a value in doing it now about what happened in the 1970s, unless someone has something new that they wanted to come forward with that has not been documented.

(Interviewee 'F')

The perception that narrating state violence can be understood as a means to an end, rather than simply as an end in itself, is central to a detailed understanding of the motivations and significances of 'going public' for former detainees. The apparent simplicity of the 'revealing is healing' mantra is complicated by the diverse and contrasting narrative experiences of those former detainees who 'went public' about state violence in Northern Ireland.

The arguments presented in this chapter have shown that there are significant problems with the popular premise that 'revealing is healing'. It is overemphasised within the literature of the social sciences, and the psychoanalytical literature is, according to Summerfield (2002: 1105) similarly 'replete with ... sweeping statements that lack validity and are pathologising and stigmatising'. More extensive research is needed to better understand why 'truth sharing' is given such a mythological status along with the perceived universality of testimony as part of healing (Herman 2001), particularly when the experiences of some survivors of violence suggest that the narration of their experiences is a painful and harmful process (Hamber *et al.* 2000). The search for personal healing though revealing also ignores the social, cultural and structural powers which may contribute firstly to an experience of violence and secondly to the silence and/or narrative sharing of those who have experienced it (see Prillelntsky 1999; Hamber 2003b). Fuelled by pop psychology, media and art, there is a popular and easy imagery of catharsis and an often uncritical perception that happiness requires a 'working through' of the issues (Hayes 1998, 2002).

However, such criticism of the popular depictions of the healing power of narratives does not mean that the revealing of personal experiences should be seen as undesirable. An argument can be made that, at times, for some people revealing *is* indeed healing. The Consultative Group on the Past (Eames and Bradley 2009: 96) reported that many of those groups and individuals it consulted with about the conflict in Northern Ireland 'advocate the cathartic nature of sharing their story'. The Group's recommendations are explored in further depth in Chapter 8 of this book. Although not explicitly using this language of healing, many of those interviewed for the current book framed their experiences of 'going public' in an otherwise beneficial way and indicated that they were always willing to narrate their experiences of state violence. They were also willing to help others to do the same:

> I have been speaking about it for thirty odd years ... I still feel that it is a story that needs to be told. It is truthful. It is honest. It is probably about man's inhumanity to man, when you can do that to another human being.
>
> (Liam)

> I spoke out all my life and still do.
>
> (Interviewee PJ)

> I think ex-detainees should continue to go public, absolutely. I think that if you have something that is relevant in a historical context, then it is remiss of you not to get it out.... So of course, if ex-prisoners have been brutalised or whatever they should speak out, totally and absolutely!
>
> (Richard)

The extent to which a positive understanding of 'going public' can equate to a 'healing' experience of revealing is difficult to measure. In conclusion then, there are no universal norms or rules about the therapeutic potential of healing through revealing. The tendency within much of the literature and also within popular discourse is to hold up 'truth' as a miracle cure, and as Hamber (2003a:

76 *Revealing as healing?*

n.p.) warns 'we should not fall into the trap of simplistically arguing that revealing (telling the truth) is instantaneously healing as it is commonly held' (see also Hayes 1998). This is not to suggest that 'revealing' *cannot* be 'healing'. Rather, it argues that there is a need for further research into the reality of 'going public' with accounts of state violence (particularly as the discourse suffers from a general absence of sociological examination and an over-reliance on the SATRC as a source of data).

'Going public' is by its nature a '*truth-sharing*' process which involves more than just one voice, and the role of audience is therefore deeply significant in Northern Ireland (and elsewhere). Furthermore, the impact of social cultural aspects such as masculinities, the language of legitimacy within the conflict, and the existence of contested and competing depictions of 'truth' may all play central roles in the narration of personal experiences of state violence and its legacy. Most significantly, survivors own interpretations of the ownership and significance of their narratives are sometimes missing from the analytical discourse, at a cost to knowledge and the understanding of lived violence. Until this balance is addressed, the easy language of 'revealing as healing' will remain and will continue to obfuscate and misappropriate the personal and political complexities of making public private experiences, particularly when those experiences are part of the subjugated knowledges and contested narratives of a conflict.

Notes

1 See Jamieson and Grounds (2002) and Jamieson *et al.* (2010) for an examination of the well-being of former prisoners.
2 For an outline of these complexities, see Laub (1992), Felman and Laub (1992) and Agger and Jensen (1990, 1996). A discussion about the repression of painful memories can also be found in Baumeister *et al.* (1998).
3 Tommy's wrists had been subjected to dorsi-flexing during interrogation, which involves repeatedly bending the hands backwards and forwards along the forearms. This places the muscles of the hand, wrist and arm under stress. The existence of such a technique was confirmed by former RUC officers in an interview with Cobain (2010).
4 Were former detainees to narrate their experiences and emphasise to such an audience that they had 'broken' under interrogation and had 'given away' valuable information, it is unlikely that they would be granted the same respect and status.

References

Agger, I. and Jensen, S. (1990) 'Testimony as Ritual and Evidence in Psychotherapy for Political Refugees', *Journal of Traumatic Stress*, 3(1), 115–130.
Agger, I. and Jensen, S. (1996) *Trauma and Recovery Under State Terrorism*. London: Zed.
Baumeister, R.F., Dale, K. and Sommer, K.L. (1998) 'Freudian Defence Mechanisms and Empirical Findings in Modern Social Psychology: Reaction Formation, Projection, Displacement, Undoing, Isolation, Sublimation, and Denial', *Journal of Personality*, 66(6), 1081–1124.

Revealing as healing?   77

Bennett Report (1979) *Report of the Committee of Inquiry into Police Interrogation Procedures in Northern Ireland* [Cmnd 7497]. London: HMSO.

Boyle, K., Hadden, T. and Hillyard, P. (1975) *Law and The State: The Case of Northern Ireland.* London: Martin Robertson.

Braithwaite, J. (2006) 'Narrative and "Compulsory Compassion"', *Law and Social Inquiry*, 31(9), 425–446.

Cobain, I. (2010) 'Inside Castlereagh: "We Got Confessions By Torture"' *Guardian*. 11 October. Available at: www.guardian.co.uk/uk/2010/oct/11/inside-castlereagh-confessions-torture (accessed 31 August 2012).

Cohen, S. (2001) *States of Denial: Knowing About Atrocities and Suffering.* London: Polity Press.

Eames, R. and Bradley, D. (2009) *Report of the Consultative Group on the Past.* (HC171) London: HMSO. Available at: www.cgpni.org/fs/doc/Consultative%20Group%20on%20the%20Past%20Full%20Report.pdf (accessed 7 January 2013)

Feitlowitz, M. (1998) *A Lexicon of Terror: Argentina and the Legacies of Torture*. New York: Oxford University Press.

Feldman, A. (1991) *Formations of Violence: The Narrative of the Body and Political Terror in Northern Ireland*. Chicago: University of Chicago Press.

Felman, S. and Laub, D. (1992) *Testimony: Crises of Witnessing in Literature, Psychoanalysis and History.* London: Routledge.

Field, S. (1999) 'Memory and the Truth and Reconciliation Commission and the Significance of Oral History in a Post-Apartheid South Africa', *The Truth and Reconciliation Commission: Commissioning the Past*. University of the Witwatersrand. 14 June.

Godwin Phelps, T. (2004) *Shattered Voices: Language, Violence and the Work of Truth Commissions*. Philadelphia: University of Pennsylvania Press.

Graybill, L.S. (2002) *Truth and Reconciliation in South Africa: Miracle or Model?* London: Lynne Rienner Publishers.

Hamber, B. (2003a) 'Rights and Reasons: Challenges for Truth Recovery in South Africa and Northern Ireland', *Strengths and Limitations of Truth Commissions: The Cases of Argentina, Chile, South Africa and Guatemala.* Centre for International Studies. Cambridge, UK. 6 March. Available at: http://ir.lawnet.fordham.edu/cgi/viewcontent.cgi?article=1893&context=ilj (accessed 2 February 2010).

Hamber, B. (2003b) 'Does the Truth Heal? A Psychological Perspective on the Political Strategies for Dealing with the Legacy of Political Violence', in Biggar, N. (ed.) *Burying the Past: Making Peace and Doing Justice after Civil Conflict.* Washington: George Town University Press.

Hamber, B., Nageng, D. and O'Malley, G. (2000) 'Telling It Like It Is: Understanding the Truth and Reconciliation Commission from the Perspective of Survivors', *Journal of Psychology in Society*, 20, 18–42.

Hayes, G. (1998) 'We Suffer Our Memories: Thinking About the Past, Healing and Reconciliation', *American Imago*, 55(1), 29–50.

Hayes, G. (2002) 'Thinking Beyond Truth and Trauma', *Flesh and Blood: Psychoanalysis, Politics and Resistance Conference.* London School of Economics, London. 20–22 April.

Hayner, P.B. (2002) *Unspeakable Truths: Facing The Challenge of the Truth Commissions.* London: Routledge.

Herman, J. (2001) *Trauma and Recovery: From Domestic Abuse to Political Terror.* London: Rivers Oram Press.

Jamieson, R. and Grounds, A. (2002) *No Sense of An Ending: The Effects of Long Term*

78 *Revealing as healing?*

Imprisonment amongst Republican Prisoners and Their Families. Monaghan: SEESYU Press.

Jamieson, R., Shirlow, P. and Grounds, A. (2010) *Ageing and Social Exclusion Among Former Politically Motivated Prisoners in Northern Ireland and the Border Region of Ireland*. Belfast: The Community Foundation of Northern Ireland.

Kerr, R. and Mobekk, E. (1997) *Peace and Justice: Seeking Accountability After War*. Cambridge: Polity.

Kitson, F. (1971) *Low Intensity Operations: Subversion, Insurgency and Peacekeeping*. London: Faber and Faber.

Lambourne, S. (2008) 'Transitional Justice and Peacebuilding after Mass Violence', *The International Journal of Transitional Justice*, 3(1), 28–49.

Laub, D. 'Bearing Witness, or the Vicissitudes of Listening', in Felman, S. and Laub, D. (1992) *Testimony: Crises of Witnessing in Literature, Psychoanalysis and History*. London: Routledge.

Linfield, S. (2000) 'Trading Truth for Justice? Reflections on South Africa's Truth and Reconciliation Commission', *Boston Review*, 25(3). Available at: www.bostonreview. net/BR25.3/linfield.html (accessed 31 August 2012).

McKittrick, D., Kelters, D., Feeney, B., Thornton, C. and McVea, D. (2007) *Lost Lives: The Stories of the Men, Women and Children Who Died as a Result of the Northern Ireland Troubles*. London: Mainstream Publishing.

Minow, M. (1998) *Between Vengeance and Forgiveness: Facing History after Genocide and Mass Violence*. Boston: Beacon Press.

Mollica, R.F. (2006) *Healing Invisible Wounds: Paths to Hope and Recovery in a Violent World*. Florida: Houghton-Miffin-Harcourt.

Oravecz, R., Hárdi, L. and Lajtai, L. (2004) 'Social Transition, Exclusion, Shame and Humiliation', *Torture: Journal on the Rehabilitation of Torture Victims and the Prevention of Torture*, 14(4), 3–15.

Paris, E. (2001) *Long Shadows: Truth, Lies and History*. London: Bloomsbury.

Parmentier, S. (2003) 'Global Justice in the Aftermath of Mass Violence: The Role of the International Criminal Court in Dealing with Political Crimes', *International Annals of Criminology*, 41(1-2), 203–224.

Prillelntsky, I. (1999) 'Critical Psychology Foundations for the Promotion of Mental Health', *Annual Review of Critical Psychology*, 1, 100–118.

Quiroga, J. and Jaranson, J.M. (2005) 'Politically Motivated Torture and its Survivors', *Torture: Journal on the Rehabilitation of Torture Victims and the Prevention of Torture*, 16(2–3), 1–112.

Ross, F.C. (2003) *Bearing Witness: Women and the Truth and Reconciliation Commission in South Africa*. London: Pluto Press.

Sangster, K. (1999) 'Truth Commissions: The Usefulness of Truth Telling', *Australian Journal of Human Rights*. 5(1), n.p. Available at: www.austlii.edu.au/au/journals/ AJHR/1999/5.html (accessed 31 August 2012).

Saunders, R. (2011) 'Questionable Associations: The Role of Reconciliation in Transitional Justice', *The International Journal of Transitional Justice*, 5(1), 119–141.

Smyth, M. and Fay, M. (2000) *Personal Accounts from Northern Ireland's Troubles: Public Conflict, Private Loss*. London: Pluto.

Stanley, E. (2002) 'What Next? The Aftermath of Organised Truth Telling', *Race and Class*, 44(1), 1–16.

Stover, E. (2005) *The Witnesses: War Crimes and the Promise of Justice in The Hague*. Philadelphia: University of Pennsylvania Press.

Summerfield, D. (2002) 'Effects of War: Moral Knowledge, Revenge, Reconciliation and Medicalised Concepts of "Recovery"', *British Medical Journal*, 325(4), 1105–1107.

Wessely, S. and Deahl, M. (2003) 'Psychological Debriefing is a Waste of Time', *The British Journal of Psychiatry*, 183(1), 12–14.

Yawar, A. (2004) 'Healing in Survivors of Torture', *Journal of the Royal Society of Medicine*, 97(8), 366–370.

5 The masculinity of 'making public'

To examine experiences of 'truth sharing' only in terms of their relationship to healing would ignore the powerful and diverse socio-cultural concepts which may enable men to take part in the production of narratives about pain, or alternatively 'close down' opportunities. The following chapter explores male former detainees' experiences alongside discussions about the meanings and significance of their own understanding of masculinity. The research compares the narrative experiences of those interviewed with the dominant depictions of gender found within the multidisciplinary literature on 'masculinities', paying particular attention to the ways in which male victimhood is portrayed within Criminological inquiry. By offering an early critical insight into men's experiences of victimisation, the chapter seeks to contribute to a refocusing of the study of male victimhood and shows how dominant understandings of gender do/do not contribute to making private memories of pain part of public history.

The meaning(s) of 'masculinity'

Despite its frequent usage, the meaning of 'masculinity' remains unclear and ill-defined (Clatterbaugh 1998). Definitions include those of positivist social science which 'yield a simple definition of masculinity describ[ing] the pattern of men's lives in a given culture' (Connell 2005: 67). This positivist approach aims to express what men are and to induce from those accounts a definition of masculinity. However, this standpoint is open to critique, in that it assumes a homogeneous community of men, who are distinct from (an equally homogeneous) community of women. As Newton (1994) acknowledges, gender is not a homogeneous entity. Rather than constructing definitions of masculinity from the outcomes of studying the many diverse and multifaceted aspects of the lives of men, positivist approaches to masculinity do not result from but *rely upon* assumptions of the binarisms of gender, and furthermore, they risk the reductionism of heterosexist biological approaches to male and female which ignore the cultural, political and socially constructed nature of 'gendered' power.

Within the epistemological framework postulated by Connell (2005), further attempts to define the meaning of masculinity can be conceptualised as a 'normative approach'. Here masculinity is perceived as a goal, as an aim of all men. This is

The masculinity of 'making public' 81

manifested through particular ways of 'doing "gender"' in relation to particular situations (Hamber 2007). Although such approaches acknowledge that masculinity is centred within a cultural framework (and furthermore, that all men might not be equally able to attain it) the concept remains deeply problematic. 'Few men actually match the "blueprint".... What is "normative" about a norm hardly anyone meets? Are we to say the majority of men are unmasculine?' (Connell 2005: 70).

Dominant definitions of masculinity often both begin and end within a local cultural framework, and most attempts at definition aim to identify the characteristics of a person who is labelled masculine. Within this localised framework, Whitehead and Barrett (2005: 15–16) suggest that masculinity signifies the 'behaviours, languages and practices, existing in specific cultural and organisational locations, which are commonly associated with males and thus culturally defined as not feminine'. The resulting essentialism 'picks a feature that defines the core of the masculine, and hangs an account of men's lives on that' (Connell 2005: 68). Within this reductionist perspective, men's experiences are reduced down to a list of core 'masculine' traits, which have often been represented in the local cultural context as aggression and so-called 'emotional illiteracy' (Goodey 1997). This both causes and results from the understanding that to show vulnerability is to show weakness and a supposedly feminine lack of self-control (Connell 2005; Harland 2009; Pelka 2004; Seidler 1994, 2007). This perspective fits neatly within an understanding of masculinity as relational, as the concept does not exist in a vacuum. Masculinity *is* what it *is not.*

Experiencing masculinities

Such theoretical and abstract discussions benefit from the detailed analysis of men's own interpretations of the meaning of masculinity, constructed in relation to their own experiences, cultures and modes of understanding. As part of the research for this book, male former detainees were asked to comment on whether their perception of their own masculinity had impacted in any way on their 'truth sharing' about experiences of victimisation. Given the opportunity to discuss the meaning and significance of masculinity, most of the interviewees referred back to a synthesis of essentialist and normative definitions surrounding what they felt were social expectations of manhood. They commented on a cultural standpoint which characterised masculinity (note not 'masculinities') as an absence regarding men's acknowledgement of personal victimhood:

> Masculinity? The cultural idea that men don't talk about their own victimisation probably is true … certainly in Ireland and Britain it's pretty universal (laughs). Men are *not supposed* to cry when they are hit and not cry out when they are hurt.
>
> (Tommy, emphasis in interview)

In his interpretation of the meaning and significance of masculinity, Tommy reflected back the powerful cultural imagery that 'boys do not cry'. From this

82 *The masculinity of 'making public'*

perspective, boys *may feel like* crying but this display of emotion is perceived as damaging and undesirable, something which should be avoided, fought against and denied (Seidler 1994). The cultural imagery of male-ness is tied up with power, invulnerability and dominance (Mac An Ghaill and Haywood 2007; Segal 2007). This leads to a lack of awareness around the impact of violence on the lives of men and has contributed to the relative absence of male victimhood from academic discourses (Stanko and Hobdell 1993). It is a form of hegemonic masculinity which Connell (2005: 76) suggests occupies a particular place in gender relations, but one which might shift and change. The concept of hegemony signifies the development of a culture in which a group can claim and sustain a position of social power through various forms:

> At any given time, one form of masculinity is ... *culturally exalted*. Hegemonic masculinity can be defined as the configuration of gender practice which embodies the currently accepted answer to the problem of the legitimacy of patriarchy, which guarantees (or is taken to guarantee) the dominant position of men and the subordination of women.
>
> (Connell 2005: 77, my emphasis)

Hegemonic masculinity therefore relates to one of a number of different meanings and interpretations of masculinity, its mechanisms and modes of control. It is tied to the depiction of masculinity which is dominant within a particular social, cultural and political field, but also to the ways in which it retains that dominance through the subordination of that deemed 'feminine' and, further, through the subordination of 'other' aspects of 'other' masculinities (Carrabine and Longhurst 1998). It need not be a form of masculinity as seen or experienced by all persons at all times in all places, but is hegemonic only in its dominant position within that particular sphere of social life (Newburn and Stanko 1994).

Within the interviews, participants often drew upon the 'culturally available notion' that vulnerability signified a threat to masculinity (Seidler 1994). Their analysis also contained personal insights into the construction and sourcing of their definitions of masculinity:

> Women expected certain things from men, macho men; they didn't want wimps in my father's day. They wanted to be swept off their feet by some big strong man, not someone who they would have to sweep away!
>
> (Interviewee 'F')

> Just grind the teeth and take it ... I think that women expect it from men in as much as men expect it from men.
>
> (Tommy)

Significantly, in this engagement with gendered power, both Interviewee 'F' and Tommy positioned women as crucially important in formulating and maintaining

The masculinity of 'making public' 83

the hegemony of particular forms of masculinity. Within this understanding, women are not passive bystanders in the construction of masculinity, but actively define (and police) what it means to be 'masculine'. For Interviewee 'F' in particular, it was *female power* that both sought out and constructed this particular form of Connell's (2005) 'culturally exalted masculinity'.

A number of interviewees thus constructed masculinity in terms of a synthesis of essentialist and normative criteria in which men were *not supposed* to talk about their own victimisation and men who spoke publicly of their victimhood risked being perceived as 'wimps', adding weight to Jefferson's (1994) observation that a failure to 'live up to' gendered ideals might lead to shame and/or stigma. Stanko and Hobdell's (1993: 403) research with male victims of assault outside the conflict/detention setting found that many participants 'admitted a reticence around speaking of the injuries they had suffered ... and their feelings related to the assaults [against them]'. In relation to the conflict in Northern Ireland, many of those former prisoners interviewed by Jamieson and Grounds (2002) also stated that displays of emotion by Republican male prisoners who had been victimised were also perceived as undesirable:

> You are never really encouraged to show any sorts of emotions as I say because you would show weakness ...
>
> (in Jamieson and Grounds 2002: 15)

> feel[ing] very low, but ... you couldn't even show that.
>
> (in Jamieson and Grounds 2002: 15)

> We had this attitude that we were rough, tough Provies, men don't cry.
>
> (in Jamieson and Grounds 2002: 15)

The comments of victimised male former prisoners reflect in part the popular cultural idea that displays of male vulnerability should be hidden in the private sphere, traditionally linked to the feminine (Seidler 1994). They represent a form of hegemonic masculinity which becomes particularly operationalised in the prison setting.

The masculinity of incarceration

Alongside the formal 'prison struggle' against state forces, there was also a struggle for masculine power akin to the 'invulnerable male' described by Stanko and Hobdell (1993). In many instances, former detainees recalled being brutalised by other men, usually male RUC officers or male prison guards ('screws'). Although both the paramilitary organisations and the security forces had female members, they were dominated by men and characterised by a hegemonic masculinity which was exaggerated by the conflict itself (Bairner 1999a, 1999b). The prison system, like all prisons, was in addition marked by the 'totality of masculinity' in its rituals and rules (Scraton *et al.* 1991). The narratives of

84   The masculinity of 'making public'

former detainees trace 'the violent encounters with the typical Goffmanesque assaults on personal identity that are associated with the total institution' (Feldman 1991: 152). This takes place in relation to the cells of the H-Blocks, the interrogation centres of Castlereagh, Gough, and Palace Barracks, and the (then unknown) destinations of the 'Hooded Men'.

State violence was used not only to gain information, but also to punish and humiliate (Aretxaga 1997). To be a male detainee or prisoner that had been 'broken' during interrogation was seen as a weakness, perhaps not only for the literal reason of giving away sensitive information (with the possibly violent consequences of being found to have done so), but also because it was in violation of a gendered hyper-masculinity. Though most of those interviewed chose to describe in detail state violence against them, none admitted to being 'broken' and would differentiate themselves from those who had. In this way, male power can be retained and its retention expressed through detainees' testimonies of resistance:

> They broke an awful lot of people and an awful lot of volunteers. They didn't break me though ... I'd say 70% of people in the H-Blocks confessed, owned up to one offence or another ... the H-Blocks were full of guys like that. I wasn't one of them. I never signed or admitted anything in my whole career as an IRA man.
>
> (Richard)

For Republican men, this kind of exemplary masculinity was articulated through the imagery of the 'Rough Tough Provo'. This presented Republicans as 'hard men' who were powerful, uncompromising, committed, strong both physically and mentally, who could be depended upon to provide resistance and to cope in any setting. The 'Rough Tough Provo' was not meant to 'crack' under the pressure of interrogations nor under the state violence of the prison regime. This idealised Republican (and also Loyalist) prisoner and would 'do their whack'[1] without displaying signs of vulnerability. In contrast to the often romanticised portrayal of solidarity between Republican prisoners, those 'conforming' prisoners who came off the 'blanket protest'[2] were given the dismissive and derogatory nickname of 'Squeaky Booters' by their fellow prisoners, due to the noise made by prison issue clothing and new rubber boots against the floors of the H-Blocks as prisoners were removed from the protest. In this way, prisoners themselves established and policed a particular form of masculinity which was closely tied to a hegemonic style of group resistance, the denial of 'weakness' and the negating (and stigmatising) of acts of individual autonomy. 'Squeaky Booters' became 'outsiders' within the framework of the protest. They were men whose strength, power, rationality and determination were taken away from them by their 'failure' to remain on the protests. Acceptance by others of their access to hegemonic forms of masculinity could be denied and their status within the community of Republican prison protesters brought into question.

Gendering 'going public' about state violence

Although the conflict in Northern Ireland adds a crucially important local dimension to this analysis, other studies of masculinities and imprisonment illustrate the problematic construction and maintenance of hegemonic masculinity across other systems of detention. In research in three prisons in England, Jewkes (2005: 53) similarly observed that male prisoners sought to reconcile feelings of fear and vulnerability with the construction and maintenance of a 'culturally acceptable masculine identity'. However, a review of the literature written by former detainees in Northern Ireland suggests that for many male Republican former prisoners, 'external work' *did* include making feelings of vulnerability part of a public history (or 'truth' in conflict). The existence of narrative testimonies detailing fear and pain articulated by male former detainees (and featured here in Chapter 2) challenges the assumption that men do not speak about their own experiences of victimisation. As shown previously, these narrative testimonies were often vividly illustrated and punctuated by expressions of emotion and vulnerability, a research finding mirrored by the secondary, edited accounts of Republican former prisoners found in Campbell *et al.* (2006):

> The bewilderment, rage, fear, hatred, powerlessness and vulnerability that consumed us was to know no respite.
>
> > (former detainee known as PC in Campbell *et al.* 2006: 64)

> I had a great fear of the beatings, I was really afraid ... and I wondered if I could take any more of this.
>
> > (former detainee known as PC in Campbell *et al.* 2006: 91)

The published detailed and emotive public narratives of victimisation written by male former detainees (and explored in previous chapters) challenge the notion that men's experiences of fear and pain are kept well hidden. Their deeply emotive recollections of their experiences of victimisation, anxiety and vulnerability contrast sharply with the powerful and popular depiction of men as emotionally illiterate (Goodey 1997). Their testimonies of victimisation are frequently deeply personal and include explicit references to feelings of fear, powerlessness and humiliation:

> They used to bang your head off the wall (laughs nervously). It wasn't funny but.... When I lay down, the room span around, [the nausea] lasted for two years and was really scary.
>
> > (Interviewee 'F')

> I could only think of an increase in the beatings and the cell searches. I didn't know if I could take anymore.... The pain was bad, but nothing compared to the humiliation I felt at that moment.
>
> > (former detainee known as JMQ in Campbell *et al.* 2006: 90)

86   *The masculinity of 'making public'*

Former detainees' accounts are indicative of a broad spectrum of victimisation in the prisons during the conflict and also reflect the similar narratives of many of those subjected to lengthy interrogations by state forces (Taylor 1980). These recollections present the reader with the minute details of dehumanising, frightening and humiliating experiences of imprisonment. Although it is deeply important to recognise that not all victims of state violence sought to narrate or publicise their experiences, the very existence of *any* personal accounts by men in the public sphere suggests that masculinity conceptualised only as emotional illiteracy represents the oversimplification of a complex concept – one which misses the ways in which masculinity might be negotiated in particular contexts (Messerschmidt 1993). Some of those interviewed sought to renegotiate masculinity by attempting to reconcile the dominant imagery of the 'Rough Tough Provo' with their experience of vulnerability and victimhood, through reference to the context of the excessive violence they felt they had suffered, which went 'beyond what *anyone* could endure' (Jim):

> Nobody screams more than me! (laughs).... But no, to be truthful, what happened to us was *so extreme* that the macho man image just didn't stand up. I cried, I pissed myself and I shit myself and I don't care who knows it.
> (Jim, emphasis in interview)

Jim's acknowledgement of vulnerability and loss of control first appears to challenge the language of 'the "John Wayne syndrome", "macho-man", "cave man", "defender", and "natural man" [which] articulates the existence of an ideal image of manhood' (Stanko and Hobdell 1993: 404) and the 'exemplary masculinity' described by Connell (2005). Yet through his re-positioning of violence as '*so extreme*' the image of the 'macho man' is not destroyed but reconfigured within the framework of Jim's narrative. For Jim, his experience went *beyond* that 'macho' imagery, thus allowing the image to remain and retain its powerful position. He understood his personal experiences as being so 'extreme' – so 'other' – as to fall *outside* the conceptual framework of masculinity, enabling that framework to survive. In this way, the concept of masculinity became little more than an irrelevance. As Seidler (1994: 154, emphasis in original) argues 'we [men] can *allow* ourselves to have these feelings [of fear] once we have been convinced we have reasons for them. This step is consonant with masculinity'.

Within this analysis, the 'Rough Tough Provo' with his 'exemplary masculinity' can be preserved, as it is only the most extreme conditions that can have any impact upon the 'macho' image. Such alternative interpretations suggest that interviewees do not imagine their accounts as records of their own vulnerability, but that they are instead attempts to reconcile their victimisation within the framework of hegemonic masculinity, partly by changing the meaning they attach to those experiences. Within this rationalising framework, boys *still* do not cry, unless they are brutalised '*beyond*' the extreme.

Humour as preserving 'The Rough Tough Provo'

These historical accounts and contemporary interviews also evidence further alternative strategies through which those who 'went public' sought to preserve an image of invulnerability. Campbell *et al.* (2006) suggest that humour was used to downplay the pains of imprisonment and this was reflected upon by two former detainees in the research for this current book:

> I would just be slagging[3] about it.... Different people would try and slag you for 'getting beaten with Mars Bars'.[4]
>
> (Harry)

> We had a laugh about it, even in the face of adversity.
>
> (Interviewee 'P')

Men's storytelling in and about prison represents a particular way of accomplishing and maintaining a sense of masculinity (Thurston 1996; Dowler 2002). For some of those who went public with accounts of the state violence they had experienced during detention, humour was recognised as a way through which victimisation could be reconstituted as something else. For Laurence, this humour was a significant element in his understanding of the legacy of his (and others') experiences:

> Sometimes you would get people together – maybe this isn't unique to Republican ex-prisoners – talking about those events and now they are done with a laugh, you know 'Ah we know what it was like'. It's a *safe way* of talking about a time when it really wasn't a laugh.
>
> (emphasis in interview)

Such an understanding is crucial to studies of victimhood and masculinity. Through the use of humour, men's experiences can be re-presented through the culturally dominant depiction of hegemonic masculinity. Furthermore, it may be that for some detainees and prisoners, the use of humour might be a way of coping with an overwhelming reality (Jewkes 2005). Through dialogue with other former detainees, experiences of suffering can be re-conceptualised as something else, something that men can speak about without shattering the image of the 'invulnerable male'.

'A group of We's'

Laurence's discussion of 'safe way of talking' refers not only to rituals of humour – particularly so-called 'black/dark humour' – that turned experiences of male victimisation into something which preserved the dominant depiction of male invulnerability, but also hinted at the network of shared support which some former detainees utilised in order to discuss their time in detention and its

88 *The masculinity of 'making public'*

legacy. The reframing of victimisation experiences can be observed in the testimonies of those who now sought to re-conceptualise their past narratives about state violence. Despite having previously 'gone public' about their experiences of state violence in detailed, visceral and strongly emotive narratives, some interviewees were now dismissive of the personal pain they had described so vividly in the past:

> It was no big deal.
>
> (Michael)

> There was no big shakes[5] about it. [Mock horror]. 'Your man did this and he stood on my face' [shrugs].
>
> (Harry)

For other interviewees, feelings of vulnerability were regularly projected or deflected onto others within their own narratives of victimisation. Some former detainees often referred to violence they had witnessed against others in detention and dismissed the violence they themselves experienced as being only relatively minor in comparison.

> I was a victim of it, as was all the blanket men. We all got beat up at one stage or another.
>
> (Richard)

> I was sort of lucky because I was taken to hospital, the rest were took back into the gaol and they had got *really bad* beatings ... I had heard about some of the others, some of them were to me quiet people, and they had got slapped all around. Some really bad beatings.
>
> (Harry, emphasis in interview)

In reference to other narratives of male victimhood outside the Northern Ireland setting, Seidler (1994: 151) asks 'are we to say that in Weberian terms, they can choose to give their experience a different meaning, for as far as they are concerned, it was nothing?' Like those prisoners featured in studies by Scraton *et al.* (1991), Evans and Wallace (2007: 488) also reported:

> softer, gentler feelings among inmates witnessing violence among prisoners and from prison guards, which suggests an ability to empathise with the powerlessness and fear of others that would normally be mocked by the traditional hegemonic male.

It would appear that it is/was the communal nature of victimisation within the detention system of Northern Ireland which significantly contributed to the creation of a 'safe space' where pain *could* be explored without fracturing hegemonic images of masculinity. Rather than engage in 'denials of self-other

The masculinity of 'making public' 89

connection' (Chodorow 1989 in Jefferson 1994: 22) the communal nature of violence experienced by former detainees allowed it to be transformed into narrative testimony in a process which was often supported by wider, shared experiences both in and outside of the detention system. The importance of a community of detainees, many of whom were able to share narratives about similar experiences, was emphasised by interviewees' frequent use of the first person plural pronoun – 'We'. This was acknowledged by one interviewee:

> Republicans speak in the 'We'. A group of 'We's' rather than a group of 'I's. You can ask someone 'Well, what happened to you?' and they will say 'We' were in the wing, … 'Aye but what happened to you?' Constantly it's a 'We'.

> (Laurence)

In this way, violence against men's bodies could be re-conceptualised as violence against a body of men. As O'Hearn (2009: 491) notes, prisoners 'appropriated and then built a solidary culture'. They created and maintained a sense of masculinity focused on willpower, determination and solidarity (Sharoni 1999), one which risked the *individuality* of the experience – both of the state violence and of the lived reality of going public – becoming secondary to the communal experience. The narratives linked to community contrasted with the H-Block regime which refused to recognise anything other than separate inmates (Feldman 1991). The shared experiences of state violence in detention also created a third space between the public and private spheres, where imprisoned men no longer had to 'mirror the unrealistic image of the superhero. Instead this space represented a home place where these men could simply be themselves' (Dowler 2002: 58). Despite – or perhaps because of – there being little in dominant masculine culture which values sharing vulnerability (Harland 2009) there was, for some, a sense of reassurance in the shared vulnerability of the prison setting (Campbell *et al.* 2006). Within the Republican community of former detainees, the communal nature of much of the state violence, and the role of others' experiences in facilitating the creation of testimony, was emphasised.

Yet there are still further complexities and contradictions evident when exploring how images of masculinity impact on former detainees, their testimonies and the legacy of state violence. The meta-narrative of the heroic struggle, the way it was used by the Republican movement outside, and the perception that Republicanism was (and is) homogeneous would benefit from critical analysis as the nature of collective and individual action within political movements further complicates any analysis of power and resistance. Polletta and Jasper (2001: 285) define a collective identity

> as an individual's cognitive, moral and emotional connection with collective identity as broader community, category, practice, or institution. It is a perception of a shared status or relation, which may be imagined rather than

90 *The masculinity of 'making public'*

experienced directly, and it is distinct from personal identities, although it may form part of a personal identity.

Such frameworks can be seen in the narrative testimonies of former detainees, particularly those featured in McKeown (2001) and in the reflections about Republicans in Sluka (1989) and O'Hearn (2009). The individual's experience is marginalised, and as Laurence indicated, the dominant narrative is that of 'we'.

The dominance of the communal narrative also reflects broader patterns outside of the prison struggle in which individual experiences of state violence were framed as attacks against the nationalist community's collective identity.[6] For Della Porta and Diani (2006), the process of creating and maintaining such an identity is linked to a shared purpose and common cause. The sense of shared experiences of state repression may have been a determining factor in recruitment to the IRA – the spikes in recruitment across the North following internment and 'Bloody Sunday' would seem to evidence this (Coogan 2000). However, real care should be taken not to universalise such responses. As the lived experiences of civil rights activist Interviewee PJ suggest, it would be foolish to portray state violence as leading all who experienced it into armed insurrection.[7]

What is clear, however, is that a sense of a collective identity emerged from and fed into the prison struggle. The imposition of power created the opportunity for resistance and this resistance was framed in collective terms. It enabled prisoners 'to turn mortifying processes into a kind of fuel for their own attempts to create a culture of solidary resistance' (O'Hearn 2009: 500). Resistance allowed prisoners the space to recreate themselves. The production, framing and dissemination of narratives of state violence further sought to consolidate this culture outside the prison walls. It formed a pattern of dialogue between the prisoners and the State, in which the authorities remained unable to fully define the meaning of imprisonment in its entirety for Republican communities. The language of criminalisation was resisted through the semantics and practices of struggle, and was made manifest through the marginalisation of individual experiences (with some exceptions, such as Bobby Sands) and the accompanying promotion of a collective and homogenised identity.

When narratives of victimhood are framed in such a communal manner, their homogeneity can form a deeply powerful resistance to the dominant narratives found in official discourse. The official discourse of the British State was one which pathologised prisoners and represented them as the 'other'. Particularly during the criminalisation period, IRA prisoners were portrayed as a part of the monolithic IRA and yet at the same time, as selfish, evil individuals who had carried out atrocities. This approach contributed to the prison protests as prisoners sought to regain a sense of both personal and political agency through acts of resistance (O'Hearn 2009). Their narratives of state violence form part of this communal resistance. However, these counter-hegemonic discourses also hide their own power to control and to subjugate alternative knowledges. As shown, Republican discourse is often portrayed as being monolithic, with dissident voices existing only at the margins. The personal is marginalised and

The masculinity of 'making public' 91

former detainees become symbols of community suffering and struggle rather than individuals with individual problems and experiences. When movements are 'seen as having a homogenous and integrated identity ... this has prevented the multiplicity of identities and allegiances among militants and movement groups from being recognised' (Della Porta and Diani 2006: 98).

Former detainees' narratives, particularly from those imprisoned in the H-Blocks during the protests, were moulded into a narrative of resistance and of 'triumph over adversity'. Though this process undoubtedly enabled many men to discuss their experiences, it both created and sustained an exaggerated, romanticised sense of community, which resulted in the exclusion of those who individualised their stories or failed to link their accounts to the wider narrative of Republican resistance. There appeared to be little space for the individualised, separated, personal narratives of former detainees. The story of 'me' became (and arguably remains) secondary to the story of 'we', along with the problems and possibilities such a process can bring. As a result of the dominant position given to the narrative of the 'Republican former prisoner community', the voice of the individual and of individualised suffering is largely excluded from the history of the prison struggle and its legacy, with some notable exceptions, for example, Bobby Sands (1998, 2001). In discussions about men's experiences of so-called non-political imprisonment, Coles (2009: 33) argues that it is possible to be subordinated by hegemonic masculinity, yet still dominate the masculinity of other men. It appears the representations of the hunger strikes of 1981 position Bobby Sands at the pinnacle of Republican masculinity, followed by the other nine hunger strikers whose masculinity is also valorised, but seemingly not to the same extent and not in as much of an individualised and personified way as that of Sands himself.

Therefore, like all communities, Republican former detainees operate within certain formalised and informal constraints. Their narrative testimonies of shared suffering can be both inclusive and seeking to exclude. The dominant depictions of 'communal suffering' may have meant that individual understandings of personal suffering were (and remain) obfuscated.[8] Some of those interviewed commented on the critical or indifferent reactions of other detainees to their public narration of their own experience of state violence:

> Within this community ... it was no big deal. Everybody knew it was going on.... It was no use telling Republicans about it, because they were likely to just say 'And so what?'
>
> (Michael)

> [F]or someone to say they were beaten up in Castlereagh – 'Big wow. It happened to lots of people.'
>
> (Interviewee 'F')

The significance of such statements can be related not only to the frequency of state violence against detainees, but also to the formal and informal pressures

92 *The masculinity of 'making public'*

operating within group dynamics. Having earlier emphasised the communal nature of many Republican narratives, Laurence recalled how:

> Someone said 'Do you not think you are bit too open?' It was someone from the Republican community. I said 'What, by saying what people really felt?' and he said 'Yes'.... To say ... what exactly happened to YOU, it's like exalting yourself above the rest of the group.

The power of the Republican discourse to marginalise the individual was strongly felt by Interviewee 'F' in particular. He commented that 'some might have said "Wimp" or words to that effect [after I went public] because everyone was being beaten, everyone was going through different degrees of abuse'. In this instance, Interviewee 'F' felt that he had been chastised by others within the Republican community, not only for going public about his experiences of victimisation and his own feelings of vulnerability, but also because in doing so, he had taken the conflict into a personal dimension. He had moved the narrative away from the communal story so dominant within the Republican depiction of the prison struggle and towards his own story. He felt a loss of ownership over his experiences and implied that they had been consumed by the wider narrative of the Republican struggle.

Conflicting interpretations about the significance and meaning of experiences of state violence erode the language of collective Republican resistance. The unity and power created through the narration of shared suffering begins to break down when experiences are given contrasting personal meanings. The imagery of shared experience (and the downplaying of individualised, personal pain) seeks to create and maintain a powerful discourse which simultaneously emphasises the suffering of all Republican prisoners and symbolically links them with the pain of the wider community from which prisoners were drawn. Emphasising the communal experience of state violence obscures any divisions, conflicts and disagreements between prisoners (and those outside) and helps to sustain an image of a homogeneous, equally committed and equally powerful group of prisoners. Most importantly, depictions of shared suffering feed into discourses around group struggle, in which a capacity for resistance is presented as equally achievable for all people. Personalising experiences of violence, particularly when the language used is that of fear and vulnerability, risks fracturing the imagined community and bringing to the forefront the diversity in detainees' responses to the harm of state violence, and to their different abilities to 'resist'.

Masculinity as resistance

However, to portray the structures of Republican discourse as omnipotent, risks constructing detainees and their narratives as powerless and passive, lacking in agency. For most detainees, a sense of agency in the ability to decide the meaning of their experiences and their testimony still remains, but is constrained by the Republican narrative. In this sense, detainees retain power, but power

The masculinity of 'making public' 93

within a limited set of discursive circumstances. Their narratives must be seen to 'fit' the communal discourse which delegitimises the British State and legitimises Republican violence. It would seem then, that it is at the juncture of shared victimhood that the dominant image of masculinity may be powerfully reconfigured. The depiction of masculinity which presents men as uniformly powerful and self-controlled (Newburn and Stanko 1994) was/is also preserved by the conceptualisation of suffering as resistance. For Bairner (1999b: 130), the paramilitarism of some former prisoners:

> has conferred on many a sense of self-esteem either directly or inasmuch as they were active members of specific organisations, or indirectly as regards those men and boys (and to a lesser extent girls and women) who have inhabited a largely imagined landscape in which being hard has been valorised.

In August 1969, violent rioting spread throughout many of Northern Ireland's towns and cities, and was experienced by many in Catholic areas as a 'Loyalist pogrom' (McKittrick and McVea (2001: 59). The phrase 'IRA: I Ran Away' is alleged to have appeared on a wall in the Falls Road area, supposedly reflecting the feelings of working class nationalists that the IRA had abandoned them (McKittrick and McVea 2001). The existence of this graffiti has since been disputed and claims have been made that the IRA was highly active in supressing further Loyalist violence in the area (see Hanley 2009; Hanley and Millar 2010). Almost a year later, on 27 June 1970, the nationalist Short Strand area of east Belfast was attacked by Loyalist groups and the injured Belfast IRA leader Billy McKee 'enter[ed] Republican folklore by reputedly holding off Protestant gunmen almost single-handed and preventing a Loyalist invasion of the Short Strand' (McKittrick and McVea 2001: 61). Thus those involved in the Republican struggle were at times valorised as the defenders of their communities. Although – like the graffiti – the precise facts about the defence of the Short Strand are now disputed (Clarke 2009), their representation, imagery and legacy reassert the hegemonic masculinity and powerful resistance narratives of the IRA.

Within the prison context, challenges to masculinity were similarly re-operationalised as resistance, and public testimonies of victimisation become reframed as images of strength and survival against all odds. Experiences and their accounts were informed and contextualised by the romanticised and poetic perception that it is 'not those who inflict the most but those who suffer the most that are victorious' (MacSwiney 1921: 26 in Bean 2002: 146). Laurence commented on the existence of narratives about state violence written by former detainees and suggested that:

> It's certainly about surviving a jail situation which includes knowledge of brutality and such like, but it is more like a celebration of victory over adversity.

94 *The masculinity of 'making public'*

Within such circumstances, the personal becomes explicitly politicised and the prison struggle becomes interpreted through a lens of symbolic continuation and the re-imaging of past struggles, with the public testimonies of victimised Republicans taking on a historical resonance and quasi-religious imagery, most visible during the hunger strikes. Men's suffering becomes represented as a form of heroism or martyrdom within Republican culture (Aretxaga 1997). Within the context of the 'prison struggle', narrative testimonies of pain now become testimonies of resistance, even when they end in death:

> If you look at Republican symbolism and Republican songs virtually all the songs ... were about suffering and people dying, about struggle.
>
> (Interviewee 'F')

The image of the invulnerable male is thus recast into the male warrior as one of the most powerful ideals of masculinity, as a figure who gains strength from his own suffering and sacrifice for his people (O'Malley 1990; Dowler 2002). Testimonies of pain reframed as victorious suffering were/are central to the Republican prison narrative and can also be seen clearly in the language of stories collected by Campbell *et al.* (2006):

> Despite the ferocity of the forced washes, men emerged with spirits steeled by the experience. There was great satisfaction that we had stood firm and fought against impossible odds. It was our victory.
>
> (former detainee known as BM in Campbell *et al.* 2006: 66)

Although many former detainees referred explicitly to emotions and feelings of vulnerability, few explored those notions in any depth as being symbolic or symptomatic of individual powerlessness. They chose instead to recast those experiences as part of a wider prison resistance in which Republican prisoners (as a group) and not simply prison officials held power. For this group of prisoners who had made their private memories of victimhood part of a contested public history, 'everything has to be seen in the context of the struggle' (Interviewee 'P'). Furthermore, as the lines between public and private blurred, the prison played an important role as 'the centre of ideological advancement and a subculture of resistance that incessantly produced collective symbols of political incorporation for insurgent communities outside the prison' (Feldman 1991: 147). Such resistance and struggle is one method through which those detained may have sought to regain and preserve hegemonic masculinity within a setting of comparative powerlessness. The conflict in Northern Ireland therefore both created and was sustained by the ideological construction of the prison system as a site of a struggle for various forms of power, including the gendered power of hegemonic masculinities. The preservation of masculinity was to be achieved through conspicuous displays of power and resistance:

> [At the end of searches] as the last cell door closed ... then someone would sing and most of the wing would join in. Bawling out the likes of 'Provos

The masculinity of 'making public' 95

March On', finishing with wild cheers and yells, getting rid of the built up tension and aggression.

(former detainee known as JMQ in Campbell *et al.* 2006: 52)

The resistance against the violence of the detention system of Northern Ireland manifested itself through protests and violence both within and outside the detention apparatus, particularly during the period 1971–1985. Men's violence could be used to negotiate power in most prison settings (Stanko 1994), but in regards to the Northern Ireland conflict, violence also manifested itself externally in the physical space outside the detention system. Prison officers were targeted by Republican (and occasionally Loyalist) groups outside throughout the 1970s and the targeting of officials continued (albeit at a slower rate) following the hunger strikes of 1980 and 1981. Twenty seven prison officers were killed by Republicans between 1974 and 1989. Some of those killed had seemingly been targeted on a personal basis due to their alleged attacks on prisoners. Others were killed for symbolic value by paramilitaries keen to support prison resistance by outward displays of their omnipotence, with the strategic aim of pressuring the authorities (McEvoy 2001). The conflict outside of the prisons added another dimension to the detention system as a site of a politicised struggle. The relationship between prison officials (predominantly male) and male Republican prisoners within the H-Blocks was commented upon by Harry, who recalled the reciprocal nature of violence and threat that often emerged from events within the prison:

One had his foot on my head pressing down on it. Another had my arm bent at the wrist trying to break it. I said to him 'What?! Are you trying to break my arm?' He said 'you're right you fucking bastard. Get down in the dirt where you belong'. I said 'Oh you will be down in the dirt with me soon enough'.

Therefore, the climate of fear and brutality which placed the British State and its agents as holders of power and control was far from absolute outside the prison. At times, including during the prison escapes of e.g. 1983 and the later shooting of Loyalist paramilitary Billy Wright within the prison in 1997 by members of the INLA, state control and power would be violently contested within prison itself. It was also uniquely challenged by violence outside of the prison by Republicans (and Loyalists on occasions). Resistance against the power of the detention system therefore manifested itself in a range of different but interrelated ways. The public narration of state violence experienced during detention was another means by which the prison struggle continued, which Feldman (1991: 119) interprets as part of a wider process through which 'the body subtracted by violence is reconstituted and re-plotted through oral history'.

96   *The masculinity of 'making public'*

Preserved images

In conclusion, the chapter has provided an analysis of former detainees' understanding of the role of masculinities in the production of their narratives about state violence. There appears to be a conflict between the perception felt by some of those interviewed that, as men, they are 'not supposed' to bring attention to their victimisation, despite the existence of so many men who violated this norm to 'go public' about their own experience of state violence and victimisation. In addition, for those who feel this norm does not/no longer exists, those occasions where male victimisation is publicly downplayed or reframed as 'black'/dark humour and/or resistance, become increasingly problematic. 'Masculinity' remains a complex concept, yet one which still retains a predictable, powerful and contemporary cultural resonance, which contrasts with the perception that masculine identity is never fixed (Segal 2007). None of those interviewed hinted at a 'crisis of masculinity' or the idea that men are in a state of 'confusion' due to consumerism, women's supposed power, and/or the alleged social and cultural disapproval of 'traditional masculinity'. Rather than depict the confusion and insecurity which dominates many definitional discussions around gender, when asked about the meaning of masculinity most responded by simply reflecting back instrumental and expressive ideals around 'toughness' and rationality:

> I have thought about that, you have men and men, and men don't cry and all that.... Maybe it is a macho thing, men are expected to do this and that, and that is it. [What about yourself?] I am macho! I spoke out, but I would do it out of ... (pauses).... If I thought I would get something out of it I would talk forever.
>
> (Harry)

For Harry, 'going public' about his experiences was a decision made based on his rational calculation of perceived costs and benefits. The meaning given to masculinity by those interviewed was not about their perception of self in terms of compassion or sensitivity, but the extent to which they 'measured up' to the image of the 'invulnerable man' which had retained for most participants, the position of 'hegemonic masculinity'. There were perceptions that challenged this position, yet these were not defined or expressed as subjugated or alternative masculinities by those interviewed. The 'ideology of masculinity which presents men as uniformly powerful, controlling and non-emotional' (Newburn and Stanko 1994: 162) was and remains preserved by the conceptualisation of suffering as resistance.

Within the literature, the different meanings of masculinity are acknowledged, and 'in some instances referring to masculinities is more helpful than referring simply to masculinity' (Newburn and Stanko 1994: 2). In addition, 'the international literature on masculinity generally suggests that masculinities are not uniform and that power relations exist within them' (Hamber 2007: 379). But for the ten volunteers in the current book, the meaning of masculinity was little more than a synthesis of normative and essentialist definitions about what they thought society 'wanted' from men. Most acknowledged the position held by the imagined invulnerable male – albeit with different degrees of explicitness – and built their 'truth-sharing' experiences around it. By recasting the violence they had suffered as extreme, by dismissing their vulnerability, by emphasising the suffering of other men, or further by conceptualising suffering as strength and resistance, many of those interviewed sought to retain something of the imagery of the 'Rough Tough Provo', even when discussing personal feelings of fear and vulnerability.

Notes

1 Colloquialism meaning to serve time in detention without complaint or upset.
2 See Chapter 2 for a detailed discussion of the various prison protests and their history.
3 Colloquial expression referring to teasing.
4 The reference to the small sweet chocolate confectionary is intended to be a humorous way of downplaying the harmful and/or serious nature of experiences.
5 Colloquialism signifying fuss or drama.
6 This is certainly not unique to the Republican movement and as the extensive literature by Della Porta *et al.* (1999), Della Porta and Diani (2006) and Melucci (1988) on social movements show, collective identities are often created and perpetuated through struggle.
7 Michael also suggested that state violence may have deterred possible recruits from joining the IRA – see Chapter 6.
8 Early discussions alongside some former prisoners who belonged to other Republican groups not featured in this book (such as the INLA) implied a growing level of discomfort surrounding the Provisional IRA's perceived ownership and dominance over the memory of the prison struggle.

References

Aretxaga, B. (1997) *Shattering Silence: Women, Nationalism, and Political Subjectivity in Northern Ireland*. Princeton: Princeton University Press.
Bairner, A. (1999a) 'Soccer, Masculinity and Violence in Northern Ireland – Between Hooliganism and Terrorism', *Men and Masculinities*, 1(3), 284–301.
Bairner, A. (1999b) 'Violence, Masculinity and the Irish Peace Process', *Capital and Class*, 69(3), 125–144.
Bean, K. (2002) 'Defining Republicanism: Shifting Discourses of New Republicanism and New Nationalism', in Elliot, M. (ed.) *The Long Road to Peace in Northern Ireland*. Liverpool: Liverpool University Press.
Campbell, B., McKeown, L. and O'Hagan, F. (2006) *Nor Meekly Serve My Time: The H Block Struggle*. Belfast: Beyond the Pale.
Carrabine, E. and Longhurst, B. (1998) 'Gender and Prison Organisation: Some Comments on Masculinities and Prison Management', *Howard Journal of Criminal Justice*, 37(2), 161–176.
Clarke, L. (1987) *Broadening the Battlefield: H-Blocks and the Rise of Sinn Féin*. Dublin: Gill and Macmillan.
Clarke, L. (2009) 'Loyalist Victim Was Shot By IRA Cross-Fire'. *The Times*. 24 May. Available at: www.timesonline.co.uk/tol/news/world/ireland/article6350922.ece (accessed 31 August 2012).

98   The masculinity of 'making public'

Clatterbaugh, R. (1998) 'What is Problematic About Masculinities?', *Men and Masculinities*, 1(1), 24–45.

Coles, T. (2009) 'Negotiating the Field of Masculinity', *Men and Masculinities*, 12(1), 30–44.

Connell, R. (2005) *Masculinities*. California: California University Press.

Coogan, T.P. (2000) *The IRA*. London: Palgrave Macmillan.

Della Porta, D. and Diani, M. (2006) *Social Movements: An Introduction*. 2nd edn. Oxford: Blackwell Publishing.

Della Porta, D., Kriesi, H. and Rucht, R. (eds) (1999) *Social Movements in a Globalizing World*. New York: Macmillan.

Dowler, L. (2002) 'Till Death do us Part: Masculinity, Friendship, and Nationalism in Belfast, Northern Ireland', *Environment and Planning: Society and Space*, 20(1), 53–71.

Evans, T. and Wallace, P. (2007) 'A Prison within a Prison? The Masculinity Narratives of Male Prisoners', *Men and Masculinities*, 10(4), 484–507.

Feldman, A. (1991) *Formations of Violence: The Narrative of the Body and Political Terror in Northern Ireland*. Chicago: University of Chicago Press.

Goodey, J. (1997) 'Boys Don't Cry: Masculinities, Fear of Crime and Fearlessness', *British Journal of Criminology*, 37(3), 401–441.

Hamber, B. (2007) 'Masculinity and Transitional Justice: An Exploratory Essay', *International Journal of Transitional Justice*, 1(1), 375–390.

Hanley, B. (2009) '"I Ran Away"? The IRA and 1969', *History Ireland*, 17(4), 24–27.

Hanley, B. and Millar, S. (2010) *The Lost Revolution: The Story of the Official IRA and the Workers' Party*. London: Penguin Books Ltd.

Harland, K. (2009) *Acting Tough: Young Men, Masculinity and the Development of Practice in Northern Ireland.* Derry: Nowhere Man Press.

Jamieson, R. and Grounds, A. (2002) *No Sense of an Ending: The Effects of Long Term Imprisonment amongst Republican Prisoners and Their Families.* Monaghan: SEESYU Press.

Jefferson, T. (1994) 'Theorising Masculine Subjectivity', in Stanko, E.A. and Newburn, T. (eds) *Just Boys Doing Business? Men, Masculinities and Crime.* London: Routledge.

Jewkes, Y. (2005) 'Men Behind Bars: "Doing" Masculinity as an Adaption to Imprisonment', *Men and Masculinities*, 8(1), 44–62.

Mac An Ghaill, M. and Haywood, C. (2007) *Gender, Culture and Society*. London: Palgrave MacMillan.

McEvoy, K. (2001) *Paramilitary Imprisonment in Northern Ireland: Resistance, Management and Release*. Oxford: Oxford University Press.

McKeown, L. (2001) *Out of Time: Irish Republican Prisoners and Long Kesh 1972–2000*. Belfast: Beyond the Pale.

McKittrick, D. and McVea, D. (2001) *Making Sense of the Troubles*. Belfast: Blackstaff.

Melucci, A. (1988) 'Getting Involved: Identity and Mobilization in Social Movements', *International Social Movement Research*, (1), 329–48.

Messerschmidt, J.W. (1993) *Masculinities and Crime: Critique and Reconceptualization of Theory*. Lanham: Rowan and Littlefield Publishers.

Newburn, T. and Stanko, E. (1994) 'When Men Are Victims', in Newburn, T. and Stanko, E. (eds) *Just Boys Doing Business? Men, Masculinities and Crime*. London: Routledge.

Newton, C. (1994) 'Gender Theory and Prison Sociology: Using Theories of Masculinities to Interpret the Sociology of Prisons for Men', *The Howard Journal of Criminal Justice*, 33(3), 193–202.

O'Hearn, D. (2009) 'Repression and Solidary Cultures of Resistance: Irish Political Prisoners on Protest', *American Journal of Sociology*, 115(2), 491–526.

O'Malley, P. (1990) *Biting at the Grave: the Irish Hunger Strikes and the Politics of Despair*. Belfast: Blackstaff Press.

Pelka, F. (2004) 'Raped: A Male Survivor', in Stombler, M., Baunach, E., Burgess, D., Donnelly, D. and Simonds, W. (eds) *Sex Matters: The Sexuality and Society Reader*. Boston: Pearson.

Polletta, F. and Jasper, J. (2001) 'Collective Identity and Social Movements', *Annual Review of Sociology*, 27(1), 283–305.

Sands, B. (1998) *Writings from Prison*. Cork: Mercier Press.

Sands, B. (2001) *One Day in my Life*. Cork: Mercier Press.

Scraton, P., Sim, J. and Skidmore, P. (1991) *Prisons under Protest*. Buckingham: Open University Press.

Segal, L. (2007) *Slow Motion: Changing Masculinities, Changing Men*. Basingstoke: Macmillan.

Seidler, V.J. (1994) *Unreasonable Men: Masculinity and Social Theory*. London: Routledge.

Seidler, V.J. (2007) 'Masculinities, Bodies and Emotional Life', *Men and Masculinities*, 10(1), 9–21.

Sharoni, S. (1999) 'Gendering Resistance Within an Irish Republican Community: conversations with Laurence McKeown'. (Unpublished) Available at: www.simonasharoni.com/Docs/IFJPconversation.pdf (accessed 31 August 2012).

Sluka, J.A. (1989) *Hearts and Minds, Water and Fish: Support for the IRA and INLA in a Northern Irish Ghetto*. London: Jai Press.

Stanko, E.A. and Hobdell, K. (1993) 'Assault on Men: Masculinity and Male Victimization', *British Journal of Criminology*, 33(3), 400–415.

Stanko, E.A. (1994) 'Challenging the Problem of Men's Individual Violence', in Stanko, E.A. and Newburn, T. (eds) *Just Boys Doing Business? Men, Masculinities and Crime*. London: Routledge.

Thurston, R. (1996) '"Are You Sitting Comfortably?" Men's Storytelling: Masculinities, Prison Culture and Violence', in Mac An Ghaill, M. (eds) *Understanding Masculinities, Social Relations and Cultural Arenas*. Buckingham: Polity Press.

Whitehead, S.M. and Barrett, F.J. (2001) 'The Sociology of Masculinity' in Whitehead, S.M. and Barrett, F.J. (eds) *The Masculinities Reader*. Cambridge: Polity Press.

6 Former detainees' narratives as 'propaganda'

As the previous chapters have shown, notions of the healing potential of revealing harmful experiences can be complicated by external factors, including perceptions of gender and masculinity. These dominant perceptions can impact on the production of narratives about violence and also on the forms those narratives take. Yet these are not the only aspects which may influence the motivation, significance and legacy of 'making public' private memories of state violence. As Curtis (1998) and Miller (1994) note, a common criticism faced by those whose allegations contrasted with the accounts of state forces was that their narratives were part of an organised propaganda strategy created by the Republican movement. The following chapter explores the extent to which interviewees were motivated to 'go public' by their own understanding of propagandist principles. It draws on political science and communication studies in order to analyse the complex meaning of propaganda in relation to narratives of state violence. These discussions suggest a diverse range of motivations, influences and understandings which have all contributed to interviewees' decisions to 'make public' their personal accounts.

The meaning of propaganda

Definitional discussions about the meaning and significance of the label 'propaganda' are undoubtedly of value. They trace the shifting perceptions, commonalities and differences in the language used to describe a range of communications and narratives. Today's dominant conceptual imagery depicts propaganda as something that is *purposefully* produced by 'others' with challenging, threatening or otherwise nefarious intentions to mislead an audience. The label propaganda is used to close down debate, to neutralise the 'truth claims' of enemies and to disempower any perceptions of the validity of their allegations or the righteousness of their alleged cause.

Critical analysis of the meaning of propaganda suggests that it is a much more complex and multifaceted concept. The study of propaganda is itself wide ranging and not limited by disciplinary boundaries, which has resulted in many different interpretations of the concept's meaning. However, as Smith (1989) suggests, there are some re-occurring themes. Most depict the label as referring

Former detainees' narratives as 'propaganda' 101

to some form of persuasion. Pratkanis and Aronson (1991: 9) succinctly state that 'we use the term "propaganda" to refer to the mass persuasion techniques that have come to characterise our post-industrial society' and it is this element which can be found throughout most definitional discussions. This is not to suggest that propaganda is a contemporary, post-industrial 'invention' as oral histories, folk tales, stories, myths and legends all have propagandist purposes which predate industrialisation. However, the changes in globalisation, communication, networks and technology have meant that attempts at mass persuasion are now able to take place through a range of diverse mechanisms and multiple channels.

Both Smith's (1989) and Pratkanis and Aronson's (1991) perceptions that propaganda contains important elements of persuasion are shared by Jackall (1995), who contends that propaganda is a term used to describe communication which aims at persuading groups of people about the value of some organisation, cause or person. For a message to be labelled as propaganda, it must be interpreted as both purposive and functional. It is a dual tiered, goal driven exercise in which the 'purpose is to send out an ideology to an audience with a related objective. The ideology that is sought endeavours to reinforce or modify the attitudes or behaviour or both of an audience' (Jowett and O'Donnell 1999: 3). It is therefore this relationship between intent and effect which differentiates propaganda from other forms of communication (Jowett and O'Donnell 1999).

Lasswell's (1971: 9) examination of the role of USA and European propaganda during the First World War suggests that 'propaganda refers solely to the control of opinion by significant symbols, or to speak more concretely and less accurately, by stories, rumours, reports, pictures and other forms of social communication'. The relationship between the message and the social body is another re-occurring element in definitions of propaganda. Yet, despite this, propaganda is not simply persuasion and persuasion not simply propaganda, even when that persuasion might arise as a consequence of a propagandist message. Propaganda is 'concerned with the management of opinions and attitudes by the direct manipulation of social suggestion rather than by altering other conditions in the environment' (Lasswell 1971: xiv). It is not propaganda itself which brings about some form of change, but the response to that propaganda which is the intended goal of the propagandist.

For Smith (1989), the concept of propaganda is best defined as 'manipulative communication'. Lasswell (1938) too, argues that clear manipulation is central to propaganda and that the concept is used not only in reference to the surreptitious influencing of ideas but is also significantly related to influencing action through the control and manipulation of representation. When framing this understanding within a politics of representation, what counts as 'the truth' (and propaganda usually aims at just one exclusive 'truth') can become dynamic and fluid. It also involves the communication of a point of view with the ultimate goal of having the recipient come to 'voluntarily' accept a position as if it was their own (Pratkanis and Aronson 1991). In this sense, propaganda can refer to attempts to persuade a person, group or organisation that a taken perspective was (and is) entirely their

102 *Former detainees' narratives as 'propaganda'*

own, without the recognition of any input or influence from external forces. Within such definitions, manipulation takes place at the most subtle of levels.

The role of narrative testimony in constructing legitimacy

Propaganda can be used to maintain the legitimacy of state institutions and their related activities (O'Donnell and Jowett 1989). During research for the current book, former detainee Tommy suggested that his public narratives about interrogation in Castlereagh were a part of his personal attempt to vividly illustrate the violence of British State forces. Through his narrative, he placed responsibility for both his treatment in detention and the wider conflict itself squarely onto the British State, whilst at the same time raising the status of the IRA into a position where that organisation's actions are seen as the *only* suitable alternative to the violence of oppression. He hoped that the legacy of his narrative about state violence might be to persuade an audience about the legitimacy of Republican aims and also the means through which those aims could be achieved. He argued that:

> I knew the RUC knew it [the details of his allegations and those of other detainees], but they had done it! And the British Government had orchestrated it, so they were not going to be concerned. I thought 'Right'. To an extent it just reinforces the view that the only answer to the British State is physical force, they don't listen to anything else.
>
> (Tommy)

In nationalist/Republican areas, agents of the British State were represented 'as brutal, merciless and uncivilised' (Ainsworth 2002: 372) in a model which clearly demonises the 'other'. Wilcox (1940) claims that in order to convince people about the legitimacy of one's violence, it is necessary to portray the enemy as a murderous, unmerciful aggressor. In support, Alonso (2001) and Sánchez-Cuenca and de la Calle (2007) discuss this concept of legitimacy at length in relation to 'reactive' acts of Republican violence and as such, it is not the intention to reproduce those arguments here. The task is instead to explore the role of narrative testimonies of state violence in constructing and/or perpetuating that legitimacy for former detainees and the extent to which this can be labelled a 'propagandist' intention. In an analysis of his motivations for 'going public', Tommy further elaborated that:

> These were not isolated reasons [for 'going public']. There was a major conflict between us on the Republican side and the British State on the other. It was a battle for legitimacy as much as anything else. So it was all part of our battle and my battle for legitimacy. So that is the greater context.
>
> (Tommy)

A further means by which narratives of state violence can seek to legitimise Republican violence is through what Lasswell (1971) labels 'kriegsgreuelpropaganda' or

Former detainees' narratives as 'propaganda' 103

'war atrocity stories', with the accompanying demonisation of enemy forces. The intention is to 'fortify the mind ... with examples of the insolence and depravity of the enemy' (Lasswell 1971: 77). During interviews with former detainees (and in the original narratives) prison officers are repeatedly referred to as 'screws' and 'evil bastards', or given powerful derogatory nicknames like 'Dr Mengele' (see for example, McKeown 2001; Campbell *et al.* 2006). These narrative testimonies, particularly those from the H-Blocks, link into the representation of IRA violence as self-defence against a menacing, murderous aggressor. 'There must be no ambiguity about whom the public is to hate' (Lasswell 1971: 47; see also Read 1938; Wilcox 1940). In these particular interpretations, the violence of the enemy British State and its agents is given primacy. This fits well with Lasswell's (1971: 195) argument that two of the main aims of propaganda concern the 'mobilisation of hatred against the enemy ... and to demoralise the enemy'. These aims of mobilisation against and demoralisation of the 'enemy' would also appear to fit within the framework suggested by Harry's recollections. He recalled 'going public' about violence he had experienced in detention after being assaulted by prison officers following an attempted escape:

I think it was highlighted and it was afterwards that they would say to you to get a solicitor. This was more or less from the [Republican] movement. 'You have to push this'. I think they were looking for the prison service to be blackened over this brutality.

(Harry)

According to Harry's recollection, the Republican movement wished Harry to tell his story as part of a wider attempt to criticise British State forces and to delegitimise the actions taken against Republicans by prison officials following the escape. Narrating and publicising the prison violence against detainees was advantageous for the Republican movement, as it offered an opportunity to publicly criticise the forces of the State and for that criticism to reach an audience which may be sympathetic towards such experiences. Through the narrative testimonies of prisoners, prison officials were demarcated not only as political opponents, but were characterised as malicious, calculating and sectarian individuals. As discussed previously, Interviewee 'P' perceived prison officer brutality as being motivated by little more than 'absolute hatred'. Harry similarly described the prison officers as 'always sectarian ... we wanted to highlight that fact ... [their] sheer badness, sheer bigotry. It wasn't justifiable, put it that way, in our eyes'. He spoke of his intentions and hopes that the narratives of his and others' experiences would have *direct* consequences in provoking action:

[Did you hope there would be any consequences?] Aye, stiff the screws. That was it ... I had heard about some of the others, some of them were to me quiet people and they had got slapped all around ... some really bad beatings. I just wanted to get hold of those screws and stiff them. I wasn't

104 *Former detainees' narratives as 'propaganda'*

> interested in highlighting anything; I just wanted to stiff them screws.... If I had got hold of them I wouldn't let them go.
>
> (Harry)

In this sense, IRA violence against prison officers was recast as retributive punishment by Harry. In his account, the political 'targeting' of prison officers by the IRA as *symbols* of a wider repressive state drops from the analysis and violence against prison officers becomes a personal act of vengeance for their actions against other prisoners, whom Harry imbued with a sense of defenceless and vulnerability. In less vivid terms, Jim also described his hopes that through his public narration, the wider knowledge of his detention experiences could become a catalyst for 'political action [pause] or military action'. These interpretations of the intentions which may lie behind public accounts of violence are distant from the subtle changing of attitudes as described by Pratkanis and Aronson (1991) and remain closer in definition to the understandings of Jowett and O'Donnell (1999) in their desire for direct consequences. As propaganda, narratives can involve changing perceptions, but furthermore, include the formulation of those perceptions into some form of action against a symbolically identifiable enemy. Narratives become the canvas upon which the image of an 'enemy' can be painted and an 'emphasis upon the aggressiveness, immorality and impropriety of the "enemy" is a sop that loosens the restraining grip of the conscience upon destructive impulses' (Lasswell 1938: 19).

The argument that definitions of propaganda require a consequence of direct action which can be seen within a clear causal relationship is further complicated by the exigencies of the conflict in Northern Ireland. To 'blacken the name' (Harry) of the State through the publication of narrative testimony may have led to a form of retaliatory violence against State forces, yet it also can be understood as a method of communicating a message to other audiences, such as those sympathetic to Republican ideologies but who may otherwise be exploring conciliation with the State. Through the publicity surrounding and emphasising the violence of British forces – diverting and/or reconfiguring the violence of paramilitaries – narratives of state brutality and violence can be constructed as possible deterrents to those who may wish to see closer co-operation with the State. Interviewee PJ argued:

> When I was lifted during internment, the whole countryside would know that I wasn't involved in any paramilitary groups, or anything to do with guns, or anything like that. And they would be all bothered and annoyed. That is what created the gunmen in this country, because then somebody out there would say 'Look at that fella there, he was never involved in anything and look what they are doing to him'.

The apparent growth in paramilitary membership following internment and 'Bloody Sunday', followed by the support offered to the hunger strikers in 1981 may add weight to the argument that the narration of violent experiences can

Former detainees' narratives as 'propaganda' 105

become a powerful and persuasive force for recruitment. Alonso (2001) posits that it is this knowledge of state violence directly experienced by the individual and indirectly through social relationships which was the catalyst for some young men to join the Republican movement, rather than the ownership of some coherent, well developed and considered Republican ideology. The form of communication described by Jim and Harry is akin to Jowett and O'Donnell's (1999) depiction of 'agitative propaganda' in seeking to rouse people into action.

Action against prison staff and the police did indeed take place. As McEvoy (2001) argues, violence against prison staff, both targeted and symbolic, outside these institutions appears to be linked to particular events, such as the changing status of prisoners and developments linked to the hunger strikes. However, the extent to which the act of *public narration* about violence experienced in detention *directly* caused the deaths of prison officers, police and other agents of the State remains unclear and difficult to quantify. Partly as a result of their relative visibility and their symbolic and actual role in the conflict in Northern Ireland, it may be likely that such individuals and groups would have been targeted with or without the narratives of former detainees being in the broader public domain.

Propaganda and Republicanism

Narrative testimonies exert a social pressure on their audiences in subtle and sophisticated ways. For example, an article about experiences of British State brutality need not make an overt appeal for support for Irish Republicanism, yet that support may still arise as a consequence. The extensive and detailed allegations of British State violence experienced during internment raids in 1971 may have provided the IRA with an effective recruiting tool, which was somewhat sarcastically acknowledged by the movement itself: 'The Republican Movement in Belfast extends to her Majesty's forces their heartfelt thanks for the magnificent recruiting drive that they have held on our behalf' (*Republican News* 9 October 1971 in Wright 1990: 36; see also Lasmar and Oliver 1998). In addition, *An Phoblacht* actively encouraged its readers to write in with allegations of state violence and abuse, reminding its audiences that:

> vague, generalised complaints about brutality or harassment and optimistic appeals for justice are no use to us or to you. The blunt facts stated tersely are far more valuable.
>
> (*An Phoblacht* 11 January 1978)

On the occasions where events and their testimonies were deemed inadequate in persuading a Republican audience to show active support for the cause and its means, *An Phoblacht*'s readership was informed that they should 'act now to save H-Block and Armagh lives…. Act now. That is your duty' (*An Phoblacht* 11 January 1978). Such emotionally coercive pronouncements may have lacked the subtlety and sophistication of former detainees' narrative testimony alone, yet they still fit clearly within the framework of 'agitative propaganda' as defined

106 *Former detainees' narratives as 'propaganda'*

by Jowett and O'Donnell (1999). When publicised by such organisations amongst a coherent and constant narrative of state violence, these accounts were a method through which the Republican movement could develop, helped by the violent and 'ill-conceived' action of the British Army and RUC (Feeney 2002: 261). Informed by the experience of internment, in 1973, a formal 'Republican Press Centre' opened in Belfast in order to increase the communication emanating from the movement. However, the collection of narratives of state violence could also have a further purpose, one linked to the operation of the IRA as a military organisation. The detailed recollections of former detainees could have been collected and used by the movement to formulate detailed anti-interrogation strategies. Yet Tommy suggests:

> The IRA had no conception whatsoever of what was happening in Castlereagh. They had publicised it many times in the paper, but the IRA Command didn't understand what was happening in the torture zones.

In this way, the narrative testimonies of Tommy and others subjected to interrogation could have acted as illustrative examples to educate and prepare people about the possible treatment captured detainees could expect to face, but they failed to do so. Coogan (2000) claims that most IRA members were largely unprepared for the possible brutality of the RUC and other State forces, particularly within the closed and confined spaces of the detention systems of Castlereagh Holding Centre. Like Tommy, he argued that 'The Green Book[1] lectures *understate* the horror which lies in store for a captured IRA man (*sic*)' (Coogan 2000: 560, emphasis in original). Although The Green Book, as featured in Coogan (2000) contains some detail regarding the methods of brutality which it suggests may be used by state forces, it gives little indication of the emotions and feelings that those methods might create in isolated detainees. Tommy recalled that:

> What they [the IRA leadership] believed was happening was the type of beating that one got at the back of the dancehall, where you got beat around the head and kicked or punched, which in comparison is actually not very difficult to put up with, believe it or not. There is a qualitative difference between being beaten up and being persistently tortured, a massive difference. One is tolerable, the other is qualitatively different – slow, agonising torture.

Despite its failures, The Green Book still shows that the Republican leadership made some attempts to prepare its 'volunteers' for the violence and brutality of highly pressurised interrogations, even if its words failed to capture the reality.[2] In 1978, 74 per cent of convictions through the Diplock Court were based on confessions of those detained, and by 1979 this rose to 79 per cent. Thus the pressure on IRA detainees to 'say nothing, sign nothing, see nothing, hear nothing' was significant (The Green Book in Coogan

Former detainees' narratives as 'propaganda' 107

2000: 570). It can be seen as persuasive propaganda in itself, as it was intended to persuade a 'volunteer' of the importance of their cause and of the kind of 'volunteer' they should actively aspire to be. In parallel, this documentation – designed to minimise both the likelihood and content of captured detainees' confessions – was further supported by the often violent actions against those who the movement thought had been 'turned' by State forces.

Aside from the IRA's own internal and informal mechanisms of social control, there are further problematic areas contained within a propaganda approach that seeks to publicise state violence against detainees. Michael argued that testimonies of brutality experienced by detainees 'might have scared a lot of people. I think it might have scared more people more than it encouraged [to join the IRA]'. Therefore, inherent in the public narration of experiences of state violence is the risk of an unintended consequence – that such testimonies may act as a deterrent against involvement, rather than encourage and sustain action against the State. Furthermore, regardless of whether conflict is represented as war or as a law and order problem, the propaganda gains made by publicising the harm caused by the 'enemy' must be weighed against the potential for such publicity to be used by the 'enemy' for its own purposes. The very *threat* of 'going to Castlereagh' (with its reputation for brutal violence and accompanying high rates of confessions) was used by the British forces to 'soften up' detainees for interrogation (Taylor 1980; Feldman 1991). Large numbers of defendants were convicted on the basis of confessions from Castlereagh alone during this mid to late 1970s period (Eisenhower 1985; Jackson 2009). From 1976 onwards:

> The RUC's Holding Centres at Castlereagh, Gough Barracks and Strand Road were having a devastating impact on the IRA … 'We'd hear of people handing over 25–30 names at a time. In the first 12–18 months of Castlereagh we suffered great damage.'
>
> (unnamed Republican source in Moloney 2007: 155)

Thus the wider context in which a conflict takes place is highly relevant to the ways in which information about violence can be created, contested, controlled and distributed. Unlike the rest of those interviewed as part of the present study who stated that, lapses of memory aside, they had made public everything that they had experienced, Jim recalled how his original public narrative about the violence he had experienced was *intentionally* fragmented with carefully chosen omissions:

> [I did not publicise everything that happened to me]. No. Because there were things that had happened that I would not want them, 'The Brits', to get knowledge of because it would allow them to – with that knowledge – perfect that technique.

Although links between detainees' public testimonies and the honing of interrogation techniques are difficult to prove, Jim's concern about fully disclosing the

108 *Former detainees' narratives as 'propaganda'*

lived impact of interrogation techniques seems logical. This shows some of the layers of complexity involved in narrating experiences of violence during times of conflict. It also illustrates how achieving the desired response from an audience sometimes required the in-depth analysis of the costs and benefits of making public one's recollections of state violence.

Targeting an 'audience'

As shown earlier in this chapter, elements of a persuasive intention re-occur within the wider literature on propaganda. Such messages can be examined from the perspective of the propagandist; however, it is the inclusion of a receiver, or group of receivers, which turns private memories into public testimonies, and furthermore into propaganda. The propagandist's audience may be the wider population or a particular segment of the public, depending on what response is being sought after (Jowett and O'Donnell 1999). Therefore, just as the semantics of truth *telling* benefit from refinement into the semantics of 'truth sharing', the language of propaganda requires further discussion in relation to the importance of audience. Indeed, it is the very existence of a real or assumed audience that is central to the dominant understanding of the power of propaganda. Propaganda cannot exist in isolation and, like all forms of communication, it is intrinsically social, requiring both message and audience. Lasswell (1938: 18) asserts that 'the propagandists' task is to identify attitudes favourable to his [*sic*] purposes, to reverse obstructive attitudes, to win the indifferent or at least to prevent them from becoming antagonistic'. In a similar vein, Tommy argued that from his perspective:

> I suppose the first audience is (or was) the Republican support base, to brief them, to let them know what was happening. I suppose also the Irish people, and I think also running with that was an awareness that there was then (and still is) a considerable group of civil libertarians in England.... And probably thereafter, the one – and I'm not sure if you could put them into a hierarchy – the United States, and two, continental Europe because we were aware, or I was aware, of the judgments rendered against Britain in the European Court and that it was necessary to impact in the European context.... There was a considerable amount of support for the Irish case in France among two different groups; the Left and the civil libertarians.

Therefore the persuasive intent which motivated the production of narratives about violence experienced by former detainees relies upon the perceived existence of a wide audience to witness to those accounts, and to contribute either through direct action, financial support, political pressure or related advocacy activities. Jim argued that:

> I think there were several audiences. There were Unionists and Brits, and the British public who I was hoping that because the ordinary working class

Former detainees' narratives as 'propaganda' 109

English are no different from any other nationality and if things were being done in their name that they knew about they would generally say 'no, this is isn't right, you are not doing this in my name'.... There was an international audience ... and there was a home audience of our own people, our own nationalist community so that they could understand what Britain was doing [to] Irish people and therefore continue to resist Britain.

Tommy and Jim thus sought to divide and label possible audiences (and attitudes to their narratives) into groupings, based on elements of a perceived shared understanding. This strengthens the argument that the publication of some of the narrative testimonies which detailed state violence was intended to build support for resistance. However, to suggest that this was the *sole* motivation and furthermore that narrative testimonies of former detainees were *always* aimed at a particular audience is to overestimate a modernist framework in which areas of overlap and/or heterogeneity become subsumed under broad politicised, oversimplified and stereotypical identities, for example, 'Unionists' or 'Brits'. Rejecting such frameworks, Liam perceived the audience for his narratives as being:

Anyone who would listen. I had no audience in mind. Anyone who wanted to listen to me I've spoken to. I've spoken to Amnesty groups, groups of journalists, groups of prisoners, their families, anyone who would listen.

Though not part of the armed struggle, Interviewee PJ also 'went public' with allegations of state violence experienced during internment. He understood his intended audience in similarly open terms to Liam, as being quite simply 'the world, whoever wanted to listen'. With the possible exceptions of Tommy and Jim (explored previously), this lack of a clearly identified audience is common throughout the remaining interviews. Both Harry and Michael argued that they had *not even considered* the significance and/or meaning of any prospective audience at any point before they went public with their accounts of state violence experienced during detention. In his own discussion about the intended audience for testimonies and reproduced at length here, Interviewee 'F' offered an analysis of the possible reasons for this apparent lack of interest in possible audiences shown by some former detainees:

As far as Republicans in the struggle were concerned ... some of the people involved in Sinn Féin would have recognised that the struggle was as much about propaganda as it was about individual actions that had taken place. There were some people there who were very astute and realised ... it was the way in which you got your propaganda together that would be most politically effective. But they were smaller in number ... [those] astute people, political propagandist types who were saying 'What will beat the British is not those actions, nothing you can do like that will beat them. It is the propaganda and the politics around this which will beat the British'.

110 *Former detainees' narratives as 'propaganda'*

> People like that thought we needed to embarrass the British internationally if the only way they can run this place is through brutality and discrimination, oppression and occupation and emergency legislation. All those things would need examples. That would have been their view on it, people like that would not have even thought about it in human terms, they would have seen it as purely another propaganda weapon. Most activists on the ground would not have been interested.

Interviewee 'F' differentiated between the armed activists of Republicanism and the political thinkers and ideologues he thought responsible for communicating some former detainees' experiences. He suggested that 'activists on the ground' would perhaps not have considered the potential benefits of raising awareness through narrative testimony and of shaming the State and its agents.

Those who did recognise the importance (and potential) of former prisoners' narratives as persuasive propaganda were able to publish testimony in outlets such as *An Phoblacht* and *Republican News*, which regularly featured articles with strongly emotive titles including 'What It Is Like In a Concentration Camp' (*An Phoblacht* 14 October 1978: 5). The audiences of these publications largely comprised those interested, sympathetic or already involved in the 'Republican movement'. Yet this was an audience which Michael argued 'already knew what was going on'. Similarly, Tommy suggested that:

> The *Phoblacht* carried these stories every week, and by and large nobody passed any remarks on what the Republican side was saying, because Republicans believed it and didn't feel there was any need to read it because they knew it was happening anyway.

However, the testimonies featured in *An Phoblacht* and *Republican News* could still convey a message to a broad audience of Republicans and, as shown earlier, could impact upon levels of morale, both positively and negatively.

Extending the 'audience'

Narratives about state violence experienced during detention not only appeared in the pages of newspapers and magazines that were marketed towards a Republican audience. Accounts were also carried by the British *Sunday Times*, which on 17 October 1971 detailed allegations of violence against internees. Almost six years later, on 2 March 1977, The British Broadcasting Corporation (BBC) transmitted further allegations of violence and brutality arising from the treatment of detainees interrogated in the Holding Centre at Castlereagh. Then, in October of 1977, Thames Television broadcast interviews with ten former detainees who had alleged they had been brutalised by the RUC during interrogations. Around this time, Irish newspapers also carried further, similar allegations (Henningan 1978; McKenna 1978; Author Unknown 1978).

Former detainees' narratives as 'propaganda' 111

Although not without problems (see Chapter 7; Curtis 1998) it is clear that the narrative testimonies of state violence were capable of being witnessed by a wide range of non-Republican audiences in Northern Ireland, the Republic of Ireland and in Great Britain. Republicans also sought to selectively use law and legal avenues to internationalise the conflict (McEvoy 2000) and the *Republic of Ireland* v. *United Kingdom* (1978) case at the European Court of Human Rights brought former detainees' experiences to a further international audience. In June 1978 the *Report of an Amnesty International Mission to Northern Ireland* (28 November 1977 to 6 December 1977) was published to a potentially global audience of human rights activists. The *Report of Amnesty International* (1978: 70) stated that 'on the basis of the information available to it, Amnesty International believes that maltreatment of suspected terrorists by the RUC has taken place with sufficient frequency to warrant the establishment of a public inquiry to investigate it'. In support of reaching the broadest possible audiences with his narratives, Liam claimed that:

> People were shocked when they heard about it, because everyone can imagine themselves in the same position. At that time, you didn't have to be in the IRA, or a gunman or anything to be arrested, to be taken to a Barracks and to beaten, to be held for days. You didn't have to be anything, you were 'Joe Public' lying in your bed and your door was kicked in and you were dragged away. That is why it had to be told, and told to ordinary people as well as journalists and stuff. They had to know. They had a right to know. A right to know what these people did and what you could expect from them.

If propaganda is 'a sub set of both information and persuasion' (Jowett and O'Donnell 1999: 46) then most of the motivations behind the narrative testimonies upon which this book is based fit neatly into those dual criteria. Recruitment for the IRA or support for its actions from a particular audience was not recalled as a clear intention or as the primary motivator for most of the detainees interviewed, even if on occasions it was a foreseeable consequence. A desire to educate was instead the most common motivation. Having been interned and subjected to state violence, despite never having been involved in armed Republicanism, Interviewee PJ described his motivation for going public as being:

> [T]o let other people know what is happening. I was attempting to have a proper democracy here.... That is all I wanted at any time, even now. So by getting all this out in the open, that you let people know what was going on behind their backs. Strengthening your own case for an open society is enough. That might lever something in their head. That is why I do that.... It is because I want that message to go across whatever way you interpret it. It doesn't matter to me. It is not [an issue] that people will seize on my story and say 'Look at what they are doing, this man was not even a Republican!

112 *Former detainees' narratives as 'propaganda'*

We can do nothing but react to that and we took up arms!' but that is not my fault. I am not in charge of what anybody else is going to say, but anything I say, I can stand over it.

Interviewee PJ thus hoped that the legacy of his narrative testimonies would be one of adding to knowledge and in changing attitudes, and although he recognised the potential for violent agitation, he distanced his own narrative from those potential consequences. Those who *were* active in the Republican struggle also explored the educative function of their narrative testimony in similar terms:

It was an attempt by me to expose what they did to us, in the hope that they wouldn't do it to anyone else.... People had to know, they had to know what happened and they had to know the type of people that did these things ... [What does it mean to you now to have told your story?] I get a certain satisfaction from making people aware of what they did and again, to get people thinking of what they could do and what they were capable of then and what they are capable of now, in terms of putting down any sort of opposition to the occupation of Northern Ireland – of Ireland.

(Liam)

I saw it as rank hypocrisy by people claiming to be upholding the law to administer this kind of thing, ostensibly claiming to have a superior moral standing than I had. I thought it was proper to expose that, to challenge it.

(Tommy)

However, the educative function of 'going public' was not an isolated intention. All of those interviewed spoke of social change as a desired legacy of their 'truth sharing' and Liam recalled the persuasive role of his testimony in bringing about what he felt was a change in the way detainees were treated:

[Going public]. It does work. Because it embarrasses governments and that is the only reason it works. Unless governments are embarrassed into doing something, they simply won't do it.... But people spoke out, people told their stories and the government was embarrassed and legally challenged into stopping it. And that is why they stopped it. Make no mistake about it. Had they not been challenged they wouldn't have stopped it. All because people went public and brought it to the attention of the wider world for want of a better word.

Other interviewees also interpreted their narrative testimony as purposive in pressuring the British State to change its approach to the conflict and the way in which the conflict was labelled as a 'law and order problem' – albeit one with special courts, powers and legislation (see Boyle *et al.* 1975; Hillyard 1993).

Since the British Government was totally indifferent to the law and that the only way to rescue the situation ... was to highlight it internationally.... So my view was ... that my contribution added to – and I wasn't the only person who was making those submissions – pressure to immediately over-turn the Diplock system and make it more difficult for the British State to dismiss the Northern Irish problem as a 'criminal outbreak' ... [I]f they were no longer able to put that veneer of respectability over it, then it rolled the situation back to one of insurrection where the British would have to come up with a qualitatively different approach. It was never admitted but it was ultimately eventually what transpired.

(Tommy)

Similarly for Michael, former detainees' narratives of state violence had to be 'made public', because of the hope that reaching a wider audience could become a catalyst for change:

It had to be told and people had to stand up and let the world know because it was on-going, and something had to be done to get it stopped. The only way really to get it stopped was by people highlighting it. And here, over a period of time, for what it is worth, it gradually pushed back their ability to do that [brutality]. Proof of the pudding was when I was taken back into Castlereagh six months later they did not physically assault me at all.

Within such interview testimony, the significance former detainees gave to seeking change through the legacy of their narrative is expressed in a subtle and sophistic-ated way. These intended aims lack the explicitly desired military agitation or 'agi-tative propaganda' (Jowett and O'Donnell 1999) evidenced earlier in the words of Harry and Jim, but they still seek an end to the state violence against detainees. By framing their public testimonies as a broad call for change, rather than as an explicit and isolated call for military action, these interviewees' narratives of state violence can be directed towards a wider audience. The testimonies could be pre-sented in such a way as to enable them to be carried by organisations who sought a form of resonance with the perceived goals, values and interests of the intended audience. Where experiences of state violence were constructed as violations of human dignity and rights, civil society and human rights organisations including Amnesty International were able to carry testimony and avoid entering potentially 'toxic' debates about the legitimacy of armed conflict, thus potentially widening the receptive audience to those who were otherwise uncomfortable giving support to paramilitary groups, such as the IRA. Narratives could be made more effective by 'harmonising' with the viewpoint of the intended audience (MacDonald 1989).

The 1981 hunger strikes and the power of propaganda

The existence of a broader audience available for the witnessing of narrative tes-timonies about state violence surrounding the conflict can be seen most clearly

114 *Former detainees' narratives as 'propaganda'*

through an analysis of the hunger strikes of 1981. Despite the deaths of ten H-Block hunger strikers, the events are regularly presented both by Republicans themselves and by those opposed to them as a huge propaganda coup which contributed to a 'groundswell' of support for Republicanism, as evidenced by the electoral successes of hunger strikers Bobby Sands to the Westminster Parliament and Kieran Doherty to the Dáil Éireann.

Narrative testimonies describing the hunger strikes of 1981 have been extensively detailed elsewhere by journalists and historians (Beresford 1987; Coogan 2000, 2002; English 2003, 2006) and references to those events appear frequently throughout the writings of former detainees themselves (McKeown 2001; Campbell *et al.* 2006). The poems and essays of Bobby Sands, the first of the hunger strikers to die during the 1981 hunger strike, have also been published extensively, both during the strike and posthumously (for example, Sands 1998, 2001). These narratives detail elements of state violence experienced during detention and can be interpreted as purposeful propaganda, intended to convince a particular audience of the righteousness of the Republican cause, as justifications for the prisoners' actions and/or a call for support or assistance – although each of these elements may exist in isolation, particularly when seen through the lens of the 'Five Demands'.[3]

Sands' (1998, 2001) emotive and vivid writings were/are capable of arousing sympathy (Crawford 2002). They were significant in the sense that the imagery they presented fulfilled a need for narratives from the prison that were 'political and analytical, but ... also had to be personal' (O'Hare 2006: 110). As likely as an intention to generate sympathy may be, the intended consequences of Sands' writings were never precisely defined in his own testimony, with the loosely framed exception of the close to one of his articles: 'With that in your mind, I will leave off. Think about it, but just don't leave it at that' (Sands 1998: 152). The receiver of the message is left to decide what action to take, but within a framework which seeks to persuade the receiver that some form of action *should definitely* be taken.

Like Wright (1990), Bowyer Bell (1994) argues that the Republican communications emerging around the events of 1981 intended to create and sustain a 'historical lineage' between the hunger strikes and detention experiences of 1981 and the Easter Rising of 1916. Such linkages at times may be problematic given the splits and conflicts within Republicanism since the Rising. However, this created sense of a historical continuity was and remains strongly imprinted upon the public narration and memorialisation of the 1981 hunger strikes. The figure of Bobby Sands is represented in books, music, murals and other cultural materials, as the latest in a line of many Irish martyrs throughout history (O'Shaughnessy 2004). Throughout the conflict, experiences of Republican detainees were portrayed through a framework tied to past state violence and abuses and this continuity with the past was emphasised in Republican publications.

Broader discussions about the nature of propaganda suggest that 'if wider circles of the public are to be touched by synthetic representations ... the form

Former detainees' narratives as 'propaganda' 115

must be personal, dramatic and literary' (Lasswell 1971: 94). One method by which the propaganda professing apparent continuity with the past was transmitted was through the use of symbolism. For Bowyer Bell (1994) all conflicts use their own stereotypes and symbols, and the conflict in and around the detention system of Northern Ireland is no exception. Barbed wire becomes the metaphor for the 'violence of incarceration', to borrow Scraton and McCullagh's (2009) phrase. A list of 'Five Demands' becomes a means of seeking the legitimation of a violent struggle for self-determination, and death itself becomes reinterpreted as an act of resistance. Such symbols do not always point to something concrete but instead retain a social and cultural meaning (O'Shaughnessy 2004). The symbols were communicated through and synthesised into 'the revolutionary songs of this nation [which] have informed, comforted, encouraged, sustained and emboldened our people through the ages, in good times and bad times' (Brolly 2006: 63–64). Ballads such as Brian Warfield's '*The Ballad of Joe McDonnell*' (n.d.) and Pat McGuigan's (1971) '*Men Behind the Wire*' suggested to their audience that anybody could become a victim of state violence.

Such cultural materials are also the means through which a persuasive intention can be communicated to an audience. These materials helped to strengthen links with the past and famously helped to cast the hunger strike as part of a historical Celtic tradition (Sweeney 1993; Crawford 2002). Similarly O'Malley (1990: 25) argues that:

> Although hunger striking is not especially Irish, in Ireland the myth of hunger striking is more powerful than the history of hunger striking itself. Hunger striking fuses elements of the legal code of ancient [Brehon] Ireland,[4] of the self-denial that is the central characteristic of Irish Catholicism, and of the propensity for endurance that is the hallmark of militant Irish nationalism.

Discussions of the apparent religious symbolism, assisted by television pictures from the H-Blocks showing bearded men wrapped in cloth, preparing to die for their beliefs and for the beliefs of those around them, may have helped to encourage the Catholic Nationalist population to support the prisoners' demands for political status (Sweeney 1993) by adding an additional level of interpretation. For Feldman (1991), it was precisely the religious and pacifist iconography of the 1981 strike which brought it such support throughout Ireland and elsewhere. The mythic interpretations of the strike(rs) infused with religious symbolism and communicated through propaganda may have 'provide[d] a common cultural vocabulary, they unite[d], they flatter[ed], they elevate[d] the argument or group that claims association with them' (O'Shaughnessy 2004: 87–88).

Propaganda of this form can act as a form of social control ensuring that 'volunteers' remain committed to the Republican movement (O'Shaughnessy 2004). Yet, significantly, the perception that such imagery sustains its supporters by

116   *Former detainees' narratives as 'propaganda'*

linking them with the past history of Irish resistance (Sweeney 1993) is power-fully challenged by research by Lloyd (2006: 233), who argues that:

> To read the survivors of the prisons and the protests now in their oral and written histories is to be struck … by how rare reference is to the whole apparatus of Celtic mythology and blood sacrifice and by how little, on their own confession the young men who entered the H Blocks even knew of the past of Republicanism and even of the so-called tradition of hunger striking.

The importance of religious symbolism which Feldman (1991) suggests represents the sacralisation of the strikes in the propaganda of this period, risks being overstated, just as the relationship between 1981 and previous historical strikes risks being overemphasised. During research for this book, detailed references were made by interviewees to the state violence surrounding former prisoners at the time of the hunger strikes, but none of the former detainees placed those events in a historical or cultural continuum alongside previous hunger strikes. A further review of the testimonies made public by former detainees themselves, largely supports Lloyd's (2006) assertion, with the exception of Sands (2001). Furthermore, the accounts of O'Malley (1990) can justifiably be critiqued for portraying and interpreting the events of 1981 only as a 'primitive, degenerative nationalism' and for overstating the religious symbolism (see Hayden 2006: 148). The framework of legitimacy emphasised through historical continuity, of Brehon laws, Irish traditions and religious symbolism appears to have been a framework largely attached *to* the prison struggle by those outside the prison, rather than emanating from within it. As Taylor (1999) states, often during conflict, the lines between myth and reality start to blur. History itself can therefore become a victim of manipulation.

This is not to suggest, however, that such historical and/or cultural frameworks are meaningless. According to Jackall (1995) these representations might only bear a passing resemblance to reality, but once internalised by a carefully targeted audience, the representation can quickly replace the reality. Propaganda remains a powerful means by which representations can be communicated. Once an audience has been chosen, symbols can be used to communicate the message. For example, from this theoretical perspective, if the intention is to persuade Christians of the 'necessity' of the hunger strike, then Christian symbolism should be used to convey the message. For Lasswell (1971: xiv), propagandists seek:

> to influence audiences whose socialisation is similarly circumscribed. At best the propagandist is selective. He [*sic*] discerns a potential reservoir of discontent or aspiration and searches for ways of discharging the discontent and harnessing the aspirations so that they harmonise with his policy objectives.

Former detainees' narratives as 'propaganda' 117

In understanding the 'world view' and values of a particular audience, propaganda can be styled and communicated to maximise the possibility of it fulfilling its persuasive intentions.

War of ideas

Feeney (2002: 290) suggests that 'Sinn Féin, its propaganda and publicity expertly and adroitly marshalled by Danny Morrison, exploited the emotionalism surrounding prisoners ... to its limits' (see also Crawford 2002) and as O'Shaughnessy (2004: 125) argues, it is difficult to imagine such a propaganda 'cleansed of victims'. However, the recasting of narratives about state violence into an emotive discourse about 'man's inhumanity to man' can be a fractured, problematic and fractur*ing* process, particularly during an ongoing period of conflict. The history of Republican attitudes towards the targeting of different audiences through the narrative testimonies of state violence involved conflicting values and attitudes, personal differences, changing political and propaganda strategies, all of which were occurring within an atmosphere of continuing violence and brutality.

In April 1977, the Relatives Action Committee (RAC) was established to provide external support for the prisoners' struggle against criminalisation (Clarke 1987). The Committee comprised mainly of the female relatives of prisoners and it attempted to raise international awareness of the prison struggle by taking part in talks, lectures and demonstrations in France, Belgium, the Netherlands and Switzerland (Corcoran 2006). Communicating detainees' experiences of state violence during these visits became part of their persuasive approach. However, Clarke (1987) argues that some members of the Republican movement within Sinn Féin were wary of attempting to reach a wider audience through the public narratives of state violence against H-Block prisoners, particular in the years 1978–1979. A Sinn Féin statement during a meeting of the Coalisland Relatives Action Committee in January 1978 argued that 'repression condemned on moral grounds isn't good enough. For while it brings sections of the population into opposition, it rarely brings them into resistance' (cited in Clarke 1987: 90). This interpretation called for those who condemned the treatment of prisoners to *act* against the repressive state in response to the published details of prisoners' narratives. Similarly, McEvoy (2001) too suggests that 'doctrinaire Republicans' insisted upon support for the armed campaign as a key aspect. The initial strictness of this discourse is particularly surprising, given that 'the Republican movement has always been an eclectic, non-cohesive body ... of militant nationalists, unreconstructed militarists, romantic Fenians, Gaelic Republicans, Catholic sectarians, Northern defenders, international Marxists, socialists, libertarians and liberal Protestants' (Tonge 2004: 2).

Thus at some late point in the Criminalisation period, there was a subtle and gradual change in the strategies and relationships and between those detained, the wider communities, the IRA, Sinn Féin and the Republican movement (see Coogan 2000; Moloney 2007). According to Feeney (2002) the Relatives Action

118   *Former detainees' narratives as 'propaganda'*

Committee struggled to be heard, and activists such as Jim Gibney and Gerry Adams had started to call for the Committee to widen its audience. The successor to the Relatives Action Committee – the National H-Block/Armagh Committee – achieved support from a broader constituency of mostly left-leaning groups, such as People's Democracy, the Communist Party, civil rights activists and trade unionists (McEvoy 2001). It did therefore not draw exclusively from the Republican movement, although there was some influence from Sinn Féin in encouraging former detainees to make public their allegations for the Committee to then publicise. As McEvoy (2001) suggests, there were many in the Committee who were in favour of the concept of a united Ireland, and there was some support for the armed struggle from such groups, but it was no longer a precondition of support for the prisoners. According to Maillot (2004: 89) 'some people even condemned the manner in which they were exploited by Sinn Féin, [yet the Committee maintained] sufficient distance from the party to enable those who were not entirely comfortable with the ideas or strategies associated with the Republican movement to get involved in the campaigns'.

The Republican strategies of the late 1970s were an 'attempt to break out Britain's successful containment and regain the initiative' (Bean 2007: 59) and the intention is not to trace all of the twists and turns of Republicanism here. Yet narratives of state violence experienced by former detainees clearly assisted in 'broadening the battlefield' (Clarke 1987). First, former detainees' experiences could be made to fit a Republican narrative and were portrayed as communal suffering against a malevolent State in publications such as *An Phoblacht*. Second, the stories of state violence could be alternatively framed as individual experiences of violence and communicated to human rights organisations and civil libertarian groups. They could widen the audience who heard accounts of state violence and garner some sympathy for the prisoners' cause and perhaps turn this into active support.

Harry commented on the importance of this communication between broader human rights/civil society audiences and the Republican movement:

> They would document it and go to civil rights and human rights people and get their backings. It would get recognised within these groups – not that it wasn't recognised but it would get more recognition with these groups.... If there hadn't have been any brutality in jail or anything like that, if you just came in, did the sentence and got out, the people, the movement would not have got half of the support it did.

The distance between the violent actions of the IRA and an individual detainee's narrative also gave human rights organisations greater room to act in publicising accounts of state violence. The relationship between Republicans and the media also changed in the late 1970s, as repeated raids on the Republican press centre inadvertently contributed to improving the Republicans' relationship with the wider media (Curtis 1998). The raids led to those involved with Republican press being identified and they then became a point of contact for journalists.

Former detainees' narratives as 'propaganda' 119

This is not to suggest that Republicans' narratives of state violence always found their way into the mainstream media, for as Curtis (1998) argues, coverage of events in Northern Ireland involving state violence was still subjected to a range of formal and informal controls. What is clear is that by framing narratives as individualised experiences of a violent state, the potential audiences for prisoners' experiences could be increased beyond those sympathetic to Republicanism. Laurence commented on the narratives of state violence emerging from the H-Blocks and their possible impact upon a non-Republican audience:

> Those interested in justice, equality, or a better society ... I think it's very difficult to [not be moved] – even if you are someone who is biased against Republicanism, I think if you were to read it with anything like an open mind, it would change your view just a bit about the state and what the state can do and get away with.

The sense in which the struggle between state violence and resistant Republicans within the semi-private sphere of the detention system could be publicly framed as a humanitarian concern about the treatment of prisoners can be seen clearly in a press release from Cardinal Ó Fiaich, released on 1 August 1978, which stated that:

> One would hardly allow an animal to remain in such conditions, let alone a human being. The nearest approach to it that I have seen was the spectacle of hundreds of homeless people living in the sewer pipes in the slums of Calcutta. The stench and filth in some of the cells, with the remains of rotten food and human excreta scattered around the walls, was almost unbearable. In two of them I was unable to speak for fear of vomiting.... They are locked in their cells for almost the whole of every day and some of them have been in this condition for more than a year and a half.
>
> (in Coogan 2002: 265–266)

Such statements 'sidestepped' questions about the legitimacy of the IRA and its actions and can be seen as possessing the educative function earlier described by Liam and Tommy. The audience is left to reach its own conclusions about what the narratives desire of them. The Cardinal's words seemingly represent a broad appeal to compassion, empathy and a sense of justice, which Lasswell (1971) and Crawford (2002) suggest are important elements of propaganda. The shifting emphasis in the public narratives of the prison struggles can be further witnessed in the 'Five Demands' of the hunger strike. As propaganda they symbolised political status and through this symbolism subtly sought to legitimise the armed conflict and IRA action. Thus the stories of State violence from this period did not ask directly for an audience to give their legitimacy to IRA actions, yet instead intended to persuade an audience that the 'Five Demands' were a reasonable and attainable request. Many of those who took part in the hunger strikes in 1981 had been convicted of 'lesser' crimes and this was thought

120   *Former detainees' narratives as 'propaganda'*

to be more amenable for those whose support for armed struggle had not been forthcoming. The resulting election successes of prisoners Bobby Sands and Kieran Doherty, along with Owen Carron on an 'Anti H-Block' ticket, strengthens the argument that the narratives of state violence and prison conditions had successfully refined the struggle into a 'human rights issue' – something aided by an international media who were mostly sympathetic to the striking prisoners and to Sands in particular (Bowyer Bell 1994).

Re-imagining propaganda

In conclusion, the period 1971–1985 can be explored as not only a violent conflict of bombings, shootings and brutality, but also as a war of ideas and interpretations. When seen as a synthesis of information and persuasion, the testimonies of former detainees about experiences of state violence can be perceived as propaganda, where this is defined as 'a consistent, enduring effort to create or shape events to influence the relations of the public to an enterprise, idea or group' (Bernays 2005: 520). Yet importantly, this shaping is not necessarily direct manipulation. As Coogan (2002) suggests, like *all* organisations, the IRA would inevitably seek to make gains from the narratives of former detainees describing state violence. Furthermore, there exists a certain level of pluralism in propaganda, as coverage of state violence in Amnesty International Reports, for example, may frame events as human rights abuses, whilst the same message in *An Phoblacht* can be coded, communicated and interpreted differently.

O'Shaughnessy (2004: 21) argues that material can be used as propaganda 'even when the intent was neutral'. However, it is unclear to what extent an intention can ever be neutral, for the concept of intention is one which is goal driven and purposeful. All propaganda, indeed, most communication itself, is usually intentional and purposeful, even if those things may not be immediately apparent. It simply may be that the intentions of propaganda/the propagandist are not achieved. Many were unresponsive, suspicious or critical towards testimonies of state violence which attempted to criticise the State, to justify the Republican cause and violence, and/or to be a catalyst for social and political change. Furthermore, attempts were made to deny the violence experienced by detainees, to reframe it as legitimate and justified, or to otherwise challenge the truth value of the persons or narratives involved (see Chapter 7).

Despite all of its complexity, the one certainty in all of this is that the stigmatising power of the label propaganda remains. The labelling of propaganda itself may signify the casting of doubt on the veracity of former detainees' accounts and on the trustworthiness of the messenger or mechanism. It can also be seen as a commentary on the legitimacy of a cause, if that cause is perceived to be only attainable through manipulation or outright deceit. When allegations of violence were described by the then Secretary of State Roy Mason's influential discourse as part of 'a propaganda wave against the success of the RUC' (in *The Newsletter* 14 April 1978) the intention was to use the power of language to control and cast doubt on the credibility of those accounts and their accuracy. It may be that some

Former detainees' narratives as 'propaganda' 121

former detainees' accounts were exaggerated, manipulated or otherwise misrepresented,[5] yet this does not mean that violence against detainees simply did *not* take place. As Chomsky and Barsamian (2001: 147) maintain, 'even the most vulgar of propaganda usually has elements of truth'. The supportive statements of academics (e.g. Walsh 1998; McEvoy 2001), respected journalists (Taylor 1980) some former State agents (in Cobain 2010), human rights organisations (Amnesty International 1978) and the partial results of actions in the European Court of Human Rights (*Republic of Ireland* v. *UK* 1978), as well as in the civil courts, all add weight to the veracity of former detainees' accounts and their consistency.

Furthermore, it is the motivations, significance and legacy of 'going public' which are the concern of this book and not the validity or otherwise of former detainees' original accounts. The dominant pejorative interpretations of the meaning of propaganda remain problematically one dimensional and myopic. Where the meaning of propaganda is perceived only as manipulation, it obfuscates the agency of an audience and patronises their own ability to deconstruct a public narrative:

> We commonly respond to persuasive messages by questioning the speaker's bias and noting how his/her self-interest is being served.... By identifying a message as biased, the audience can prepare to defend its position and either to scrutinise carefully the contents of the message or reject it out of hand.
>
> (Pratkanis and Aronson 1991: 94)

Audiences are not blind dupes, but will deconstruct the message in a way which they see fit. As Jowett and O'Donnell (1999) rightly assert, an awareness that a message may be propaganda does not necessarily mean that an audience dismisses it outright. An audience can choose to assist the propagandist in achieving their intentions, even if that audience is aware of a supposedly hidden agenda. The problem with propaganda is that the term has become symbolically linked and stained with an 'unpleasant connotation' (Bernays 2005: 48). Miller (1994: 3) describes the effects of the label as being 'insidious and unconscious', and it is, as O'Shaughnessy (2004: 3) argues, now perceived merely as a 'term of opprobrium'. This was recognised by two of the former detainees who took part in the present study:

> [Going public] was just part of the thing we could do to blacken their name – and I don't mean propaganda as telling lies. You couldn't afford to tell lies, because if you were caught telling lies then the whole lot was out of the window. You had to stick to the exact truth.
>
> (Harry)

> So [I] feel good that the story has got out there, that it's not propaganda, it's just the story of someone saying this is what happened to me and this is what I was thinking at the time.
>
> (Laurence)

122 *Former detainees' narratives as 'propaganda'*

Thus it remains very difficult to reach an agreed upon definition of propaganda cleansed of all this stigma (Jowett and O'Donnell 1999). The label of propaganda conveys a judgement made by an audience about their interpretation of a message and its apparent source. It is a deeply political judgement. Discussions with former detainees about the motivation, significance and legacy of their narrative testimonies about state violence suggest that, at times, their narrations were indeed motivated by propagandist intentions. However, this simply means that their testimonies were purposive, like most communication. For the majority of those former detainees interviewed, this purpose was linked to educating their audiences about what they had experienced in detention in the hope that this would bring about increased awareness and, in time, social change.

Notes

1 IRA training manual for 'new volunteers'.
2 See Scarry (1987) and Feitlowitz (1998) on the inability of language to communicate pain.
3 See Chapter 2 for an analysis of the meaning and significance of these demands. They essentially symbolised political status for paramilitary prisoners.
4 As interpreted by Sweeney (1993), elements of Brehon traditions involved a wronged individual situating themselves close to those suspected of that wrong, and then engaging in a hunger strike. Any harm caused to the wronged individual would then be the responsibility of the suspects.
5 For example, Clarke (1987) alleges that an account entitled 'Day in the Life of the H Blocks' is often featured in Republican publications with names and locations changed to better resonate with the respective publication's local audience.

References

Ainsworth, J. (2002) 'Kevin Barry, the Incident at Monk's Bakery and the Making of an Irish Republican Legend', *History*, 87(287), 372–387.
Alonso, R. (2001) *The IRA and Armed Struggle*. London: Routledge.
Amnesty International (1978) *Report of an Amnesty International Mission to Northern Ireland 28 November–6 December 1977* [AI Index:Eur 45/01/78/].
An Phoblacht (1978) 'Act Now To Save H Block and Armagh Lives', 11 January.
An Phoblacht (1978) 'What It Is Like In a Concentration Camp', 14 October.
Author Unknown (1978) 'Recruited Men to Make Bombs for the North', *Irish Independent*, 17 June.
Bean, K. (2007) *The New Politics of Sinn Féin*. Liverpool: Liverpool University Press.
Beresford, D. (1987) *Ten Men Dead: The Story of the 1981 Hunger Strike*. London: Harper Collins.
Bernays, E. (2005) *Propaganda*. Brooklyn: Ig Publishing.
Bowyer Bell, J. (1994) *The Irish Troubles: A Generation of Violence 1967–1992*. Dublin: Gill and MacMillan.
Boyle, K., Hadden, T. and Hillyard, P. (1975) *Law and The State: The Case of Northern Ireland*. London: Martin Robertson.
Brolly, F. (2006) 'The H-Block Song', in Morrison D. (ed.) *Hunger Strike: Reflections on the 1981 Hunger Strike*. Dingle: Brandon.

Former detainees' narratives as 'propaganda'   123

Campbell, B., McKeown, L. and O'Hagan, F. (2006) *Nor Meekly Serve My Time: The H Block Struggle*. Belfast: Beyond the Pale.

Chomsky, N. and Barsamian, D. (2001) *Propaganda and the Public Mind: Conversations with Noam Chomsky*. London: Pluto.

Clarke, L. (1987) *Broadening the Battlefield: H-Blocks and the Rise of Sinn Féin*. Dublin: Gill and Macmillan.

Cobain, I. (2010) 'Inside Castlereagh: "We Got Confessions By Torture"' *Guardian*. 11 October. Available at: www.guardian.co.uk/uk/2010/oct/11/inside-castlereagh-confessions-torture (accessed 31 August 2013).

Coogan, T.P. (2000) *The IRA*. London: Palgrave Macmillan.

Coogan, T.P. (2002) *The Troubles: Ireland's Ordeal 1966–1996 and the Search For Peace*. New York: Palgrave.

Corcoran, M.S. (2006) 'Talking About Resistance: Women Political Prisoners and the Dynamics of Prison Conflict, Northern Ireland', in Barton, A., Corteen, K., Scott, D. and Whyte, D. (eds) *Expanding the Criminological Imagination: Critical Readings in Criminology*. Devon: Willan.

Crawford, M.K. (2002) *Creating the Ideal Republican: Northern Ireland Prison Writings as Propaganda*. Unpublished Thesis. Haverford College, Pennsylvania [Online] Available at: http://triceratops.brynmawr.edu/dspace/bitstream/10066/673/5/2002Crawford M.pdf (accessed 31 November 2012).

Curtis, L. (1998) *Ireland: The Propaganda War*. Belfast: Sásta.

Eisenhower, J.J. (1985) 'Interrogation and the Admissibility of Confessions in Northern Ireland', *Temple International and Comparative Law Journal*, 1(1), 16–34.

English, R. (2003) *Armed Struggle: A History of the IRA*. London: Pan Macmillan.

English, R. (2006) *Irish Freedom: The History of Nationalism in Ireland*. London: Pan Macmillan.

Feeney, B. (2002) *Sinn Féin: A Hundred Turbulent Years*. Dublin: O'Brien Press.

Feitlowitz, M. (1998) *A Lexicon of Terror: Argentina and the Legacies of Torture.* New York: Oxford University Press.

Feldman, A. (1991) *Formations of Violence: The Narrative of the Body and Political Terror in Northern Ireland*. Chicago: University of Chicago Press.

Hayden, T. (2006) 'Dead Men Live' in Morrison, D. (ed.) *Hunger Strike: Reflections on the 1981 Hunger Strike*. Dingle: Brandon.

Hennigan, A. (1978) 'Judge Heads North Torture Inquiry', *Irish Press*, 17 June.

Hillyard, P. (1987) 'The Normalisation of Special Powers: From Northern Ireland to Britain', in Scraton, P. (ed.) *Law, Order and the Authoritarian State.* Milton Keynes: Open University Press.

Hillyard, P. (1993) *Suspect Community: People's Experience of the Prevention of Terrorism Acts in Britain.* London: Pluto.

Jackall, R. (ed.) (1995) *Propaganda*. London: Macmillan.

Jackson, J. (2009) 'Many Years on in Northern Ireland: The Diplock Legacy', *Northern Ireland Legal Quarterly*, 60(2), 215–230.

Jowett, G.S. and O'Donnell, V. (1999) *Propaganda and Persuasion*. London: Sage.

Lasmar, P. and Oliver, P. (1998) *Britain's Secret Propaganda War*. Stroud: Sutton Publishing.

Lasswell, H.D. (1938) 'Propaganda', in Jackall, R. (ed.) (1995) *Propaganda.* London: Macmillan.

Lasswell, H.D. (1971) *Propaganda Techniques in World War One*. Boston: Massachusetts Institute of Technology.

124 *Former detainees' narratives as 'propaganda'*

Lloyd, D. (2006) 'The Myth of Myth', in Morrison, D. (ed.) *Hunger Strike: Reflections on the 1981 Hunger Strike*. Dingle: Brandon.

MacDonald, F.J. (1989) 'Propaganda and Order in Modern Society', in Smith III, T.J. (ed.) (1989) *Propaganda: A Pluralistic Perspective*. London: Praeger.

Maillot, A. (2004) *The New Sinn Féin: Irish Republicanism in the Twenty-First Century.* London: Routledge.

McEvoy, K. (2000) 'Law, Struggle and Political Transformation in Northern Ireland', *Journal of Law and Society*, 27(4), 542–571.

McEvoy, K. (2001) *Paramilitary Imprisonment in Northern Ireland: Resistance, Management and Release*. Oxford University Press: Oxford.

McKenna, P. (1978) 'Derry Murder Raises Fears of A Violent Weekend', *Irish Independent*, 17 June.

McKeown, L. (2001) *Out of Time: Irish Republican Prisoners and Long Kesh 1972–2000*. Belfast: Beyond the Pale.

Miller, D. (1994) *Don't Mention the War: Northern Ireland, Propaganda and the Media*. London: Pluto Press.

Moloney, E. (2007) *A Secret History of the IRA.* London: Penguin Books Ltd.

O'Donnell, V. and Jowett, G. (1989) 'Propaganda as a Form of Communication' in Smith III, T.J. (ed.) *Propaganda: A Pluralistic Perspective*. London: Praeger.

O'Hare, R. (2006) 'Those Cherished Pictures' in Morrison, D. (ed.) *Hunger Strike: Reflections on the 1981 Hunger Strike*. Dingle: Brandon. ·

O'Malley, P. (1990) *Biting at the Grave: the Irish Hunger Strikes and the Politics of Despair*. Belfast: Blackstaff Press.

O'Shaughnessy, N.J. (2004) *Politics and Propaganda: The Weapons of Mass Seduction*. Manchester: Manchester University Press.

Pratkanis, A. and Aronson, E. (1991) *Age of Propaganda: The Everyday Use and Abuse of Persuasion*. New York: WH Freeman and Company.

Read, J.M. (1938) 'Atrocity Propaganda and the Irish Rebellion', *American Association for Public Opinion Research*, 2(2), 229–244.

Republic of Ireland v. *United Kingdom* [1978] 2 EHRR 25.

Sánchez-Cuenca, I. and de la Calle, L. (2007) 'The Dynamics of Nationalist Terrorism: ETA and the IRA', *Journal of Terrorism and Political Violence*, 19(3), 289–306.

Sands, B. (1998) *Writings from Prison*. Cork: Mercier Press.

Sands, B. (2001) *One Day in my Life*. Cork: Mercier Press.

Scarry, E. (1987) *The Body in Pain: The Making and Unmaking of the World.* Oxford: Oxford University Press.

Scraton, P. and McCullagh, J. (eds) (2009) *The Violence of Incarceration*. Abingdon: Routledge.

Smith III, T.J. (ed.) (1989) *Propaganda: A Pluralistic Perspective*. London: Praeger.

Sweeney, G. (1993) 'Self Immolation in Ireland: Hunger Strikes and Political Confrontation', *Anthropology Today*, 9(5), 10–14.

Taylor, P. (1980) *Beating the Terrorists: Interrogation in Omagh, Gough and Castlereagh.* London: Penguin.

Taylor, P.M. (1999) *British Propaganda in the Twentieth Century: Selling Democracy*. Edinburgh: Edinburgh University Press.

The Newsletter (1978) 'MPs Warned of Big Anti-RUC Campaign'. 14 April.

Tonge, J. (2004) ' "They Haven't Gone Away, You Know" Irish Republican "Dissidents" and "Armed Struggle" ', *Paper presented to the Political Studies Association of the United Kingdom Annual Conference*, University of Lincoln, Lincoln. 6–8 April.

Walsh, D. (1998) 'The RUC: A Law Unto Themselves', in Tomlinson, M., Varley, M. and McCullagh, C. (eds) *Whose Law and Order? Aspects of Crime and Social Control in Irish Society.* Belfast: The Sociological Association of Ireland.

Wilcox, F.O. (1940). 'The Use of Atrocity Stories in War'. *American Political Science Review*, 34(06), 1167–1178.

Wright, J. (1990) 'Provisional IRA Propaganda: The Construction of Legitimacy', *Conflict Quarterly*, 10(3), 24–41.

7 Discourse, denial and dehumanisation

The previous chapters of this book have examined the meanings and motivations which underpin the production of narratives of state violence, or make that production problematic. The following chapter moves deeper into these problems and explores the legacy of 'official discourse' for those detainees who have made public their accounts of state violence. It explores the sociology of denial and the manner in which 'truths' are constructed and legitimated. Using material from a series of interviews with former detainees, it critically analyses the inter-relationship between social control and information control, and examines the techniques of neutralisation which may have impacted upon former detainees' experiences of narrating state violence. Mechanisms of denial form lenses which shape the perception of narratives of state violence. They are identified and analysed in order to illustrate the different ways in which official discourse is constructed and deconstructed. The chapter shows how the three interrelated levels of denial described by Cohen (2001) can be observed in the official discourse surrounding the conflict and argues that the legacy of those denials are experienced by former detainees in a number of different ways.

As outlined earlier, an extensive and growing literature exists across a range of disciplines that explores the role of narratives in post-conflict society and their role in healing, reconciliation and peace-building (see Minow 2000; Hayner 2002). However, there is little consideration of the role played by discourses of truth *during* conflict, or more precisely, the exact nature of truth *in* conflict. These issues remain important as conflicts do not exist in a vacuum but are instead shaped and moulded by contrasting conceptions of truth, denial, disinformation and dehumanisation, each of which impact on our understandings of ourselves and our apparent enemies. 'Truth' as an instrument can be used to justify or delegitimise ideologies, individuals, events and their narration.

Literal denial

As research 'from below' (Stanley 2009) concerned with those more often subjected to official interpretations with relatively less access to discursive power, the analysis of official discourse should be supported by a greater understanding of the lived consequences of such language from the perspective of those whose

Discourse, denial and dehumanisation 127

subjugated knowledges form part of these contested public narratives. Cohen (2001) adapts Sykes and Matza's (1957) 'techniques of neutralisation' in order to construct a sociological framework of 'state denials'. The existence of state denial can be seen most clearly in the official discourse offered by states, particularly against allegations of wrongdoing and/or criminality. In many instances, state denial may be 'literal' and claim that the alleged event literally did not happen. This official discourse denies outright that state harm occurs (Cohen 2001) and can be witnessed most frequently in the public pronouncements of 'less open' societies (Morgan 2000), in areas where civil society organisations/human rights groups may lack power and opportunities, and where the government can act without any accountability in ways which suppress dissent. Yet the literal denials of harms caused by agents of the state can also be observed in other so-called 'open' and 'liberal' states. Such states are often under political pressure to respect human rights, not least in order to add greater strength to their critiques of the human rights records of other states deemed 'less democratic'. The difference may be that within so-called 'democratic' states, literal denials are more difficult to maintain, partly as a result of greater press freedom and increased opportunities for dissent within both civil and political spheres of influence. In February 2009, the British Government apologised for previously denying that it had knowledge that aircraft flights arranged by the Central Intelligence Agency (CIA) of the United States of America (involving the rendition of prisoners) were using UK territories (Norton-Taylor 2009). The literal denials of the British Government were thus found to be in conflict with the truth. A further example of the literal denials of state harm can be seen in Israel's use of white phosphorus in Gaza during January 2009. The use of these controversial munitions by the Israeli Defence Forces (IDF) was initially denied outright by the Israeli Government, yet later confirmed by the IDF spokesperson Avital Leibovich, albeit with the added qualification that their use of white phosphorus had been 'in accordance with international law' (in Hider and Frenkel 2009).[1]

Thus even the most literal of denials may not always be permanent, but are instead temporal and dynamic. Despite later pronouncements, the original attempt at literal denial retains some significance and is illustrative of the nature of the state and its relationship to truth and violence. Furthermore, as Cohen (2001: 126) argues, the breaking down of literal denial is 'not to say that all mass atrocities and suffering are known about. But once exposed, they are more difficult to deny'. As shown by the use of social networking and internet communication concerning state violence following a disputed election in Iran in 2009 and revolutions in a number of Arab States in 2011, globalisation and the development of technology can play an important role in challenging official discourse and in distributing allegations of state violence to a wide audience.

The sociology of literal denial can also be seen in the detention system of Northern Ireland. As shown in previous chapters, the security forces of Northern Ireland were frequently accused of using violence as part of their response to the perceived threat from paramilitary and non-violent groups involved in civil

128   *Discourse, denial and dehumanisation*

unrest. Between 1975 and 1978, there were approximately 7,538 recorded complaints made against the RUC alone. Of these recorded complaints, 21 per cent (1,562) concerned alleged assaults during interview (Bennett 1979). One of those former complainants recalled:

> The times I had been in Castlereagh I made official complaints but nothing ever happened. You made it to the Police and they investigated it themselves and would always 'find that it was untrue'.
>
> (Interviewee 'F')

According to Interviewee 'F', the results of an internal investigation conducted by those presented as experts disputed the truth of his testimony. Through such mechanisms, the primary definers of the state and its agents seek to shift the focus of an allegation back onto the alleged victim, in order to send out a powerful message that what (s)he says simply *cannot* be true. In other instances, this reconfiguration can be more subtle, for example, the allegations of detainees are represented as being 'lacking in substance' rather than simply labelled as 'untrue'. Michael recalled that:

> I followed through my complaint ... I had to meet this 'Complaints Officer' who was in theory a neutral. I met him in an RUC barracks, gave him the full statement within a few weeks of getting out, [when] I still had marks on me. He looked at me, did the investigation, took my evidence and a few other things that I had told him.... That man ... sent me a letter after a month or two telling me that 'there was no substance to my allegations'.

Within the internal inquiries and internal complaints procedures of the RUC, these allegations of state violence could be disputed and attempts made to destroy their truth value. However, when the narratives of state violence in detention became public, a further mechanism of denial could then be employed, as another former detainee recalled:

> I met this miner[2] ... he said to me, 'I never believed it [narratives about state violence]. I thought it was Republican propaganda and lies and bullshit about our boys and our police'. I remember saying to him [sarcastically] 'Aye right, it is all make-believe and I'm not sitting here in front of you.'
>
> (Interviewee 'P')

Therefore not all instances of literal denial are framed in clear and explicit terms. It may be that official findings which suggest that 'nothing happened' are more likely to be challenged by former detainees and by those who believe in the substance of their allegations. Yet for a regime of denial to operate 'successfully', there need not be an official finding which claims that the violence 'simply did not happen', for as Interviewee 'P' shows, the labelling of an allegation as propaganda will transmit a similar message. Articles in *The Newsletter*[3] (14

Discourse, denial and dehumanisation 129

April 1978) stated that Members of Parliament had been warned about the 'IRA's anti-RUC propaganda campaign' in relation to violence during interrogations in Castlereagh, Gough and Palace Barracks. Furthermore, any rejection offered by former detainees of the possible value of testimonies to the Republican movement then appears naive, and within the official discourse this adds further power to existing perceptions that former detainees' narratives are false or exaggerated. As the recollections of Interviewee 'P' imply, it may be that disproving the propaganda value of allegations against the security forces remains more difficult than combating the explicit denials which were experienced by Interviewee 'F' and Michael.

The claims that former detainees' allegations were IRA propaganda were often repeated within the British establishment and by sections of the media (Hoggart 1973). The pejorative power of propaganda was used as a euphemism for politically inspired lies. Powerful language was re-employed within the official discourse in order to cast doubt on the veracity or 'truth value' of a detainee's claims. This dominant pejorative meaning of propaganda symbolises a challenge to the 'truth' of a detainee's assertions and the label is difficult to shift, particularly when narrative testimonies can be seen to have some kind of political purpose (see previous Chapter 6). Furthermore, given the historical, political and socio-cultural nature of the conflict in Northern Ireland, any criticism of the police or Army could be framed as resulting only from hostility to their presence (Hegarty 2002) thus any real discussion of the truth of former detainees' accounts becomes obfuscated. Interviewee PJ felt that:

> Some people would be completely disbelieving. Some people would have thought that I was some front for some terrorist groups just to blacken the security forces.

Therefore, an accusation which is labelled and stigmatised as propaganda within the dominant discourse stifles and undermines the allegations, and recasts the narratives of detainees as little more than a calculated attack on the agents of the state, its institutions and its values – and all for a political purpose. This stifling can be observed in the text of the Bennett Inquiry (1979: 7 para. 19) into allegations which emerged from a number of RUC Holding Centres:

> We have seen ... abundant evidence of a co-ordinated and extensive campaign to discredit the police. We have been shown literature in which the intemperate language and the character of the illustrations leaves no doubt that it was designed to destroy the reputation of the police at home and abroad. The propaganda is principally concerned with allegations of ill-treatment of prisoners in the course of their interrogation by the police.

To label the narratives of former detainees as propaganda is to employ a semantic 'gag' which attacks the detainee, their testimony and their perceived political motivations in 'going public'. Testimonies then become a discursive quicksand

130 *Discourse, denial and dehumanisation*

which ensures that any public re-interpretation of experiences becomes difficult. Rather than being simply a technique of neutralisation, the use of the label 'propaganda' can be understood as coding detainees and their narratives as little more than a deliberate and purposely misleading attack on the state and its agents. Although not as overt as other forms, the framing of narrative testimonies as propaganda can therefore be understood as a form of literal denial that seeks to destroy the truth value of a detainee's allegation.

Conceptualising communities

The allegations and the British State's responses to those allegations are highly significant for our understanding of the legacy of state violence, particularly when synthesised within the wider battle for legitimacy and definitional power which has underpinned the conflict in Northern Ireland (Tomlinson 1998). Within this context, the attitudes of audiences again become important. Interviewee 'F' felt that: 'I imagine Unionists did not believe me.... The Unionists would have said "He is a liar".' He suggested that the responses of his audience could be split into clearly defined political groups and communities, and that this division would result in generalised, predictable responses and denials. His analysis is complicated somewhat by Crawford (1999) who briefly alludes to the recognition shown by Loyalist former prisoners to the violence against Republican prisoners – violence carried out by the (overwhelmingly Protestant) security forces. In a similar way to the popular representations of ethno-religious dimensions about the conflict, the easy depictions of Unionism as universally disbelieving or even acquiescing in the violence of the state, and of nationalist audiences as universally critical of the actions of the state against those labelled 'terrorist suspects', remains deeply problematic. Such depictions ignore the role of Protestant groups in the development of Irish Republicanism (and also constitutional nationalism) and the presence of Protestant members (such as Harry) in Republican paramilitary groups. It also fails to consider Catholic support for the Union or Catholic involvement in the security forces. As Tonge (2002) suggests, although attitudes might have hardened later, some Unionists were initially supportive of calls for greater rights for Nationalists in the late 1960s. The extent to which these limiting, caricatured depictions of politicised and divided communities remains powerful may call into question the potential of 'truth sharing' for purposes of reconciliation. Interviewee 'F' felt that Unionists depicted him and his (politicised) community as 'the other', would not listen to his narrative of state violence and would not perceive his testimony to have any validity whatsoever. The label 'Unionist' was used by many former detainees as a form of political 'shorthand' to signify those they felt would not consider the 'truth value' of detainees' experiences. They constructed opposing monolithic, homogeneous communities in which all of those deemed to be 'Unionist' would be automatically disbelieving of any narrative which criticised the actions of the security forces.

Despite this, the 'expected' lack of belief in his narrative testimony was not experienced as problematic for Interviewee 'F' and the literal denials offered by

Discourse, denial and dehumanisation   131

the police in relation to his case were not recalled as having a particularly powerful impact upon his experience of narrating state violence. His lack of concern about official denials was widely shared amongst most of the interviewees. Interviewee PJ was particularly philosophical and dismissed as unimportant any denials contained within the British State's response to his narrative of violence experienced during internment. He argued that:

> It doesn't matter. Really doesn't matter.... It doesn't matter what the security forces thought about me. What matters to me is what I think about them.... It doesn't matter to me. It doesn't matter whether they deny it or whether they do not deny it. I know what happened and I can say it. Independent people can judge.
>
> (Interviewee PJ)

Yet Interviewee PJ also acknowledged that this was a deeply personal conviction and one that not everyone would share. He suggested that the families and friends of those who 'went public' with allegations of state violence may have experienced the denials of others in a different and much more significant way:

> Put it this way, my wife would get annoyed sometimes with peoples' reactions to what I would say. I would talk to her and say 'What are you getting annoyed about? What odds what they say?[4] It does not matter'. You would know you were telling the truth. That is alright, people are entitled to not believe me. Why should somebody believe me?
>
> (Interviewee PJ)

The apparent indifference of some former detainees to the denials witnessed in parts of the official discourse is in sharp contrast to the perceptions of Jim, who experienced the denials of the British State and its agencies as intensely frustrating. He recalled the proceedings of the *Republic of Ireland* v. *UK* (1978) case at the ECtHR and passionately argued that:

> [A Special Branch officer] said the white noise was really just because it was beside an airplane hangar and it was just the noise of the aircraft that we had heard. It was stuff like that. I suppose I was laughing about it, at the stupidity of it but at the same time being angry and frustrated about it because you knew at that stage that there would be people who believed him, because they wanted to believe him, because it justified it for them and that made them sleep easier. So on that level there was frustration around that.

In this sense, Jim experienced state denials concerning the use of 'white noise' as personally significant. He was angry and frustrated about what he felt was the high likelihood that the public would uncritically accept the narrative offered by agents of the State, and consequently felt that this would adversely impact upon

132   *Discourse, denial and dehumanisation*

the 'truth value' of his experience of state violence and its perception. He argued that he could foresee people accepting the official discourse as the primary definition of what he had experienced and that his testimony would then be transformed into something 'other' than an account of state violence. Jim also viewed the denials of Special Branch as an attempt to justify any action taken against him by portraying him only as a violent and dangerous individual. Here, the discursive intent which underpins state denials becomes more complex than the simple assertion that something just 'did not happen'. For Liam, the language of the British representatives was also important:

> All they said was 'It wasn't as bad as he is making out to be'. That was it, it was a play on words again. But all I did was tell it as it happened and you make your own mind up then from there being a listener.

In this way Liam felt that his suffering was being diminished by the language 'games' around the meaning of torture and brutality. He recognised the importance of official discourse in defining what he had experienced, but in contrast to Jim, he suggested that his audiences were capable of reaching their own conclusions and that there was little he could do to influence the way his experiences were interpreted.

Injuries as self-inflicted

Denials thus take many forms and can include the denial of responsibility. This can involve the shifting of responsibility within organisations, for example, the claim that any abuse by members of state agencies was not systematic or planned but was the work of a few 'rotten apples'. Alternatively, denials may shift responsibility between organisations, for example, that the abuse of detainees was not carried out by the British Army en route to detention, but by the RUC or Prison Service on arrival. Harry suggested that if there were any visible signs of violence on the bodies of detainees, 'the "peelers"[5] would say "Oh it was the 'screws' that did that, not us"'.

Yet within the context of the conflict in Northern Ireland, the denial of responsibility offered by state agencies (the RUC in particular) was often expressed in such a way as to avoid any state responsibility whatsoever for the visible injuries to detainees. The text of the Compton Inquiry (1971: 22 para. 96) suggested that detainees were responsible for their own treatment, stating that it was 'difficult to give credence to the far more serious allegations by some detainees that they were denied food and water for long periods, and think it was they who failed to take such food and drink as was offered to them'. The Inquiry also claimed that for one detainee, 'the handling ... was more forcible because of his active resistance' (Compton 1971: 22 para. 98). In this way any visible, recordable signs of violence were represented within the official discourse as being 'self-inflicted'. The precise nature of this denial and its personal impact was commented on by several detainees:

Discourse, denial and dehumanisation   133

The suggestion from the RUC in general to all of this was that [any injuries] were self-inflicted, which seemed so ridiculous. You would have to be really messed up in your brain – I know people do self-harm, but that's because of psychological problems. The suggestion that I would do that, I just think it is daft. Some people might have believed that [my injuries were self-inflicted] and clearly there are still people who believe that in society. That is the problem.

(Interviewee 'F')

For Interviewee 'F', the RUC sought to contest and neutralise the power of his narrative by counter-claiming that his injuries were self-inflicted. Such official discourse absolves the state of any clear responsibility and could also impact upon the image of the wider Republican movement by presenting suspected members as, in the words of Interviewee 'F', 'suffering from psychological problems'. When framed within the stigmatising discourses of 'mental illness' which were common at the time, such a label firstly presented detainees as depoliticised individuals, driven to self-mutilation, irrational in thought and action, and as vulnerable and lacking in individual agency. It drained their testimonies of the wider context of state violence in the conflict. Second, by re-classifying the physical signs of state violence as self-inflicted, the official discourse helped to subtly depict detainees as so fearful of an unmerciful IRA outside that they would self-harm and make up allegations of state brutality as a means of self-preservation, perhaps as an attempt to justify any 'breaking' during interrogation.[6] In addition, a third layer of neutralisation can be identified within the official discourse which presented injuries as self-inflicted, one which shifts the focus from the individual to the wider Republican movement. The discourses which suggested that 'calculating' IRA members were given awards and gifts for injuring themselves in detention sought not only to neutralise allegations of state violence, but also to puncture the romantic imagery of the principled, selfless Republican patriot and to delegitimise their role in the wider conflict.

These denials are not simply abstract language games or matters of symbolism. Where truth is in conflict, due process safeguards must retain their strength if there is to be any possibility of both procedural and substantive justice for those alleging state violence. Several detainees were critical of the official discourse which claimed that their experiences were self-inflicted and also comment on the impact of that discourse within a system reliant on confessions, 'Diplock' juryless courts, special powers and extensive detention:

Now for a long time what was happening was people who were the interrogators claimed that they were self-inflicted injuries and because the courts were just one judge and no jury, all the judges went along with it.

(Laurence)

The weight of evidence was changed, the length of detention was extended and there was quite obviously, a blind eye turned to what was clearly brutality.

134 *Discourse, denial and dehumanisation*

The judiciary routinely said, suggested and maintained that any evidence of brutality was self-inflicted and done maliciously to tarnish the so-called good name of the RUC. It was sort of a bizarre claim that someone was willing to mutilate themselves and spend a lifetime in prison just to tarnish the reputation of the police force, but that was taken as quite a plausible excuse for what was happening.

(Tommy)

For Laurence and Tommy, the official discourse which redefined their injuries as 'self-inflicted' was problematic, particularly as they felt that the judicial system often seemed to accept such official explanations without question or proper investigation.

Interpretive denial

The political control of truth and the manipulation of knowledge can take place in a number of different ways (Des Pres 1996). A further means through which denials can operate is in the re-interpretation of harmful experiences. Therefore, another semantic device through which official discourse can attempt to neutralise the power of allegations against the state is through the employment of a series of mechanisms Cohen (2001) calls 'interpretive denials'. He argues that within this form of denial, 'raw facts (something happened) are not being denied. Rather they are given a different meaning from what seems apparent to others' (Cohen 2001: 7). Within the context of the conflict in Northern Ireland, detainees may have indeed experienced harm, yet the interpretive denial communicated through official discourses contests the interpretation given to those experiences by former detainees themselves. It is this form of denial which can be seen most frequently within the official discourse in regards to the allegations of state violence in Northern Ireland. It represents language 'games' which are equivalent to different 'conceptualisations' of truth (Smyth 2007). These interpretive denials utilise semantic devices to manage and maintain the imagery which language can invoke. Within this discursive regime, 'persons' become 'suspected terrorists', and 'interrogations' become 'interviews'. This official discourse then becomes the formal way of defining and labelling experiences (Gilligan and Pratt 2004).

The documentary analysis of official documents, public records and press releases suggest that an extensive and multiple-layered regime of interpretive denials operated in regards to state violence in Northern Ireland during the period 1971–1985. The denials sought to avoid or deflect the moral censures which were (and are) a crucial part of the rhetoric of 'human rights' and are equally central to the discourse around democracy and justice. The hegemonic framework of interpretive denials represent, as Cohen (2001) suggests, the social, political and cultural operationalisation of Sykes and Matza's (1957) 'techniques of neutralisation' on a macro-scale. Examples of interpretive denial can be seen in the texts of public inquiries launched by the British Government

Discourse, denial and dehumanisation   135

into allegations of state violence. As Conroy (2000: ix) argues, 'accounts of torture often burden the reader with some doubt as to whether the survivor is telling the truth, [yet] in the Northern Ireland case, however, the government admitted the abuse but denied that it constituted torture'. Compton (1971) examined allegations of brutality arising from internment in relation to so-called 'intensive questioning' and found that there *was* some evidence of ill-treatment, but that such treatment did not amount to torture and that any resulting pain experienced was not intended by state forces and thus did not fall under the Inquiry's own definition of brutality. In describing this official discourse related to the internment cases he had been directly involved in, one former detainee recalled that:

> The Brits didn't deny it. They didn't deny it. It went to the ECtHR and they went 'Well, ok, we put hood on peoples' heads but I mean, what's that?!' They omitted to say that they beat the shit out of us (excuse the language) and they frightened the lives out of us and the only time the hood was removed was for a KGB type interrogation with two floodlights in your face and a silhouette of a figure screaming obscenities at you during what they called 'interviews' – which were what we would call interrogations.
>
> (Liam)

At the most basic level, this official discourse in Northern Ireland enabled and perpetuated powerful attempts at re-ordering and re-coding the narratives of detainees as something *other* than state violence. Euphemisms were employed to distract from the lived reality of state violence. A further re-ordering can be observed in the semantic battles between the signifiers of 'torture' and the lesser 'ill-treatment', and in the long-standing use of the techniques themselves by British forces (Conroy 2000; Rolston and Scraton 2005; Cohen 2006). The apparent simplicity of this interpretive denial – one which recognises that something occurred but denies the power of that occurrence – is shown by Liam's comments. His vivid and detailed recollections of fearfulness and vulnerability (explored in depth in Chapter 2) reflect an empirical dimension that challenges the reductionism of terms like 'ill-treatment'.

Within official discourse then, the reconstruction of state violence 'cannot be divorced from the political and ideological circumstances in which "exceptional" measures were granted legitimacy and the authority of powerful institutions had to be protected' (Rolston and Scraton 2005: 553). Discourse becomes a way of maintaining a particular narrative, as the production and control of 'truth' is located within wider aspects of control. As Scraton (2004: 62) acknowledges:

> The Compton Inquiry [was] held in secret ... detainees were refused legal aid, and, after protesting, were granted a lawyer. Yet the police and military witnesses were legally represented. All but two detainees boycotted the Inquiry. In contrast, [Compton] consulted ninety five Army personnel, twenty six police officers, eleven prison officers, five regimental medical officers, two medical staff officers and four civilian doctors.

136   *Discourse, denial and dehumanisation*

Given these circumstances, it is perhaps surprising that 'ill-treatment' was recognised *at all* within the discourse of Compton (1971), particularly as the Inquiry's report preceded most of the international pressure and publicity which followed Ireland's commencement of proceedings against the UK at the ECtHR and long before the emergence of narratives from Holding Centres and prisons following the end of Special Category Status in 1976. These regimes of interpretive denial were often constructed through official discourse in the shape of public inquiries on those occasions where allegations of state violence were particularly powerful and potentially damaging. Official inquiries are an important tool through which dominant narratives about state violence can be constructed and disseminated at both the national and international level (Cohen 1996). After Compton (1971) and against a context of increasing international interest in Northern Ireland following events on 'Bloody Sunday', the Government launched a further inquiry designed to explore the legal status of interrogation techniques, which according to Rolston and Scraton (2005: 558) was 'not established to restore public confidence in the impartiality of the rule of law *within* the North of Ireland, but rather to give that appearance to a British and international audience'. The resulting Parker Inquiry (1972) came to the majority conclusion that interrogation methods used against a number of detainees were unlawful, but that they were necessary in times of civil unrest and were therefore morally justifiable. The Government was thus able to avoid total censure for its use of the 'Five Techniques'.

However, in contrast, the minority report of Lord Gardiner (in Parker 1972) derided the methods used during internment as unlawful, immoral and counterproductive. The very presence of public inquiries and of contrasts within and between inquiries, provides evidence that official discourse is not omnipotent, homogeneous and monolithic, but is instead better understood as part of a hegemonic process of construction. In essence, it is the *appearance* of allowing dissenting voices which may grant legitimacy to the British State. Inquiries and the like allow the Government to argue that they have 'responded to' and 'investigated' allegations. Opportunities for counter narratives still exist within these limited and limiting circumstances, even if they are subjected to a greater set of controls than the dominant narrative. Thus the narrative of official discourse remains incomplete and gaps in the power and legitimacy of official interpretations remain. Counter narratives might often be denied, controlled, restricted or rendered invisible through censorship, yet they are rarely destroyed entirely. They can become part of a cultural memory, rather than the official re-imagining of events by the state. When understood as a socio-political process concerned with the production of 'legitimate' knowledges, official discourse may not *always* represent the omnipresent silencing of alternative interpretations, but is instead the working through of a particular narrative into a position of primary definition, through the utilisation of discursive power.

Public inquiries often seek to justify or minimise the violence of the state whilst at the same time construct an official version of events (Hegarty 2002). Therefore understanding the role of inquiries in contesting narratives and subjugating knowledges is central to any analysis of truth in conflict. Public inquiries can create and sustain a dominant narrative, whilst simultaneously retaining the power to delegitimise and subjugate other knowledges. This power can be seen within the official discourse of Northern Ireland, through the British State's 'capacity to impose its regime of truth on its citizens, particularly in those states of intervention where state authority and political legitimacy are challenged' (Rolston and Scraton 2005: 550). Through public inquiries into allegations of state harms, Cohen's (2001) triumvirates of denial – literal, interpretive and implicatory – all have the potential to reach a wide audience, and to form part of a hegemonic discourse which seeks to neutralise any dissenting narratives, or render them extraneous.

Yet, not all official discourse concerned with allegations of state violence experienced during detention engages so identifiably with the regimes of interpretive denial described by Cohen (2001). The Bennett Inquiry (1979: 55 para. 163) which centred on allegations of abuse during interrogations at Castlereagh, concluded that:

> There can however, whatever the precise explanations, be no doubt that the injuries inflicted in this last class of cases were not self-inflicted and were sustained during the period of detention at a police office.

It would be erroneous therefore to argue that Bennett's (1979) findings are in complete conflict with the accounts of former detainees, given that the Inquiry *does* assert that (some) detainees *were* injured by someone/something else during detention. This recognition still forms part of the official discourse and its power should not be underestimated. Yet even within this interpretation which at first appears to be a strongly worded condemnation of the RUC, detainees' allegations of state harm slip into a semantic 'black hole'. Bennett (1979) recognised that something happened, but does not acknowledge nor comment on the 'why', 'what' and 'by who' questions. The official discourse thus suggested that *something* happened, but the responsibility for naming and labelling those occurrences is shifted onto the audience. The loose language of 'injuries' refrains from depicting the occurrences as torture, ill-treatment, or brutality – terms which have a greater power and significance, as shown in Chapter 3 of this book. Furthermore, despite its stated aims and scope 'to examine police procedures and practice in Northern Ireland relating to the interrogation of persons suspected of scheduled offences' (Bennett 1979: 1 para. 1), the resulting report of the Inquiry avoided any explicit discussion of responsibility. As observable in the text of Bennett (1979), the official discourse only *implies* that the RUC *could* be responsible for a selected number of injuries through the omission of other alternatives. By subtly avoiding 'the precise explanations' which might describe how detainees were injured (and by whom), the public record of Bennett (1979) is indicative of wider official discourses which utilise a wide range of interpretive denials.

Official discourse acts as an additional layer of social control, demarcating enemies, reaffirming expert knowledges and emphasising absolute boundaries

138   *Discourse, denial and dehumanisation*

between truth and lies. These frameworks are not unique to the state but are closely related to the production of knowledge and its legitimacy. Within the context of Northern Ireland, knowledge about the conflict was tied into particular representations of 'truth'. These meta-narratives depicting events as part of a struggle, civil unrest, the 'Troubles' or as a 'law and order' problem mark out not only operational decisions or political rhetoric, but also are the means through which legitimacy can be granted – or denied – to particular interpretations of violence and victimhood.

Constructing 'the victim'

Another means by which official discourse can deny the interpretation (and also the implications) of former detainees' narratives is through a selective reading of the meaning of 'victimhood'. Some of those former detainees interviewed for the current book discussed the contested nature of their victimhood, and its communication and control through different mechanisms of state denial. Political prisoners are amongst some of the most studied victims of torture (Green and Ward 2004) and the relative visibility of Republican former prisoners within Northern Ireland should conceivably mean that their detention experiences frequently enter the debate about the nature of 'victimhood'. However, with the exception of the hunger strikes, there has been comparatively little debate post-conflict about the prison victimisation experiences of detainees and prisoners. Discussions about the nature of victimhood in Northern Ireland have instead focused on the victimhood or alleged ineligibility of those killed or seriously injured by both non-state and state forces (and are explored in Chapter 8 of this book). This focus is understandable, but arguably it need not be exclusive.

Outside the context of the conflict in Northern Ireland, the significance of the label 'victim' is evidenced by the growth of victimology (and victimologies) as an academic sub-discipline. The key foundational premise of much victimological discourse involves the discussion of:

> victim status [as] something that has to be achieved and involves a process from the individual recognising that they have been victimised and thus may claim the label through to being socially, and/or in policy terms being recognised as a victim.
>
> (Walklate 2007: 28)

Yet this process remains problematic. As Fattah (1992) suggests, people are rarely willing to stand 'against victims'. However, studying the Northern Ireland conflict through a victimological framework involves the further recognition of the often blurred distinctions between 'victim' and 'perpetrator' (Goodey 2005). Several detainees discussed the impact and significance of these problematic, subjective categorisations which, as Stanley (2005: 584) observes, are 'cultural representations … central to how state crimes come to be legitimised and how those involved as perpetrators or victims come to be viewed and responded to'. For example:

> The Unionists would have said ... 'He is attacking our police force, attacking our state, we want nothing to do with him, he should just be put into a jail.'
>
> (Interviewee 'F')

> Unionists were basically our enemies in a sense. If anything happened to us they would have cheered. They wouldn't have cared.
>
> (Harry)

Again, political labels were employed to symbolise what were perceived by detainees as inevitable reactions from those who wished to see Northern Ireland remain part of the UK, and whose members were disproportionately represented within the RUC and Police Service of Northern Ireland. These two groups were often involved as perpetrators in detainees' allegations of state violence. McAuley (1994) argues that for some Unionists there was a feeling of being under siege and being pushed into retaliation. Physical and symbolic attacks by Republicans on the RUC and Prison Service furthered this feeling and may have been interpreted as violence against the wider unionist community, as the RUC in particular was liked and supported by most Unionists (see Smyth and Ellison 1999; Ryder 2000b; Tonge 2002).

Official discourse seeks to 'undo' the blurring of boundaries regarding victimhood and to annihilate the 'other', whilst at the same time proclaiming the righteousness of state 'justice' (Burton and Carlen 1979; Hegarty 2002). Evidence for such arguments and of the oversimplification of supposedly partisan binaries of victimhood can be seen within the political literature of the conflict. The hunger strikes of 1980 and 1981 represented a particular challenge to the official discourse and its depictions of 'victims' and 'perpetrators', a contest which was made manifest through the bodies of the condemned. The hunger strikes and surrounding protests are a form of Foucaultian spectacle, as acts of symbolic and actual resistance against the victimising bio-power of imprisonment with its control over the bodies of prisoners. Here, within limited circumstances, the prisoners 'chose' not to be the object of punishment, but the creators of an additional narrative of resistance. During the strikes, Peter Robinson[7] of the Democratic Unionist Party published a twelve page booklet entitled 'Self Inflicted: An Exposure of the H-Blocks Issue'. Beginning with an emotive and vivid poem allegedly written by 'a young mother left a widow by the actions of one the "Dirty" protestors', the document aimed to present the prison protests 'in perspective ... against the backcloth of over 2,000 people who have been murdered and more than 20,000 who have been maimed or mutilated during this present IRA campaign' (Robinson 1981: 1). The booklet also contains distressing images of the burnt and charred remains of some of those supposedly killed by the IRA and the word 'murder' is emblazoned ten times in bold and dramatic text around one such image. Throughout the document, Robinson (1981: 4–6) argues that 'the inmates of the H-Blocks are the perpetrators of some of the most heinous atrocities known to civilisation', and that allegations that 'the criminals

140 *Discourse, denial and dehumanisation*

in the H-Blocks have been convicted by *induced* admission statements and an unjust court system ... could not be further from the truth' (my emphasis). The document asks the reader 'With whom is your sympathy? Their disgusting campaign has no moral appeal to anyone outside their own murder gangs' (Robinson 1981: 8), thus seeking to perpetuate a binary distinction between those it deems deserving of empathy and those 'fellow travellers' of 'murder gangs' it feels require only retribution.

Many of the paramilitary prisoners in the H-Blocks were indeed involved in acts of violence, but the Robinson (1981) document explicitly illustrates the purposeful exclusion of victimised prisoners from the wider 'moral community' (Kelman 1995). The apparent reductionism of Robinson (1981) may lack any sophistication and subtlety, yet this re-ordering can be followed by layer upon layer of shifts in language, significance and meaning which act to re-present the vulnerable victim seen in detainees' narratives as a mass-murdering 'evil terrorist' apparently deserving of retributive punishment. This constructed distance and false dichotomy between the idealised images of the 'innocent victim' and the 'violent terrorist' is dependent on constructions of violence and legitimacy which see 'some people being viewed as deserving victims, that is, acquiring the label "victim" very readily and easily, and other people being viewed as undeserving victims who may be never labelled as victims' (Walklate 2007: 28).

State violence as 'deserved punishment'

The apparent ease with which prisoners can be excluded from discourses about victimhood results in part from the depiction of prisoners as dehumanised 'others' whose assumed lack of humanity means that they are no longer deserving of dignity, protection and recognition (Morgan 2000). The nature of imprisonment itself furthers the dehumanisation process, as Interviewee 'P' recalled:

> The screw would force me against a wall at the top of the wing and order me to tell him what my prison number is in an attempt to dehumanise me. I knew the number because they would quote it to me (and to us all) ad nauseam but I would never give them it. It is still ingrained like in the Nazi concentration camps,[8] I could tell it to you now.

The attempted dehumanisation within prisons reflects a wider apathy towards prisoners in most external audiences, which was commented upon by another former detainee:

> If a prisoner goes to the press and says 'this happened to me' how many people are going to believe them? They are just prisoners.
>
> (Interviewee 'F')

Such arguments are further evidenced by the absence of public inquiries into conditions within which H-Block prisoners were held. Given the levels of

Discourse, denial and dehumanisation 141

national and international interest in the prison, this lack of investigation might be surprising, but is also illustrative of a lack of concern regarding brutality against the prisoners (Rolston and Scraton 2005). The general public's lack of concern and the weak or absent official responses to the violence of incarceration can also be seen outside the context of the Northern Ireland conflict. It is illustrative of wider discourses which appear unable – or more accurately unwilling – to countenance the idea of state violence against prisoners as representing an injustice.

Some detainees recalled feeling hurt or frustrated by some of the perceived reactions to testimony about their experiences of state violence within detention. In the months after the introduction of internment, British Defence Minister Lord Peter Carrington denounced Jim and 13 internees as 'thugs and murderers' despite a lack of evidence (in Conroy 2000). In response to his depiction within this official discourse, Jim recalled:

> The thing that annoyed me was Lord Carrington, who said that all the people involved in it were mass murderers and he could stand over it. I think he singled me out in particular and said … that I 'had killed more people in Northern Ireland than anybody else at the time'. Something ridiculous like that. He said it … and it just went down into history. [How do you feel about that now?] That would still frustrate me now.

For Jim, Lord Carrington's reaction to his story was still experienced as problematic almost 40 years after his original narrative testimony. His experience is far from unique, for as Kelman (1995: 31) argues:

> the main source of dehumanisation of the victims [of state violence] is their designation as enemies of the state who have placed themselves outside the moral community…. They are described as terrorists, insurgents or dissidents who endanger the state. They are perceived [and presented] as menacing destructive elements, bent on undermining law and order and destroying the community.

As recalled by Jim, Lord Carrington's statement is therefore not unusual, but characteristic of a wider framework of interpretive denial which sought to prevent detainees from acquiring the label of 'victim'. The greater the distance from perceived 'innocence' and 'passivity', the easier it becomes for the interpretive denial of detainees' victimhood. This denial of the victim and the shift of focus upon the alleged crimes of those who were harmed not only provides official justification for state violence, but also acts as a form of personal exoneration for those who have carried it out (Korn 2004). Jim becomes a 'mass murderer' within the dominant official discourse, and far from the 'innocent victim'. Thus not only can the state deny outright its own violence or recast that violence as something else, it can also deny individuals the label of 'victim'.

142 *Discourse, denial and dehumanisation*

Similarly, the Bennett Inquiry (1979), which recognised that some detainees had been injured, also engaged with interpretive denial in relation to victimhood. Rather than describe those who alleged state violence with neutral language such as 'the complainant', Bennett (1979: 5 para. 5) depicted those who had made allegations against the RUC as 'prisoners', explaining that:

> We have chosen the world 'prisoner' to describe a person kept in police custody who has either been arrested by a police officer or who has been delivered into police custody after arrest by some authorised person.

Such language is deeply value-laden and in the battle for truth in conflict these semantics become highly significant and symbolic. The popular imagery of the prisoner implies someone who has been tried fairly and within guarantees of due process, convicted within a legitimate setting and justly found guilty of causing harm. By labelling detainees with the language of 'prisoner', the official discourse both reflects and sustains the assumption that the victims of state violence are factually guilty of some crime. The question of their *actual* guilt never arises (Kelman 1995). Thus the consequences of the label of 'prisoner' (even in Northern Ireland where the term takes on added significance) are different to that of the less value-laden term 'suspect' or even further still 'complainant', although such language is itself still reductionist, as Interviewee 'F' observed:

> People take sides. You would prefer that people saw you as a person, not as a 'suspect'. But I agreed to do it [go public] and I remember that the overriding reason that I did it was that I wanted to let people know that their state wasn't this benign state that was trying to curb these terrible terrorists.

Distanced from the less pejorative (and often more accurate) label 'complainant', the language of 'prisoners' and 'suspects' seeks to disempower testimonies of state violence and cast doubt on the veracity of allegations, in part by linking in to the reductionism of wider popular discourses which dehumanise those incarcerated. In relation to the lived reality of experiencing such powerful labelling, Interviewee 'F' argued that:

> How do you convince people around you? Who are already opposed to you anyway because you are a Catholic, and secondly because you are a Republican or they claim you are a Republican? Now you are a 'suspect' and 'maybe he did do it'? Therefore 'He is entitled to it'? That 'He is lucky that that was all that he got?'

The denial process operates at this juncture on two related levels. The 'state of exception' creates and sustains the construction of a suspect community, where guilt is implied and against whom state violence may take place via a range of systems and institutions (Hillyard 1993). This can clearly be seen in Northern Ireland and marks the blurring of distinctions between those perceived to be

Discourse, denial and dehumanisation   143

directly involved in violence and those labelled as supporters (Crelinsten 2003). Secondly, Interviewee 'F' suggestion that others may feel that 'he is entitled to it' reflects the interpretive denial that recognises that something happened, but gives those events a different meaning (Cohen 2001). Through denials communicated throughout official discourse, detainees were recast as 'prisoners' *deserving* of violent treatment. Here, the violence they experienced was not really violence, but rightful retaliation and justice. 'By a subtle alchemy the [offender] moves himself [sic] into the position of an avenger and the victim is transformed into a wrong doer' (Sykes and Matza 1957: 667). The power of such labelling re-presents state violence as retributive justice against non-state actors and those who were alleged to have violated dominant norms of acceptable behaviour. Just like Interviewee 'F', Tommy also suggested that some people may have viewed his experiences as 'just deserts' and as the manifestation of warranted punishment:

> One negative reaction would be those who believed it and said 'You deserved it'. I would make a defence, but they'd say 'Well, he would say that, wouldn't he?' I was in the IRA and I take a particular view of the world, but the only thing is that I don't any longer expect everyone else to take the same view. But that is it. Oddly enough, when I heard those who were suggesting 'Well you deserved it', it was a little bit more hurtful.

For Tommy it was these interpretive denials and the suggestion that his narrative of state violence was accurate, but had happened as punishment for his perceived wrongdoing, which was experienced as the most destructive. The literal denials 'that "you are telling lies" were always felt with a little bit of sourness' (Tommy) and yet it was the suggestion that he had *deservedly* been subjected to state violence which he felt had been the most harmful. The idea of being 'deserving of punishment' hints at just deserts and proportionality (Morgan 2000). In this way, victims of state violence have to overcome two levels of denial in proving to an audience that a) their narratives are true and b) that the violence against then was unjustified (Cohen 2001).

Understanding detainees' experiences (e.g. Tommy's at Castlereagh) as being 'punishment' destroys the dominant depiction of violence during interrogations as being 'necessary' information seeking. It also casts aside any supposed utilitarian justifications for the torture of detainees. The United Nations Convention against Torture (1984) for example, recognises the presence of torture as an instrument of punishment, not simply interrogation. Ashworth (1998) describes how the deliberate imposition of pain is usually accepted as the 'just deserts' of those convicted of offences. Concepts such as 'just deserts', notions of 'deserving' and the quantification of punishment are problematic in themselves, furthermore, as detainees' narratives (and the reactions to those narratives) have shown, the imposition of pain is not something which occurs exclusively post-conviction. The perception of state violence against detainees as being 'deserved punishment' reflects back the flexible nature of morality and an exaggerated penal retributivism which blurs the line between 'suspect' and 'offender'.

144 *Discourse, denial and dehumanisation*

Idealised images

Another way in which denial can work is by representing the perpetrators of state violence as being more acted upon than acting. As shown in previous chapters, State forces were a target of Republican groups and were also killed by Loyalists on occasion. Between 1966 and 2001, 1,112 members of the police and Army were killed (McKittrick *et al.* 2007) with some 29 prison officers killed between 1974 and 1993 respectively, 27 of whom were killed by Republicans (McEvoy 2001: 114). The Bennett Inquiry (1979: 6 para. 17) lists the significant number of RUC members killed by paramilitaries and claims that:

> Even these statistics do not fully convey the personal tragedies inflicted on the RUC. The extent of their sacrifice is brought home … by accounts of such family tragedies as of father and daughter, both police officers, killed in separate incidents and of officers shot down in a most cowardly way in performing such routine work for the community as shepherding children across the street outside their school.

The binary categorisations of modernity, of innocence *or* guilt, of good *or* evil are central to such a polarising framework. Interpretive denials can be seen within an official discourse which emphasises the non-state violence of the 'other' and deny any commonalities or relationships between this and state violence. Official discourse also renders explicit a hierarchy of victims and seeks to protect perpetrators of state violence (Walklate 2007). Such mechanisms of denials often contain resonances of Christie's (1986) idealised victim – the innocent female out helping the community who is attacked by an unknown and faceless stranger. There are clear parallels here with the imagery of killed RUC officers presented by the Bennett Inquiry (1979: 6 para. 17), particularly in the included description of a female officer 'shot down in a most cowardly way in performing such routine work for the community as shepherding children across the street outside their school'. This narrative of sacrifice, suffering and victimhood is a core aspect of the RUC's official discourse (Mulcahy 2005). The police officers of the RUC are recast as noble, gentle, community-orientated individuals, in an imagery which contrasts sharply with the allegations former detainees made against them. The state can therefore use official discourse to create its own heroes. Those depicted as violent, sectarian, brutal abusers by the testimonies of former detainees now became the brave men and women of the RUC/Army/Northern Ireland Prison Service (NIPS). Within such discourses, themes of courage and selflessness dominate (Mulcahy 2005) and the police are lauded as the 'guardians and defenders of society' who took real risks to save others (Bennett 1979: 6 para. 17).

Compton (1971: 30 para. 134) too, presents similar images in relation to the British Army, who it argues displayed nothing other than 'thoughtlessness on the part of those who directed the movement on 9th August not to realise that the going was rough in places'. The Inquiry suggested that there had been 'a lack of judgement here, but not cruelty or brutality' (Compton 1971: 36 para. 160). Furthermore, the report emphasised the training and supervision of the Army and noted 'the absence of any record of *significant* physical damage in the medical record made for each of the [complainants]' (Compton 1971: 22 para. 97, my emphasis). Within the official discourse therefore, any violence experienced by detainees was represented as unintentional, unplanned and certainly not systematic. Such subtle interpretive denials trivialise and challenge the truth value of detainees' accounts and the seriousness of their experiences. Thus, the official discourse about state violence experienced during internment sought 'to allay, suspend and close off popular doubt through an ideal and discursive appropriation of a material problem' (Burton and Carlen 1979: 13–14). Within such a discourse, responsibility is diverted back towards detainees. The state is presented as virtuous and beyond reproach, more victimised than violent, and the notion of victimhood is controlled and constrained not only by the representation of detainees' alleged actions, but also by a benign and gentle depiction of the state and its agents.

Implicatory denials

Adapting Sykes and Matza's (1957) framework for understanding neutralisation, Cohen (2001) identifies a third major technique through which violence can be re-conceptualised. Sharing many features with interpretive denial, 'implicatory denial' shifts the focus from state offender onto external forces and can be understood as an attempt to rationalise, justify or otherwise deflect criticism (Cohen 2001; see also McLaughlin 1996). The present research explored the ways in which former detainees experienced these techniques which sought to change the cultural meaning and legacy of their narratives. These implicatory denials involve the use of carefully chosen language in order to reconstruct and downplay the 'significance of what is known' (Cohen 2001: 503). Within such a framework, there can be no literal denial and an additional layer of obfuscation must be added to the interpretive denials which are communicated through the official discourse. Both implicatory and interpretive denials share a need to reframe or recast harmful events and to dehumanise and delegitimise those who have made their private experiences of state violence part of a contested public history.

Implicatory denial can be observed within official discourse concerning the treatment of 'suspected terrorists' throughout the world. Israeli security services famously have admitted to and attempted to justify using what they called 'moderate physical pressure' against those in detention (Morgan 2000), the implication being that such acts were morally permissible. In essence, action against detainees as 'suspected terrorists' can thus be recast as 'necessary', something carried out in a controlled, civilised manner by agents of the state who are motivated only by a perceived need to protect the public. Within such a framework, an alternate reality must be maintained that allows and justifies state violence (Crelinsten 2003). Implicatory denials attempt to shift responsibility for

146 *Discourse, denial and dehumanisation*

state violence away from state forces and re-distribute it not only towards the 'suspect' but also to the wider community. In already divided communities that have long been engaging in mass stereotyping, discrimination and panic, implicatory denials may gain greater hold (Kauzlarich *et al.* 2001). In support, Crelinsten (2003: 296) suggests that:

> Laws are directed against [the] enemy, labels to describe them are promulgated and disseminated via the mass media and people are divided into us and them, for us or against us. If such groups happen to include violent insurgents or separatists at their radical fringe, so much the better, since the threat will be more easily depicted as real.

The depiction of an 'enemy within' – a threatening menace disguised within a created and falsely homogenised 'suspect community' – is deeply powerful, particularly when applied to those who do not share the same community background and/or are not part of the dominant sector of society (Kelman 1995). Through implicatory denial, the wider community shares the responsibility for the violence against detainees: it was for 'your safety' that such violence against 'suspected terrorists' occurred. Within such discourses, the violent treatment of detainees may not only be interpreted as deserved, but also as *necessary* to prevent harm to the rest of society. The violence of the state is thus presented as justified, in part by the apparent acquiescence of the general public. These implicatory denials sustain the perception of a risk society and attempt to justify state violence against suspects through a fog of utilitarian predictions, which contributes to the 'aggrandisement of "terrorism"' as an imminent threat (Korn 2004: 214). In discussing allegations of state violence during internment in Northern Ireland, the official discourse evident in Compton (1971: 13 para. 52) claimed that:

> For a small number of persons … it was operationally necessary to obtain [information] as rapidly as possible in the interest of saving lives, whilst at the same time providing the detainees with the necessary security for their own persons and identities.

Thus Compton (1971) explicitly engages with implicatory denials, in contrast to Morgan's (2000) perception that attempts at such justification are usually subterranean and hidden. As Rolston and Scraton (2005) have rightly observed, the authoritarianism usually implicit in 'liberal' states like Britain was made explicit throughout its involvement in Northern Ireland and was repeatedly framed as necessary on the grounds of 'state security'. The Compton Inquiry (1971) clearly attempts to recast 'ill treatment' as necessary in order to protect the public, thus conferring a 'respectable status' upon such activities and re-emphasising distinctions between the 'at risk' and 'innocent' community/British State on the one hand, and the 'threatening' and 'guilty' suspect on the other. Similarly, the Parker Inquiry (1972: 6 para. 18 and 24) into the legal status of interrogation techniques, argued that:

Discourse, denial and dehumanisation   147

There is no doubt that when used in the past these techniques have produced very valuable results in revealing rebel organisation, training and Battle Orders ... There is no doubt that the information obtained by these two operations directly and indirectly was responsible for saving the lives of innocent civilians.

Implicatory denials are therefore central to the preservation of state power and its institutions, particularly in so-called 'open' and 'democratic' societies where the opportunities for publicising state violence may be greater. They represent an appeal to:

> higher loyalties [in that the] deviation from certain norms may occur not because the norms are rejected but because other norms, held to be more pressing or involving a higher loyalty, are accorded precedence.
>
> (Sykes and Matza 1957: 669)

Thus implicatory denials represent an opportunity to hide illegal or deviant acts by elevating and encouraging concerns about national security over human rights, civil liberties and due process safeguards (Kauzlarich *et al.* 2001). The foreword to the Inquiry into allegations of brutality during internment does precisely this, stating that 'in considering the Committee's Report, it is important to have in mind the circumstances in Northern Ireland' (Maudling in Compton 1971: iii). Compton (1971) praises the actions of state forces (and demonises detainees) by providing an extensive list of arms finds discovered by state forces which were believed to belong to Republicans, despite such information falling outside the Inquiry's own limited remit. The inclusion of such information (and its implications) is highly significant, centralising the importance of 'risk'. Its position at the beginning of the report intends to add a subtle layer of denial to the Inquiry's findings. Within this context of implicatory denials, some stoic former detainees recognised that such official responses were inevitable and were simply an intrinsic and necessary way in which the British State sought to create and sustain its legitimacy:

> From their point of view they had a job to do, which was to pull us down, to destroy Republicans. Their hands were tied in many ways, in the sense that the IRA was going out and shooting them – if they were to go out and shoot the IRA, they had to do it a certain way ... [The RUC] believed it was a war but their propaganda was telling them it was just crime and criminals to be put away ... so whatever they did, they had to do surreptitiously.
>
> (Interviewee 'F')

The representation of 'threats to national security' underpins the utilitarian justifications of state violence and is popular with security forces (Morgan 2000). Violence against detainees becomes self-defence – something 'forced by circumstance' rather than brutality (Bandura 1990). Within the context of official

148   *Discourse, denial and dehumanisation*

discourse about interrogation techniques, Bennett (1979: 6 para. 16) repeatedly affirmed that:

> Our duty of considering police practices and procedures in the interrogation of prisoners suspected of scheduled offences cannot be considered in isolation from the situation in which the police must carry out their task.

Equally, despite its narrow remit, the Parker Inquiry (1972) made reference to wider circumstances as part of its – to borrow Stanley's (2005) phrase – 'tactical storytelling'.

> We think that such expressions as 'humane', 'inhuman', 'humiliating' and 'degrading' fail to be judged in the light of the circumstances in which the techniques are applied, for example, that the operation is taking place in the course of urban guerrilla warfare in which completely innocent lives are at risk; that there is a degree of urgency; and that the security and safety of the interrogation centre, of its staff and that of the detainees are important considerations.
>
> (Parker 1972: 7 para. 30)

Thus the perception of threat was amplified and utilised as a means through which violence against people ('prisoners') could be understood and, consequently, the potential for social and moral censure dispersed. At the centre of discussions about the use of violence are inevitable questions of justification and legitimacy (Cavanaugh 1997). Implicatory denials control the boundaries of this debate about what is or is not justifiable. It is, as Cohen (2005: 24) describes:

> 'Voodoo talk': 'Yes, we understand and affirm that a total prohibition on torture means just that: there can be no exceptions, not under any circumstances. But what we are doing isn't torture and anyway is morally justifiable under the special circumstances we find ourselves in (*in these terrible times*)'.
>
> (emphasis in original)

However, such utilitarian excuses and attempts at justifications for violence against suspects cannot be analysed in the same way as violence against incarcerated prisoner populations, as within such a framework there is a difference between supposedly preventing 'greater' harm through the gathering of information in comparison to violence as punishment. Violence against detainees within the prison, as narrated by male prisoners (and also by female prisoners, see Corcoran 2006a, 2006b), could not be argued as being necessary to collect information or to save lives, but instead was part of a disciplinary instrument which was being used to 'break' the resistance of prisoners to the prison regime under which they lived:

Discourse, denial and dehumanisation   149

[After the 25 September 1983 escape] the regime that the block staff imposed … was extremely strict and uncompromising … Some might say that this was an over the top reaction, but the staff felt that this was the only response that could restore control and discipline within H7.

(Challis 1999: 74)

Yet such an interpretation, which former Governor Challis (1999) suggests tells the 'truth' of events within the H-Blocks, clearly blames detainees for the violence against them. The shift of condemnatory attention from the state and its agents towards those *alleging* state violence and brutality is itself a form of implicatory denial. The focus on those deemed to be 'the enemy' is perpetuated through their actions of 'disorder' and/or 'ill-discipline'. The state violence they experienced within prison is justified by Challis (1999) as necessary to restore order. Yet former detainees describe the violence in a different way, linking it to wider struggles for power within the prison system and as a failed attempt to 'break' the prisoners and their legitimate protests. Although feeling that some of the violence he had experienced and the legacy of accompanying denials were 'part of the way of war' Harry still felt that the state violence following the 1983 prison escapes:

wasn't justifiable, put it that way…. There was an awful lot of brutality there going on. Fellas were naked, and screws were getting drunk, coming in absolutely drunk and maybe four or five going into a cell and giving out a beating. People got their jaws broken, different things happened to them.

However, Harry also suggested that at other points during his experience of imprisonment, the state violence against him and the accompanying denials of official discourse were interlinked and equally inevitable due to his own political actions:

You accepted this as part of the way of war. There are people there – I was one of them – that fought back. But then you accepted that you were in a position and you had to either give in to it and come off the blanket or just take it, and stick with it … I am *not* saying it was considered a part of prison life, but well, 'I am here and I have to take what is given to me'.

(Harry)

It was a feeling shared by Tommy, who had been victimised during interrogations at Castlereagh:

The other thing about it is that – while I would have been outraged to an extent about the hypocrisy of it all – on the other hand I had been engaged in an insurrection against the British State. So part of it wasn't entirely unexpected … I suppose I viewed myself as an insurgent, combatant, part of the IRA. It was part of a conflict, part of a battle, so you take hits and you

150   *Discourse, denial and dehumanisation*

give hits. Like anything, when you get knocked over you just have to gather yourself and go on.

(Tommy)

Thus, some detainees recognised that they had been identified and labelled as the 'other' and expected to be treated as such by all instruments and agencies of the amended 'criminal justice' system which was operating in Northern Ireland at the time. This is not to suggest that they were 'accepting' of the state violence against them, more that there was a feeling that such violence was an inevitable part of the detention system and another potential site of personal and political struggle.

Condemnation of the condemners

Cohen's (2001) depictions of literal, interpretive and implicatory denial are of immense value to sociologists, criminologists and others interested in conflict. They establish an analytical method of understanding much official discourse and are a useful way in which the inter-relationships between different forms of truth in conflict can be deconstructed. It is also important to note that literal, interpretive and implicatory denials are not mutually exclusive categories. They are perhaps better understood as changes of emphasis, as something more complex than a linear shift from literal, through interpretative, to implicatory denial. For example, the same aspects of denial can be perceived simultaneously within particular elements of the official discourse of Northern Ireland. The suggestion that detainees were 'not tortured, but were ill-treated' is clearly interpretive denial, yet it also *remains* a literal denial that torture did not take place and is *equally* a denial of the socially and morally censorious implications linked to a hierarchy of state harm. Therefore a particular denial can engage with all three aspects of Cohen's (2001) framework simultaneously, avoiding the false dichotomy that denial must be one of either literal, interpretive or implicatory denial.

Returning to Sykes and Matza's (1957) original techniques of neutralisation, the 'condemnation of the condemners' can be explored as a further element of denial. Rather than focusing upon the victims and their possible disenfranchisement, the perpetrators and the legitimacy of their actions, or the wider justifications for actions taken against constructed threats, the 'condemnation of the condemners' shifts attention away from alleged acts and onto those who 'go public' with their disapproval. The continued presence of testimonies condemning the actions of the state suggest that for some, the literal, interpretive and implicatory denials contained within official discourse *failed* to change the understanding and meaning given to events, and therefore further attempts at neutralisation become necessary. The condemnation of the condemner:

attack[s] the reliability, objectivity and credibility of the observer. Victims are lying and cannot be believed because they have a political interest in discrediting the government. Witnesses are untrustworthy or drawn from the

Discourse, denial and dehumanisation   151

political opposition. Journalists and human rights organs are selective, biased, working from a hidden political agenda or else naive, gullible and easily manipulated.

(Cohen 1996: 524)

For example, within the official discourse of the public inquiry, Parker (1972: 2 para. 8) condemned those who critiqued the 'Five Techniques' by suggesting that they must have felt that 'it was better that servants of the State and innocent civilians should die that the information which could save them should ever be obtained by such methods'. By reframing any disagreement which criticised violence against detainees in such a way, the Inquiry's Majority Opinion condemned the opposition of Lord Gardiner and attempted to undermine his moral position on the use of the Techniques.

The 'condemnation of condemners' takes place at a local, national and international level. In Northern Ireland, an increasingly explicit condemnation can be witnessed in the allegations made against some of those who published detainees' accounts of state violence. Father Denis Faul and Father Raymond Murray collected the statements of detainees and published extensive allegations of abuse (1971, 1972, 1973, 1974, 1975a, 1975b, 1978, 1979, 1981). Both men were subjected to campaigns designed to delegitimise their criticisms of the British State. Father Faul was labelled as a Provo Priest, despite his statements criticising violence and his opposition to the hunger strikes (McHardy 2006). Thus the narratives of Faul and Murray were not perceived as neutral narratives fuelled by a concern with human rights abuses – a position shared by this book – but were instead labelled as part of a Republican political strategy to discredit British action in Northern Ireland. The legitimacy of the priests' concerns became lost in a discourse which framed their work as politically motivated and as being solely linked to the constitutional question, as Tommy recalled:

At that stage the British Government and State was dismissing the priests as being pro-IRA and the lawyers were seen as pro-IRA.... This type of thing was dissembling the civil liberties, they were saying that they were supporters of terrorists and terrorism, all of the usual, we still hear it today.

The battle for truth in conflict situations may not always display such direct levels of explicitness. In relation to allegations about state violence experienced during internment, the *Irish Times* (24 November 1971 in Curtis 1998) reported that the BBC had been given approval to interview a small number of internees, but not to talk to the doctors who might corroborate their allegations. The control of access to information thus remains highly important within the context of conflict, even if such things are more difficult within societies which claim to be democratic. The narratives of the detainees were one of a long list of 'sensitive' issues observable in the history of media coverage of the conflict (Taylor 1978; Millar 1994; Curtis 1998). Overt censorship may be unpopular and difficult to police (as evidenced by the 'Broadcasting Ban'[9]), therefore the state must instead

152 *Discourse, denial and dehumanisation*

invoke, alongside denial, instruments which aim to delegitimise challenges to the dominant discourse. Through condemning those who support allegations against the state, the power and influence of such damaging allegations can begin to be subjected to greater controls.

The shifting of the discourse from the state as condemned to the condemners also occurred following accounts of state violence which were emerging from Castlereagh Interrogation Centre from 1976 onwards. The literal denials that the torture alleged by detainees 'simply did not happen' were challenged on occasions where clear evidence of injuries was recorded by medical experts, including the RUC's own doctors. Dr Robert Irwin identified and publicised evidence of state violence experienced by detainees (Taylor 1980). The faceless body charts showing the locations of physical injuries and trauma contrasted with the dehumanised depiction of 'the terrorist other' which had been operationalised against detainees. Here, the featureless white figures were drained of all those images and could simply show 'victims'. They were free of any political context or interpretation. The construction of the 'other' was (and is) challenged by these simplistic drawings of the human body which identified the sites and severities of injuries.

However, it was Dr Irwin, and not just his narratives, who became the subject of condemnation. In addition to recording the injuries of detainees, he had been involved in 'going public' with detainees' experiences. Following his appearance on the *Weekend World* television programme, stories began to appear in the *Daily Telegraph* and *Daily Mail* (both right-leaning British newspapers). According to Coogan (2002) the stories had been fed to the media by the Northern Ireland Office. The articles implied that Irwin's wife had been raped by a British soldier, and that his anger at the RUC's failure to arrest the perpetrator underpinned his allegations of state violence against detainees (Taylor 1980; Curtis 1998; Coogan 2002). As an attempt to 'condemn the condemner', the accuracy of the lurid media stories was irrelevant and unimportant, as its purpose was solely to deflect any criticism of the RUC back onto Dr Irwin by calling into question his reliability as a witness. Laurence found such an approach particularly dishonourable:

> The *Sunday Times* the next week did a report that the only reason he was saying this was because he had a grudge against the RUC because British soldiers had raped his wife and they hadn't brought them to trial. Now, it wasn't publicly known that his wife had been raped, so it shows you the extent to which they went to just blacken his name, and that was it. So whereas his coming out and saying this was creating a real stir, it was just dead within a week because it was just thought that 'Oh, he would say that because [of what happened to his wife]'.

The condemnation of the condemners witnessed by Laurence attempts to ensure that contested narratives can become subjugated further. Through the 'targeting' of those criticising the state, the power of dominant discourses may act as a deterrent against possible future challenges to the approved truth:

Discourse, denial and dehumanisation   153

It is probably a lesson to others not to come out, because if there is anything about them, then [it will be used against them]. I thought it was particularly brutal, not really on him, but on his wife. But that was the argument; 'He's only saying this because he's disgruntled with the RUC who haven't been able to bring these British soldiers to account'.

(Laurence)

The condemnation of those with conflicting understandings about the value of narratives of state violence are not only visible at the domestic level, but can also be witnessed in inter-state discussions. The possibility and presence of shaming maintains a level of power at an international level and thus nation states may seek to invoke various regimes of denials across wide audiences and also in their relationships with international bodies. In the months prior to the *Republic of Ireland* v. *UK* (1978) case at the European Court of Human Rights – where the applicant state argued that the UK was guilty of subjecting detainees to torture in violation of Article 3 of the European Convention on Human Rights and Fundamental Freedoms (1950) – representatives of the UK discussed the possibilities of a change in the legislation on nationality (to exclude Irish citizens from claiming British nationality) and the deprivation of British voting rights to Irish citizens living in the UK. The possibility of using the Irish Governments' opposition to abortion as a possible method of pressuring the Irish State was also discussed (Author Unknown n.d., Document 'E40' *The Irish Case at Strasbourg*: 5 para. 17–22). Through highlighting the problematic aspects of the Irish State's approach to human rights and in claiming that the Irish legal action was detrimental to the fight against the IRA, the UK's representatives hoped to call into question the suitability of the Irish State to offer criticism of the way in which the UK treated those 'terrorist suspects' it deemed a threat to law and order. Through this technique, the condemner could be condemned.

In the context of the conflict in Northern Ireland, those who vocalise allegations about state violence become 'outsiders', those who support the testimonies become interlinked and stained by their association, or are instead recast as individuals driven by personal vengeance. Within this framework, the testimonies themselves become lost, their truth value and their consequences never directly explored. Thus 'knowledge is no longer the mind's ground of judgement but a commodity for hire' (Des Pres 1996: 3). Within such a framework, the integrity of the accuser becomes the subject of concern and the notion of state violence and accountability drops from the discourse.

'Truth' in conflict

In conclusion, the construction of regimes of truth in Northern Ireland involves all aspects of the state's official discourse. Any action taken by the state has to fit within the dominant ideological paradigm that it wishes to maintain in order to be perceived as legitimate. Such paradigms impact upon the construction of enemies, allies and their supporters, and have real, lived consequences, as shown

154 *Discourse, denial and dehumanisation*

by the former detainees in this book. Narratives can become part of a battle for truth in conflict, as stories told by survivors of state violence seek to compete with a version of the truth promoted by the state (Hegarty 2003), often with different levels of success. It may be that memories of state violence are long, and that these subjugated knowledges will always form part of a contested narrative. Official discourse can never achieve a total condition of domination, nor is it an omnipresent and omnipotent discourse. It must constantly challenge, co-opt and suppress the alternative version (Burton and Carlen 1979).

The permanent and total destruction of alternative narratives therefore remains difficult, as the contemporaneous growth in 'Truth Commission' type mechanisms illustrate (Teitel 2000; Hayner 2002). Dominant discourses might represent the 'official management of recognition' (Stanley 2002) at a particular moment in time and place. They may seek to 'establish an implicit perspective whence authoritative judgement can be made regarding first, what actually happened at the time, *and second, what those events really mean* for all time' (Burton and Carlen 1979: 69–70, emphasis added). However, this process is a constant battle for truth both in times of conflict and beyond, and it is always unfinished and always under threat. The public testimonies of those who allege state violence are a constant challenge to official regimes of truth (Rolston and Scraton 2005). The role of the audience takes on an added significance, for, as Interviewee 'F' observed, 'when you go public, you take on something that is powerful'.

For some former detainees, the narration of their own suffering and the State's inevitable denials had also led them to consider the suffering of others and the recognition of those experiences by Republicans. One interviewee concluded:

> But you have to learn to say to yourself 'Well, these things happen'. We weren't particularly charming either when we got our hands on policemen, so you have to take a balanced view of things as well.
>
> (Tommy)

Tommy's observation hints at Republicanism's own complicated relationship to victimhood, its own discourses of denial and their legacy. As previous chapters have shown, the historical narrative of Republicanism is replete with images of selective victimhood, resistance and of strength gained through suffering. Within this historical narrative, there was, and to an extent still is, limited space for acknowledging the suffering of 'other' victims, particularly when they came from outside the Republican community or were part of organisations which carried out violence against Republicans. Tommy's recognition of the suffering of British forces might not be an apology for the violence of the IRA, but is an acknowledgement of the violence of armed conflict and his desire for 'taking a balanced view on things'.

His desire for balance has so far not been reflected by the official discourse of the British State, which is yet to respond to the legacy of its central involvement

Discourse, denial and dehumanisation   155

in the conflict. With the exception of the British Government's response to the Saville Inquiry (2010), the British State has rarely publicly and unequivocally apologised for its role in the conflict and has not fully acknowledged its responsibility for the deaths of civilian and paramilitary victims in particular (see Chapter 8). The study of official discourse illustrates that this continuing denial occurs through a range of semantic mechanisms, as important aspects of information control synthesise with broader patterns of social control. It is simply one approach amongst many in the process of reproducing and maintaining particular ideological social relations (Burton and Carlen 1979). Denials may obfuscate incidences of state violence, recast harmful events as legitimate or downplay their significance. They may also call into question the veracity of truth claims made about state violence, or cast negatively framed judgements on the motivations of those who make their private experiences part of a public narrative. They remain a powerful part of official discourse and play a role in subjugating knowledges and contesting narratives. Yet, despite all of this, and the presence of labels that mould and shape the dominant depiction of victimhood, the majority of those interviewed as part of the present study attached little or no significance to the legacy of the denials which were operationalised around their narrative testimonies of state violence.

Notes

1 The *Report of the United Nations' Fact Finding Mission on the Gaza Conflict* (2009) criticised this interpretation and recommended that Israel (and Hamas) be investigated for war crimes and possible crimes against humanity.
2 As part of British Prime Minister Margaret Thatcher's 1984 Conservative economic plan, plans were announced to close twenty coal mines across England, Scotland and Wales. As a result of the plan 20,000 jobs would be lost and often in areas where coal mining and related industries entirely dominated employment. In the 'Battle of Orgreave' between police and picketing miners in South Yorkshire,

> an out-of-control police force ... charged pickets and onlookers alike on terraced, British streets. The full brutality of the police was only revealed later as prosecution after prosecution of 'rioting' miners was thrown out. Instead, the South Yorkshire police force ended up with a huge compensation bill.
>
> (Hunt 2006)

Similar events also took place at Armthorpe, where police 'behaved like "animals". They were hitting anyone they could find.... There were six policemen and the lad they were chasing was on the floors. They were knocking hell out of him' (Armthorpe witnesses in Scraton 1985: 4–5). In the present series of interviews, Interviewee 'P' positions a British miner as someone initially disbelieving of the British State's violence in Northern Ireland, despite the miner's membership of a community which had experienced violent policing.
3 Northern Ireland newspaper with a generally Unionist readership.
4 Phrase suggesting unimportance.
5 The police.
6 In 1976 IRA Volunteer Michael Kearney was shot dead by the IRA for 'imparting information of vital importance to the British war machine'. Although initially it was argued that Kearney had been an informer, in 2003, representatives of the IRA admitted that he had in fact been 'broken' under severe interrogation at Castlereagh (see

156 *Discourse, denial and dehumanisation*

Moloney 2007: 155–156; McKittrick *et al.* 2007: 790). Despite this documented violence, the public history of the Republican movement and the present interview data contains conflicting accounts in relation to the extent of violence, stigma or sympathy experienced by former detainees known to have 'broken' under interrogation.

7 Northern Ireland's First Minister (at the time of writing) sharing power with Sinn Féin and other parties in devolved administration.

8 Allusions to the major genocide of the mid twentieth century are erroneous in terms of scale and context, but are often present in former detainees' accounts. These representations assist in depicting the 'other' (security forces) as being akin to Nazi guards. These 'concentration camp' allusions are strongly critiqued by Graham and McDowell (2007: 357) as being 'myopic self-delusions'.

9 The 'Broadcasting Ban', also known as the 'Northern Ireland Notice', came into being in 1988 until 1994. It banned journalists from broadcasting any direct material that supported, solicited or invited support for illegal organisations, or any words spoken by a person who represented or purported to represent those organisations. Miller (1994) and Curtis (1998) describe how the ban was really targeted at Sinn Féin and show that it was deeply unpopular with journalists, who undermined it by dubbing possibly problematic coverage with actors' voices.

Bibliography

Ashworth, A. (1998) *The Criminal Process: An Evaluative Study*. Oxford: Oxford University Press.

Author Unknown (n.d.) *The Irish Case at Strasbourg*. Outline of HMG Policy and Commission Procedure Document 'E40'.

Bandura, A. (1990) 'Selective Activation and Disengagement of Moral Control', *Journal of Social Issues*, 46(I), 27–46.

Bennett Report (1979) *Report of the Committee of Inquiry into Police Interrogation Procedures in Northern Ireland* [Cmnd 7497]. London: HMSO.

Burton, F. and Carlen, P. (1979) *Official Discourse: On Discourse Analysis, Government Publications, Ideology and the State*. London: Routledge & Kegan Paul.

Cavanaugh, K.A. (1997) 'Interpretations of Political Violence in Ethnically Divided Societies', *Terrorism and Political Violence*, 9(3), 33–54.

Challis, J. (1999) *The Northern Ireland Prison Service 1920–1990: A History*. Belfast: Northern Ireland Prison Service.

Christie, N. (1986) 'The Ideal Victim' in Fattah, E. (ed.) *From Crime Policy to Victim Policy*. New York: St Martin's Press.

Cohen, S. (1996) 'Human Rights and The Crimes of the State: The Cultures of Denial', in McLaughlin, E. Muncie, J. and Langan, M. (eds) *Criminological Perspectives: A Reader*. London: Sage.

Cohen, S. (2001) *States of Denial: Knowing About Atrocities and Suffering*. London: Polity Press.

Cohen, S. (2006) 'Neither Honesty nor Hypocrisy: The Legal Reconstruction of Torture', in Newburn, T. and Rock, P. (eds) *The Politics of Crime Control: Essays in Honour of David Downes*. Oxford: Oxford University Press.

Compton Report (1971) *Report of Inquiry into Allegations Against the Security Forces of Physical Brutality in Northern Ireland Arising out of Events on the 9th August 1971* [Cmnd 4823]. London: HMSO.

Conroy, J. (2000) *Unspeakable Acts, Ordinary People: The Dynamics of Torture*. London: University of California Press.

Discourse, denial and dehumanisation   157

Coogan, T.P. (2002) *The Troubles: Ireland's Ordeal 1966–1996 and the Search for Peace*. New York: Palgrave.

Corcoran, M.S. (2006a) *Out of Order: The Political Imprisonment of Women in Northern Ireland, 1972–1998*. Collumpton: Willan.

Corcoran, M.S. (2006b) 'Talking About Resistance: Women Political Prisoners and the Dynamics of Prison Conflict, Northern Ireland', in Barton, A., Corteen, K., Scott, D. and Whyte, D. (eds) *Expanding the Criminological Imagination: Critical Readings in Criminology*. Devon: Willan.

Council of Europe (1950) *European Convention for the Protection of Human Rights and Fundamental Freedoms, as amended by Protocols Nos. 11 and 14*, 4 November.

Crawford, C. (1999) *Defenders or Criminals? Loyalist Prisoners and Criminalisation*. Belfast: Blackstaff Press.

Crelinsten, R.D. (2003) 'The World of Torture: A Constructed Reality', *Theoretical Criminology*, 7(3), 293–318.

Curtis, L. (1998) *Ireland: The Propaganda War*. Belfast: Sásta.

Des Pres, T. (1996) 'On Governing Narratives: The Turkish-Armenian Case', *The Yale Review*, 75(4), 517–531.

Fattah, E.Z. (1992) *Towards a Critical Victimology*. New York: St. Martin's Press.

Faul, D. and Murray, R. (1971) *The Hooded Men: British Torture in Ireland*, Dungannon: The Authors.

Faul, D. and Murray, R. (1972) *British Army and Special Branch RUC Brutalities, December 1971–February 1972*. Dungannon: The Authors.

Faul, D. and Murray, R. (1973) *Whitelaw's Tribunals, Long Kesh Internment Camp, Nov.1972–Jan. 1973*. Dungannon: The Authors.

Faul, D. and Murray, R. (1974) *Long Kesh – The Iniquity of Internment, August 9th 1971–August 9th 1974*. Dungannon: The Authors.

Faul, D. and Murray, R. (1975a) *The RUC: The Black and Blue Book*. Dungannon: The Authors.

Faul, D. and Murray, R. (1975b) *The Shame of Merlyn Rees: 4th Year of Internment in Ireland, Long Kesh 1974–1975*. Dungannon: The Authors.

Faul, D. and Murray, R. (1978) *The Castlereagh File: Allegations of Police Brutality 1976–77*. Dungannon: The Authors.

Faul, D. and Murray. R. (1979) *H-Blocks: British Jail for Irish Political Prisoners*, Dungannon: The Authors.

Faul, D. and Murray, R. (1981) *The British Dimension – Brutality, Murder and Legal Duplicity in Northern Ireland*. Dungannon: The Authors.

Gilligan, G. and Pratt, J. (eds) (2004) *Crime, Truth and Justice: Official Inquiry, Discourse and Knowledge*. Devon: Willan.

Goodey, J. (2005) *Victims and Victimology: Research, Policy and Practice*. Harlow: Pearson Education.

Graham, B. and McDowell, S. (2007) 'Meaning in the Maze: The Heritage of Long Kesh', *Cultural Geographies*, 14(3), 343–368.

Green, P. and Ward, T. (2004) *State Crime: Governments, Violence and Corruption*. London: Pluto.

Hayner, P.B. (2002) *Unspeakable Truths: Facing the Challenge of the Truth Commissions*. London: Routledge.

Hegarty, A. (2002) 'Government of Memory: Public Inquiries and the Limits of Justice in Northern Ireland', *Fordham International Law Journal*, 26(4), 1148–1192.

Hider, J. and Frenkel, S. (2009) 'Israel Admits Using White Phosphorous in Attacks on

158 *Discourse, denial and dehumanisation*

Gaza', *The Times*. 24 January. Available at: www.timesonline.co.uk/tol/news/world/middle_east/article5575070.ece (accessed 31 August 2011).

Hillyard, P. (1993) *Suspect Community: People's Experience of the Prevention of Terrorism Acts in Britain.* London: Pluto.

Hoggart, S. (1973) 'The Army PR Men of Northern Ireland', *New Society.* (n.d.) October.

Hunt, T. (2006) 'The Charge of the Heavy Brigade'. *Guardian.* 4 August. Available at www.guardian.co.uk/theguardian/2006/sep/04/features5 (accessed 6 October 2012).

Kauzlarich, D., Matthews, R. and Miller, W. (2001) 'Towards A Victimology of State Crime', *Critical Criminology*, 10(3), 173–194.

Kelman, H.C. (1995) 'The Social Context of Torture: Policy, Process and Authority', in Crelinsten, R.D. and Schmid, A. (eds) *The Politics of Pain: Torturers and their Masters.* Boulder: Westview Press.

Korn, A. (2004) 'Israeli Press and the War Against Terrorism: The Construction of the "Liquidation" Policy', *Crime, Law and Social Change*, 4(3), 209–234.

McAuley, J.W. (1994) *The Politics of Identity: A Loyalist Community in Belfast.* Aldershot: Avebury.

McEvoy, K. (2001) *Paramilitary Imprisonment in Northern Ireland: Resistance, Management and Release.* Oxford University Press: Oxford.

McHardy, A. (2006) 'Obituary: Monsignor Denis Faul'. *Guardian.* 22 June. Available at: www.theguardian.com/news/2006/jun/22/guardianobituaries.mainsection1 (accessed 12 December 2012).

McKittrick, D., Kelters, D., Feeney, B., Thornton, C. and McVea, D. (2007) *Lost Lives: The Stories of the Men, Women and Children Who Died as a Result of the Northern Ireland Troubles*. Mainstream Publishing: London.

McLaughlin, M. (1996) 'Political Violence and the Crimes of the State' in Muncie, J. and McLaughlin, M. (eds) *The Problem of Crime.* London: Sage.

Miller, D. (1994) *Don't Mention the War: Northern Ireland, Propaganda and the Media.* London: Pluto Press.

Minow, M. (2000) 'The Hope for Healing: What Can Truth Commissions do?' in Rotberg, R. and Thompson, D. (eds) *Truth* v. *Justice: The Morality of Truth Commissions*. Princeton: Princeton University Press.

Moloney, E. (2007) *A Secret History of the IRA*. London: Penguin Books Ltd.

Morgan, R. (2000) 'The Utilitarian Justification of Torture: Denial, Desert and Disinformation', *Journal of Punishment and Society*, 2(2), 181–196.

Mulcahy, A. (2005) 'The "Other" Lessons from Ireland: Policing, Political Violence and Policy Transfer'. *European Journal of Criminology*, 2(2), 185–209.

The Newsletter (1978) 'MPs Warned of Big Anti-RUC Campaign'. 14 April.

Norton-Taylor, R. (2009) 'Britain Aided Iraq Terror Renditions, Government Admits'. *Guardian.* 26 February. Available at www.guardian.co.uk/world/2009/feb/26/britain-admits-terror-renditions (accessed 1 August 2012).

Parker Report (1972) *Report of the Committee of Privy Counsellors Appointed to Consider Authorised Procedures for the Interrogation of Persons Suspected of Terrorism* [Cmnd 4901]. London: HMSO.

Report of the United Nations Fact Finding Mission on the Gaza Conflict, 2009 [A/HRC/12/48] Available at: www2.ohchr.org/english/bodies/hrcouncil/docs/12session/A-HRC-12-48.pdf (accessed 31 August 2011).

Republic of Ireland v. *United Kingdom* [1978] 2 EHRR 25.

Robinson, P. (1981) *Self Inflicted: An Exposure of the H-Blocks Issue.* Belfast: Democratic Unionist Party.

Rolston, B. and Scraton, P. (2005) 'In the Full Glare of English Politics: Ireland, Inquiries and the British State', *British Journal of Criminology*, 45(4), 547–564.

Ryder, C. (2000b) *The RUC 1922–2000: A Force Under Fire*. London: Arrow Books.

Saville Report (2010) *Report of the Bloody Sunday Inquiry*. London: HMSO.

Scraton, P. (1985) *The State of the Police*. London: Pluto Press.

Smyth, J. and Ellison, G. (1999) *The Crowned Harp: Policing Northern Ireland*. London: Pluto.

Smyth, M.B. (2007) *Truth Recovery and Justice After Conflict*. London: Routledge.

Stanley, E. (2005) 'Truth Commissions and the Recognition of State Crime', *British Journal of Criminology*, 45(4), 582–597.

Stanley, E. (2009) *Torture, Truth and Justice: The Case of Timor Leste*. London: Routledge.

Sykes, G. and Matza, D. (1957) 'Techniques of Neutralisation: A Theory of Delinquency', *American Sociological Review*, 22(6), 664–670.

Taylor. P. (1978) 'Reporting Northern Ireland', *Index on Censorship*, Vol. 7(6), 3–11.

Taylor, P. (1980) *Beating the Terrorists: Interrogation in Omagh, Gough and Castlereagh*. London: Penguin.

Teitel, R. (2000) *Transitional Justice*. Oxford: Oxford University Press.

Tomlinson, M. (1998) 'Walking Backwards into the Sunset: British Policy and the Insecurity of Northern Ireland', in Miller, D. (eds) *Rethinking Northern Ireland: Culture, Ideology and Colonialism*. Harlow: Longman.

Tonge, J. (2002) *Northern Ireland: Conflict and Change*. Harlow: Longman.

United Nations (1984) UN Convention Against Torture and Other Cruel, Inhuman or Degrading Treatment or Punishment. Available at: www.ohchr.org/EN/ProfessionalInterest/Pages/CAT.aspx (accessed 13 May 2013).

Walklate, S. (2007) *Imagining the Victim of Crime*. Maidenhead: McGraw-Hill/Open University Press.

8 Seeking accountability for state violence

State violence against detainees rendered explicit the violent and coercive power of the criminal justice system in Northern Ireland, albeit a criminal justice system with amended rules of evidence and reduced due process safeguards. Yet the British State was rarely held to account for state violence and abuse, not only against detainees but against the wider population. The following chapter traces the possible ways in which survivors of state violence might be able to seek some form of redress. It illustrates how the lack of accountability for detainees' experiences is linked into a broader lack of accountability for other acts of state violence, particularly the state's own lethal violence which led to one in ten of all deaths in the conflict.

Between 1976 and 1979, Northern Ireland's non-jury courts were achieving an unusually high conviction rate in 94 per cent of cases. Most of these successful prosecutions depended wholly or mainly on confessions signed during police interrogation (Bishop and Mallie 1988). Yet in recent years, as Northern Ireland seemingly transitions towards a post-conflict society, the safety of these convictions has been subject to closer scrutiny. Though the issue of unsafe convictions does not often feature in many of the transitional justice discussions about 'making peace with the past', the use of criminal appeals is becoming one method through which former detainees are attempting to address the legacy of state violence (Quirk 2013). The Criminal Cases Review Commission (CCRC) was established in 1997 following the recommendations of the Criminal Appeal Act 1995. It emerged following a number of high-profile miscarriages of justice linked to the conflict in Northern Ireland, including what became known as 'The Guildford Four', 'Maguire Seven' and 'Birmingham Six' cases. These referred to a series of criminal cases which followed a spate of pub bombings in England in 1974. Fifteen men and two women from Northern Ireland were charged, found guilty and sentenced to imprisonment ranging from four years to life. During their imprisonment, questions began to be raised about the safety of the convictions, particularly after IRA defendants in another trial claimed responsibility for the bombings. Yet it was not until years later, in 1990 and 1991, that the convictions were ruled unsafe following the discovery of evidence not admitted to the original trials, the police fabrication of statements and the discrediting of forensic evidence once thought central to the prosecution (Quirk 2013). These three cases, along with that of Judith Ward,[1] highlighted the weaknesses of the established appeals process and contributed to the creation of the CCRC (Joyce 2013; Quirk 2013).

The CCRC is therefore one way in which former detainees who have experienced state violence in detention might be able to begin to challenge the safety of their convictions.The CCRC can refer a case to the Court of Appeal if there is a 'real possibility' that the conviction would not be upheld. This might be on the basis of the admission of new evidence or legal argument which was not available (or not disclosed) at the time of the original trial or appeal (Walker 2002). Applicants need to have tried to appeal previously or have clear 'exceptional circumstances' for not doing so. Thus far the CCRC has given little precise indication of what such circumstances might involve, but it has still made a number of referrals to the Northern Ireland Court of Appeal (NICA) in cases linked to the conflict. According to Quirk (2013) applications from Northern Ireland have been referred at about three times the rate of applications from elsewhere.

One legacy of the violent and oppressive interrogations in places such as Castlereagh might therefore be an increase in the number of applications to the CCRC in coming years, as awareness of its work grows (Cobain 2010). The investigative journalism of Cobain (2010, 2012a) and RTÉ Investigations Unit's (2014; see also Reilly 2014) examination of state violence against the 'Guinea Pigs' during internment has shown that, rather than being the result of 'bad apples', violence against detainees was a regular occurrence throughout the 1970s (in particular). There is therefore a strong possibility that many more former detainees might seek to have their convictions overturned. Within the 31 conflict-related cases which have been decided at the time of writing, the NICA raised doubts about the reliability of confession evidence in 26 of the 28 cases that were quashed (Requa 2014). Almost half of these cases make reference to ill-treatment and police violence during interview. Despite this, at the time of writing, allegations of physical mistreatment *alone* have raised sufficiently significant doubts about the safety of conviction in very few of cases in which they were raised as a specific area of concern. In the overturned cases of *R.* v. *Mulholland* (2006), *R.* v. *McCartney and MacDermott* (2007), and *R.* v. *Livingstone* (2013), the accused supported their claims with evidence that other former detainees had lodged very similar complaints against the exact same police officers. The language of the judgments shows concern not with the violence itself, but the extent to which its use undermined particular officers' 'credibility'. This individualised approach to state violence can also be seen in the remainder of the overturned cases which emphasise former detainees' particular 'vulnerability', rather than the state violence against them. Care must therefore be taken not to exaggerate the role of the CCRC in responding to the legacy of state violence against detainees.

For those falsely convicted, the overturning of convictions will not undo the violence of incarceration and its legacy. The CCRC is also not designed or suited to being a transitional justice mechanism, or a way of 'making peace with the

162 *Seeking accountability for state violence*

past'. Nor is it a panacea for the physical and psychological damage which might be caused by a wrongful conviction (Joyce 2013). Former prisoners have described their feelings of isolation post-release and the problems they have experienced in maintaining good relationships with their families (Shirlow *et al.* 2005; Jamieson *et al.* 2010). They have also hinted at a range of mental health difficulties (Jamieson and Grounds 2002; McEvoy *et al.* 2004) and it is reasonable to believe that such things may become particularly pronounced when one is falsely convicted. Rolston's (2011: 12–13) review of the literature featuring/ about former prisoners suggests that:

> a substantial number of ex-prisoners experience poor health as a result of their prison and pre-prison experiences. A substantial minority of ex-prisoners display symptoms of serious psychological trauma, including PTSD (Post Traumatic Stress Disorder): depression, hyper activity, hyper alertness, negative self-appraisal, loss of sleep, deep-seated emotional stress. Although many prisoners were unmarried when first imprisoned, half of those who were married later divorced. Release from prison was often highly traumatic, with worries about personal security, emotional problems, relationship problems with partners and children. Difficulties in readjusting to life outside prison included anxiety, depression, anger, fear and isolation. Alcohol dependency and attempted suicide were sometimes the result.

The legacy of imprisonment – wrongful or otherwise – means that rates of unemployment are four times higher for former prisoners than for the general population, partly as a result of statutory rules which enable employers to discriminate against former prisoners (Rolston 2011). Financial difficulties are commonplace and continue to contribute to the socio-economic marginalisation of many former prisoners. The CCRC is unlikely to be able to fully alleviate many of these problems, particularly as rendering a conviction unsafe is not the same as declaring a person innocent. Furthermore, the CCRC works slowly and requires that cases fulfil strict criteria in order to avoid being filtered out. Of the 16,333 applications completed by April 2014, 15,779 (96.6 per cent) have been dismissed without being referred to the appeals courts. The 'real possibility ... that a conviction would not be upheld' is therefore a high threshold which many applications fail to reach. For the small proportion of cases which *are* referred back, there is no guarantee that the conviction will be rendered unsafe. Nor is it likely that former prisoners will be automatically entitled to compensation (see section 133 of the Criminal Justice Act 1988) if their convictions are eventually ruled unsafe. For some Republicans who refuse to recognise the Courts, any engagement with the British legal system still remains problematic – though as McEvoy (2000) shows, this practice of 'non-recognition' has been declining since the late 1970s. Nor should it be assumed that all of those convicted following state violence wish to revisit their experiences of interrogation and imprisonment. There are those who just want to 'move on' from the conflict and/or do not wish to apply to the CCRC for personal reasons (Requa 2014).

Seeking accountability for state violence 163

The CCRC therefore does offer some limited potential for shaping to the legacy of state violence, but it should not be seen as an easy panacea for this element of the conflict.

During interviews for this book, not one of the former detainees made reference to the CCRC or its work. Nor did they express any explicit desire to seek retribution – through the Courts or otherwise – against individuals who had committed acts of state violence against them. Interviewee 'F' and Tommy were particularly stoic:

> The sentence can't be overturned, the RUC has been disestablished or whatever they did with them. Politics have moved on. There might be a positive outcome but I can't imagine what it would be.... That's in the past, it's over and done with and now so what? It doesn't leave me feeling any cosy rosy glow towards the RUC or those interrogators! I don't like them any better now than I did then! (laughs). But I just say to myself, it is over, it is done.
>
> (Tommy)

> There is peace now, so I don't see me having an enemy now – I don't see RUC people [as enemies] now. I can honestly turn round and say I don't want anything to happen to this guy in the RUC who took out a gun and stuck it between my legs during interrogation. He did what he had to do during the conflict, maybe he operated under much stronger controls than Republicans operated under.
>
> (Interviewee 'F')

There is a tendency to see the legacy of state violence in Northern Ireland only in terms of a search for legal accountability. This was rarely referred to by former detainees. Instead, they hoped that the legacy of their narrative would be an end to the use of torture by British forces. Rather than seeking to have their convictions overturned, or involving themselves in difficult attempts to achieve punitive justice through cases against agents of the British State, most of the former detainees hoped that the legacy of their narrative could be linked to prevention and deterrence. Laurence spoke of his hope that 'by exposing stuff you can say something about the whole policy in general you could either deter people or educate them by saying this isn't the right approach to adopt'. There are echoes here of a wider belief, one often found in transitional justice discourses which seek to prevent the re-occurrence of a violent past through the sharing of stories about pain and suffering (see e.g. Nunca Más (meaning 'Never Again') 1984). Former detainee 'P' hoped that the idea of 'never again' would indeed be the legacy of his narrative. He hoped that by telling the story of the pain, fear and vulnerability he experienced, he might be able to dissuade people from treating others inhumanely:

> Now, I would like to think that some of those people who inflicted this on us might just think or realise that religious and political bigotry is an appalling

164 *Seeking accountability for state violence*

mind-set that others can use and abuse. Also, anyone who cares to read this will come to appreciate that bigotry and hatred serve only to injure and hurt us all; victim and perpetrator both.... What would I like out of it is that I would like things like that to be known not for any reason other than for hopefully getting individuals who would be of a mind to do that or get caught up in that business of hurting someone to take a step back and not do it. That is what I reckon and what I would like to come out of this; to make us all that bit more appreciative of each other and not be cruel or vindictive to others.

(Interviewee 'P')

Despite still hoping that their narrative might somehow contribute to preventing British state violence in the future, most detainees were pessimistic about its real ability to do so. Tommy drew parallels with British involvement in Northern Ireland in the 1970s with the post 9/11 'War on Terror':

What happened to me and many others in custody is important for several reasons. I think it useful to have an accurate historical record, for if people understand what happened before there is a small chance they may not make the same mistake again – although I would not be too optimistic about that.... Unfortunately, the British Army has ... participated in some nasty incidents in Iraq – maybe not to the same extent as the Americans, but the British have supported the US Government. What was happening in Abu Ghraib and [Bagram] and other places like that is known to the British Government. The torture being perpetrated by the US – and the obscene contracting out of torture – is known to the British government. There is *no way* that happens without the Government knowing, without their intelligence picking up what is happening and what their allies are doing. So you become a bit disenchanted about the lessons.

(Tommy)

The parallels between British State involvement in Northern Ireland and in the post-9/11 'War on Terror' have been examined in depth by a range of authors, such as Campbell (2005); Campbell and Connolly (2006) and Pantazis and Pemberton (2009) and it is not the intention to revisit those arguments here. What is of significance for the purpose of this chapter is the understanding that former detainees felt that their narratives had not 'taught the British any lessons' (Tommy). The International Criminal Court is currently considering a complaint relating to the involvement of British forces in war crimes in Iraq. Aspects of the complaint relate to violence in detention and include the torture, cruel, inhuman or degrading treatment carried out against 400 Iraqi detainees. British forces were also responsible for the death of Baha Mousa in 2003 following the invasion of Iraq. Baha was an Iraqi hotel receptionist who was beaten, hooded, forced into stress positions and given very little food or water – techniques which have much in common with those used against detainees in Northern Ireland. Baha died within 36 hours of being detained. One British soldier pled

Seeking accountability for state violence   165

guilty to inhuman treatment and was sentenced to one year imprisonment, whilst six others had the case against them dropped. The Ministry of Defence later paid out £2.83 million in compensation to Baha Mousa's family and to the families of nine other detainees who had alleged similar treatment at the hands of the British Army. Such cases strengthen Tommy's argument that little has been learnt from former detainees' experiences in Northern Ireland.

The broader legacy of state violence in Northern Ireland

The narratives of former detainees hint at a lack of faith in the ability of the legal system to hold state actors to account. This is understandable given the State's response to wider aspects of state violence. This book has focused on the lives of former detainees and explored in detail their experiences and the reasons for their narratives. Yet these narratives represent one small element of the history of state violence and its legacy in Northern Ireland. Approximately one in ten deaths during the conflict came as a result of state violence (McKittrick *et al.* 2007). Such statistics do not include those who are thought to have been killed as a result of collusion, which is itself a form of state violence. During the period 1969–1974, alternatively characterised as the 'militarisation phase' by Ní Aoláin (2000) or 'reactive containment' by McEvoy (2001), 24 per cent of those killed died in what Ní Aoláin (2000) labels 'gun battles'. The majority of the dead were killed by the British Army, with only 12 per cent known to be armed at the time of their death (Ní Aoláin 2000). Some 64 per cent of those killed were civilians with no involvement in armed conflict and were often killed in circumstances such as during riots, rallies or at checkpoints (Ní Aoláin 2000). For 17 per cent of the deaths caused by British State violence in this period, little information exists (Ní Aoláin 2000), illustrating the ease with which experiences of state violence can be marginalised.

Inquiries

Yet the marginalisation of experiences of state violence is, as shown in previous chapters, an incomplete process which can be resisted in part by the publication of narratives and by increasing public awareness. In relation to the conflict in Northern Ireland, the Government often used public inquiries in response to sustained pressure from survivors, their families and community groups. Thirteen people were killed by the Parachute Regiment of the British Army on 'Bloody Sunday' (30 January 1972) during a march by the Northern Ireland Civil Rights Association. A fourteenth would later die as a result of the injuries he received on that day (Pringle and Jacobson 2002). Such examples of state violence are broadly indicative of the State's involvement in the conflict during the period 1969–1974, and are symbolic of the primacy given to the British Army following its deployment in 1972. The events of 'Bloody Sunday', however, quickly gained international attention and within eleven weeks the Government published the findings of the Widgery Inquiry (1972 at CAIN n.d.) which had been

166 *Seeking accountability for state violence*

swiftly set up to examine the events of 30 January 1972. The Inquiry concluded that there was

> no reason to suppose that the soldiers would have opened fire if they had not been fired upon first.... At one end of the scale some soldiers showed a high degree of responsibility; at the other, notably in Glenfada Park, firing bordered on the reckless ... there is a strong suspicion that [members of the crowd] had been firing weapons or handling bombs in the course of the afternoon and that yet others had been closely supporting them.
>
> (Widgery 1972 at CAIN n.d.)

However, following sustained public pressure, in 1998, the new Labour Government announced that there would be a fresh inquiry into those events. Twelve years later, the Saville Inquiry (2010) published its Report which absolved the dead of any responsibility for the events of that day and stated that 'the immediate responsibility for the deaths and injuries on "Bloody Sunday" lies with those members of Support Company whose unjustifiable firing was the cause of those deaths and injuries'. The Prime Minster of the Conservative–Liberal Coalition Government, David Cameron, apologised for the shootings, describing it as 'unjustified and unjustifiable' (BBC 2010). The ways in which Saville (2010) contrasted with the earlier findings of Widgery (1972) provides a clear example of the temporal nature of denials and adds support to the power of alternative public narratives in challenging interpretations of state violence. Had the families of those affected by 'Bloody Sunday' accepted Widgery's (1972) version of events, it is unlikely that sufficient pressure would have been placed on the British Government to revisit the killings and to apologies for state violence.

An investigation by the Police Service of Northern Ireland (PSNI) into 'Bloody Sunday' is underway at the time of writing, but one dominant theme of the conflict has been the failure to bring prosecutions – successful or otherwise – against agents of the British State (Rolston 2002). The lack of desire to seek convictions for state violence is symptomatic of a system in which the separation of powers remains little more than a myth, where the law in both design and function perpetuates particular understandings of the conflict, and where the language of 'reasonableness' and 'force' remains open to political manipulation. Ní Aoláin (2000: 34) asserts that 'the courts and attendant legal process were playing a minimalist role in the management of the conflict' and it is this continued minimalism which illustrates the extent to which the state functions through violence and need not even engage with the law fully in responding to allegations or in needing to reassert its 'legitimacy'.

The families of those victimised by the State play a role in pushing for an end to impunity and for greater accountability for state violence. They are often assisted in this endeavour by community groups and Non-Government Organisations. The family of Patrick Finucane and the Pat Finucane Centre, for example, have played a central role in increasing awareness of the close relationship between State forces and Loyalist paramilitary groups (Rolston 2005; Punch

Seeking accountability for state violence 167

2012; McGovern 2013). This relationship involved shared membership between state forces and pro-state paramilitaries and the protection of informers in what Tomlinson (1998) suggests is clear evidence of 'partisanship'. It also extended to collusion, as is strongly argued by the third report of the Stevens Inquiry (2003), suggested repeatedly in the reports into the deaths of Pat Finucane, Robert Hamill, Rosemary Nelson and Billy Wright (Cory 2004a, 2004b, 2004c, 2004d) and unequivocally confirmed by the Report of the Police Ombudsman (O'Loan 2007).

Following the publication of the Cory Reports (2004a, 2004b, 2004c, 2004d) the Government pledged to begin public inquiries into all four deaths, and in 2010 the first report was released. The Report of the Billy Wright Inquiry (MacLean 2010) found no evidence of collusion as it understood the term, but criticised a number of state agencies including the police and Prison Service for their negligence and failings. The inquiry into the death of Rosemary Nelson (Morland 2011: 465) also failed to reach an explicit finding of collusion, but instead hinted at the existence of 'bad apples' and argued that the report 'cannot exclude the possibility of a rogue member or members of the RUC or the Army in some way assisting the murderers to target Rosemary Nelson'. It also acknowledged that Rosemary had been abused and assaulted by the police, that there had been a leakage of intelligence and that abusive and/or threatening remarks had been made about the lawyer by the RUC to her clients. It also stated that 'there were omissions by state agencies, which rendered her more at risk and more vulnerable' (Morland 2011: 465). Although critical of state agencies, both the MacLean (2010) and Morland (2011) inquiries constructed the meaning of collusion in a much narrower way than the Cory (2004a, 2004b, 2004c, 2004d) investigations which preceded them. As McGovern (2013: 13) notes, the MacLean Inquiry decided at an early stage that actions such as ' "turning a blind eye", which might include "wrongful acts or admissions", "intentional acts that could have facilitated the death" all could "amply be covered by the [Inquiry's] terms of reference without attempting to analyse them in terms of collusion' (MacLean 2010: 9). The inquiry could then examine the Wright case 'without having to resort to the words "collusion" or "collusive"' (MacLean 2010: 9). Similar obfuscatory language games can be seen in the Morland Report (2011).

A full public inquiry into the death of Pat Finucane is yet to take place and now seems unlikely. The British Government instead ordered a review of pre-existing evidence, rather than establishing a full public inquiry. The De Silva Review was published in 2012 and asserted that this evidence had left De Silva with

> no doubt that agents of the State were involved in carrying out serious violations of human rights up to and including murder. However, despite the different strands of involvement by elements of the State, I am satisfied that they were not linked to an over-arching State conspiracy to murder Patrick Finucane.
>
> (De Silva 2012: 23–24 para. 116)

168   *Seeking accountability for state violence*

Again, rather than being seen as symptomatic of wider systems, processes and cultures in which state agents can operate with relative impunity, events linked to the RUC and/or Army are drained of the wider context of state violence and reduced down to the acts/omissions of individual 'bad apples'. The Inquiry into the death of Robert Hamill is yet to release its full report, but had recommended the Department of Public Prosecutions reconsider a decision not to prosecute former RUC officer Robert Atkinson for conspiracy to pervert the course of justice (Jowitt *et al.* 2010). Charges against Atkinson were reinstated in March 2014 following these recommendations, yet were dropped again in September 2014 after Craigavon Magistrates Court ruled that the witness who gave evidence against Atkinson was unreliable and therefore that there would not be a realistic prospect of conviction (BBC 2014).

The legacy of public inquiries being used as a means to hold the state to account for its violence has therefore been problematic both during the conflict and since its apparent cessation. Established by the British Government, such inquiries often emerge when attempts to suppress alternative accounts of state violence have failed and where the discursive challenge to the legitimacy of the state is at its most overt. Although the claim is that such inquiries are independent, objective and open, the reality is that they often function to provide a veil of democratic process over state abuses. The Public Inquiries Act 2005 has also increased the possibility of greater Ministerial influence over the content and publication of inquiries (McGovern 2013). As argued by Rolston and Scraton (2005: 558), inquiries and the laws around them can be part of a 'calculated move by government, in consultation with powerful state institutions and the judiciary, to give the appearance of scrutiny while protecting state interests'. With few exceptions – the recent Saville Inquiry (2010) being a pertinent example – such inquiries are often muted in their criticism of state agencies. At other times, such as in the unpublished Stalker inquiry in relation to a possible 'shoot-to-kill' policy, those charged with carrying out the investigations can be removed or put under pressure to step down. Prosecutions of members of the security community following public inquiries therefore remain rare. As a means for survivors of state violence to hold the state to account, they are often hamstrung by narrowly defined terms of reference, a seeming lack of objectivity and independence, along with the length of time taken to release reports (Rolston and Scraton 2005; McGovern 2013).

Inquests

State violence in Northern Ireland thus encompassed a wide remit, from on-street harassment, house searches and raids to internment, detention violence and lethal shootings. The legal response to violence and its legacy in Northern Ireland is illuminating and shows the ways in which the history of the conflict is formed through a conflicting bricolage of differing interpretations of events. As chapters in this book have evidenced, the role of official discourse in perpetuating particular understandings of the conflict cannot be ignored. The narratives of former detainees are but one way of challenging the dominant discourses which seek to legitimise acts

Seeking accountability for state violence   169

of state violence. Other mechanisms include the use of inquests, as well as other courts at both the domestic and international level. Like much of the legal regime around detention and interrogation, inquest powers in Northern Ireland have also been considerably amended from those available in England and Wales. Coinciding with the emergence of a seemingly 'shoot-to-kill' policy, from 1981, coroners could only reach findings of facts, such as who died and when, rather than culpability. As Leckey (2005: 1–2) notes, the remit of inquests has been 'strongly criticized by many bereaved families; the person suspected of causing the death was not a compellable witness and the short-form verdicts available at inquests in England and Wales – such as lawful and unlawful killing – were not available'. The use of Public Immunity Interest Certificates also prevented the appearance of witnesses or the production of evidence (Rolston 2002). These certificates have been used in Northern Ireland with a frequency Ní Aoláin (2000: 164) likens to 'a scattering of confetti' over the legal process. In comparison to England and Wales, the executive also has greater powers to decide which cases are eligible for inquests, all of which further compromises the supposed separation of powers thought so crucial to liberal democracy. The European Court of Human Rights (ECtHR) has strongly criticised the inquest system's response to state violence in Northern Ireland, particularly in relation to restrictions on available verdicts, the compelling of witnesses, the time taken to begin proceedings and the absence of legal aid (*Jordan et al.* v. *UK* 2001). Following this criticism, there have been some changes to rules regarding inquest procedures in Northern Ireland, which include allowing the inquest 'to compel a person suspected or charged with causing the death of the deceased person to appear before an inquest as a witness' (McEvoy 2013: 48).

Yet these reforms represent only limited changes to the inquest process and are far from the major re-haul the ECtHR implied was required (Bell and Keenan 2005). Witnesses who may be suspected or charged with causing the death can be compelled to attend, but are protected against answering any questions which might incriminate themselves or their spouses. The reforms have also done substantively very little to change the lengthy delays and adjournments also found in inquests in England and Wales, but which have always been particularly pronounced in Northern Ireland. At the time of writing, there are 46 inquests currently outstanding, many of which concern events from the 1970s. Since his appointment in 2010, Attorney General John Larkin QC has directed 30 of these inquests, recently restarting them in 2014 following a four month suspension over legal concerns he may have exceeded his powers in 21 of the cases. Further complexity surrounds the relationship between the inquest system and the procedural obligations under Article 2 of the ECHR. In 2011, the UK Supreme Court ruled that Article 2 would apply to

> the 16 'legacy inquests' (involving 26 deaths) currently outstanding on the coroner's books, a further six incidents (involving eight pre-2000 deaths) referred by the Attorney General … and a further seven deaths (between 1994 and January 2000) not yet the subject of inquests.
>
> (Brown LJ in Re McCaughey 2011: para. 102)

170   *Seeking accountability for state violence*

It remains to be seen whether this can be broadened out to include other deaths caused by state violence much earlier in the conflict.

Criminal courts

If the findings of inquests have in the main proved unable or unwilling to critique the role of State agents during violence in Northern Ireland, the criminal court system has further consolidated an official history in which the state is portrayed as neutral peacekeeper. The acts of British State agents were/are rarely framed as 'possible crimes' necessitating a criminal justice investigation. The rarity of convictions and the broader inaction (or limited action) of the criminal justice system against the 'security community' filters through the official discourse to further construct the power of the state and the legitimacy of its actions. Whereas convictions for violence by State agents were rare in comparison to the number of deaths, conviction rates for those accused of involvement in paramilitarism (particularly Republicanism) were high. The Diplock, juryless court system, which by 1979 had convicted 79 per cent of cases involving paramilitaries on the basis of confessions alone, had an acquittal rate of 100 per cent for accused members of the security forces regardless of the types of evidence used (Boyle *et al.* 1980). In the period 1974–1994, only 24 prosecutions involving 34 persons took taken place in relation to lethal force incidents, with only eight members of the security forces being convicted (Ní Aoláin 2000). These few successful prosecutions included the cases of James Ward[2] (shot outside North Queen Street RUC station in December 1972) in which a soldier pleaded guilty to manslaughter; and the guilty of murder verdicts given to two soldiers following the killings of Michael Naan and Andrew Murray[3] in Fermanagh in the same year. Later cases include that of Ian Thain, convicted of the murder of Thomas Reilly in 1984, and the convictions of James Fisher and Mark Wright for the murder of Peter McBride. All three returned to the British military following their release, with Ian Thain serving only two years of his life sentence in custody.

Cases involving the use of lethal force illustrate the relationship between the criminal courts and the legitimacy of state violence. As Ní Aoláin (2000) has argued, the criteria under Section 3 of the Criminal Law (Northern Ireland) Act 1967 has been interpreted in such a way as to allow for the broad definition of 'reasonable force' in Northern Ireland. The Act states that '(1) A person may use such force as is reasonable in the circumstances in the prevention of crime or in effecting or assisting in the lawful arrest of offenders or of persons unlawfully at large' (Criminal Law (Northern Ireland) Act 1967 section 3.1). This has resulted in the key principle of 'reasonableness' being stretched to include a range of events in which the use of force was seemingly neither proportionate or necessary and yet was still framed as 'reasonable'. The death of Patrick McElhone, a Tyrone farmer who had been shot dead in 1974 after running from soldiers who were questioning him, is symbolic of a wider rationale in which the judiciary could claim 'that the soldier *reasonably believed* that he might be dealing with a paramilitary seeking to escape and that his action was reasonable under the circumstances' (in McKittrick *et al.* 2007: 470, my emphasis). In acquitting the soldier responsible for the death of Patrick McElhone, the definition of reasonableness was further stretched to centralise the notion of the accused's 'reasonable belief' and to include a broad interpretation of the common law right to self-defence. In this way, successful lethal force prosecutions are rendered more difficult, as the background context of conflict drawn on by the accused might be able to persuade an audience that s/he honestly believed themselves (or those around them) to be under threat (Ní Aoláin 2000). The legacy of state violence cases in Northern Ireland suggests that there was often 'a discrepancy between the promise of reliability, impartiality and integrity within institutions and the reality of poor functioning, serious malfunctioning, illicit manipulation and systematic bias' (Punch 2012: 148).

The European Court of Human Rights

The British State can also seek to legitimise its violence through regional court systems. The European Court of Human Rights (ECtHR) has also been involved in constructing the legacy of the conflict in Northern Ireland, yet care must be taken not to exaggerate the extent of its rulings. At the Committee stage, 94 per cent of all applications are declared inadmissible, often with the suggestion that the domestic system provides an effective remedy for any violation which may have taken place (Steiner *et al.* 2000).

State violence in Northern Ireland was not limited to violence in interrogations, collusion or the shooting of a crowd with live rounds. It also included the use of plastic and rubber bullets. Although designed to be non-lethal, the frequent recourse to the use of these bullets led to the deaths of seventeen people during the conflict, eight of whom were children (CAIN 2012). In 1976, 13-year-old Brian Stewart died as a result of damage to his brain and skull after he had been shot with a plastic bullet by a member of the British Army. The circumstances in which this had taken place were, like many other events during the conflict, contested by agents of the British State, who alleged the 13-year-old had been leading a group in rioting and throwing stones at an isolated soldier. The existence of a riot was dismissed by all eyewitnesses, yet the resultant (civil) case ruled that the soldier's action had been 'reasonable in the circumstances' and this was later supported by the European Commission of Human Rights, which ruled the case inadmissible. As before, the legal (criminal, civil and European) system was reluctant to apportion responsibility for violence onto the agents of the British State. The 'emergency' regime with its modified courts assumed the guilt of non-state actors, but sought to deny (or at least reframe) the illegal or 'barely legal' actions of State agents.

Those cases that do continue to the ECtHR are often responded to over the course of five or six years, at a pace slower than what the Court has itself criticised individual states for. In relation to the conflict in Northern Ireland and particularly in relation to the lethal forms of state violence, the Court is yet to rule

172 *Seeking accountability for state violence*

conclusively that the force used in a particular case violated the right to life under Article 2 of the ECHR (Dickson 2010). Rulings have concerned themselves with procedural issues, such as questions about whether proper planning preceded the use of force, or issues around the investigations of state killings. The *McCann* v. *UK* (1995) case is broadly indicative of the response of the ECtHR to allegations against the UK, and shows the extent to which the Court is an unsuitable avenue for addressing the legacy of British state violence. The Court rulings can obfuscate seemingly clear instances of illegitimate state violence. In 1988, three suspected members of the IRA – Mairead Farrell, Daniel McCann and Sean Savage – were killed by the SAS in Gibraltar. The three had been under surveillance by the security forces for some time and bomb making equipment would later be found in a car rented by Mairead in Marbella. However, all three were unarmed at the time of their death and no attempt had been made to arrest them prior to the shootings. The car they had parked in Gibraltar contained no explosives and it was argued that the SAS who carried out the shootings were aware that this was the case before the three were shot dead (McKittrick *et al.* 2007). The judgment made at the ECtHR was that there had been a breach of Article 2 paragraph 2, but this was framed only in relation to the planning and control of the operation and not in relation to the actions of the SAS soldiers themselves:

> The Court accepts that the soldiers honestly believed, in the light of the information that they had been given … that it was necessary to shoot the suspects in order to prevent them from detonating a bomb and causing serious loss of life. The actions which they took, in obedience to superior orders, were thus perceived by them as absolutely necessary in order to safeguard innocent lives … [therefore] the actions of the soldiers do not, in themselves, give rise to a violation.
>
> (quoted in Connolly 2007: 8)

Thus, although the ruling from the ECtHR in the case of *McCann* v. *UK* (1995) confirms a breach of Article 2, it does so in such a way as to remove the very act of state violence. It is not a comment on the illegitimacy of the killing of Farrell, McCann and Savage itself, but a judgment about the extent to which such seemingly pre-planned operations can be compatible with the provisions of Article 2. Similarly, following the killings at Loughgall,[4] the Court ruled not that there had been unlawful killing, but that the British State's response to that killing had violated Article 2 of the ECHR. This case of *Kelly and Others* v. *UK* (2001), alongside *Jordan et al.* v. *UK* (2003), *McKerr* (2002) and the Ulster Freedom Fighters (UFF) collusion linked killing of *Shanaghan* (2003) and *Finucane* (2003) plus the similar verdict in *McShane* (2002) have done little to suggest a change in the Court's approach to the conflict. Such verdicts suggest that justice for those killed by the state remains a very incomplete form of justice, one which maintains the state's monopoly on the use of force and its power to frame the circumstances in which its use is legitimate.

Post-conflict mechanisms

Inquiries, inquests, national and regional courts all operated during the conflict itself, yet they still continue to construct the memory of the conflict and its legacy post-Peace Process. The question of how best to 'make peace with the past' has become increasingly central as Northern Ireland transitions, and has led to the production of vast amounts of literature on the subject (see e.g. Hegarty 2002; Bell 2002; Lundy and McGovern 2006; Connolly 2006; McGrattan 2009; Lundy 2009a, 2009b, 2011; McEvoy and McConnachie 2013). Yet, at the level of official discourse, this question largely remains unanswered and in its place a number of piecemeal approaches have developed. The most discussed mechanisms which have emerged since the Peace Process inevitably focus on deaths in the conflict and one such approach can be seen in the work of the Historical Enquires Team (HET). The Team is a unit of the Police Service of Northern Ireland (PSNI) tasked with re-examining the 3,268 deaths which have been attributed to the conflict, including deaths linked to state violence (Gawn 2007; Aiken 2010; Lundy 2009a, 2009b, 2011; Lundy and McGovern 2008; McGovern 2013).

One of the HET's vaguely stated aims is to 'assist in bringing a measure of resolution' to families affected by the conflict (Lundy 2009b). At the end of a process of case review, families are given a Review Summary Report which seeks to provide answers to some of the questions that they might have regarding the death of their loved one. Where the HET has uncovered 'evidential opportunities', cases can be referred on to other elements of the PSNI for further investigation and eventually, to the Public Prosecution Service (PPS) for consideration under both the evidential and public interest tests required to seek trial. Despite these opportunities, the HET's work is unlikely to result in a high number of convictions, given the time which has passed in historical cases (Lundy 2009a). There are significant limitations to the HET's ability to make 'peace with the past' and these become particularly pronounced in regards to victims of state violence. The HET's reports do not engage with the wider context of the conflict, as events described in its Review Summary Reports are individualised, separated off and fragmented from the wider circumstances in which they took place. Though this personalised approach might undoubtedly be of value to some families, it also enables the British State and its agents to 'fudge' the acknowledgement of its own role in the conflict and the legacy of the structural and systematic violence it was involved in. The HET also lacks the independence necessary to adequately review cases of police violence, as former RUC officers are currently employed in a range of positions within the HET, including in influential roles such as Lead Senior Investigating Officers (Lundy 2009a). Given the composition of the RUC historically and its role in relation to state violence and collusion, this lack of independence sits uncomfortably with the HET's aim of 'commanding the confidence of the wider community' (quoted in Lundy 2009b: 333). There are also further problems with the HET's examination of deaths caused by other agents in the security community, in regards to its

174 *Seeking accountability for state violence*

reluctance to refer cases on – particularly in relation to cases involving the British Army. In June 2013, a report by the Her Majesty's Inspectorate of Constabulary (HMIC 2013: 11) found that:

> State involvement cases appeared to be treated less rigorously in areas such as: how interviews under caution are conducted; the nature and extent of pre-interview disclosure; and the way claims made by state agents about being unfit for interview under caution were verified. We consider that these practices may seriously undermine the capability of the HET's review process to lead to a determination of whether the force used was or was not justified in state involvement cases, and to the identification and punishment of those responsible. They may also undermine the effectiveness of the PSNI and the Public Prosecution Service to the extent that state involvement cases relating to the British Army are not routinely referred to these agencies.

Though the HMIC Report (2013) suggested that this discriminatory approach was based on 'misunderstanding of the law' rather than anything more systematic, it remains a damning critique of the HET's attempt to respond to the legacy of state violence. Soon after its publication, the Policing Board issued a vote of no confidence in the HET and at the time of writing, an embargo is currently in place regarding the release of HET reports (*Belfast Telegraph* 2014). Research by Bill Rolston in January 2014 found that the majority of families – including those victimised by non-state agents – felt that the HET should be disbanded (Rolston 2014). Although it might have succeeded in 'bringing a measure of resolution' (its own words) to some families, the HET seems unwilling to fully engage with the legacy of state violence in Northern Ireland, and poorly equipped to respond to the wider demands of 'making peace with the past'.

The HET is not the only body in Northern Ireland whose role in responding to state violence is vulnerable to criticism. A further feature of the transition in Northern Ireland has been the work of the Historical Investigations Directorate of the Office of the Police Ombudsman for Northern Ireland (OPONI), though only in cases involving allegations against the police force. Despite publishing reports strongly criticising the RUC's involvement in collusion (O'Loan 2007), in later years the OPONI seemingly underwent a period of what McGovern (2013) justifiably calls 'retrenchment'. During the tenure of Ombudsman Al Hutchinson, a report (OPONI 2011) into the deaths of six people killed by the UVF in a pub in Loughinisland was finally published – almost two years later than expected and some 17 years after the Loughinisland killings themselves. It stated that although there was evidence of what it called 'numerous police failings', it could find no evidence of collusion. The families of the dead claimed that the report was inadequate and that there *had* been collusion between the RUC and the UVF. They argued that neither the RUC at time nor the later OPONI had carried out sufficient investigations into the killings and the related allegations of collusion. The OPONI's own staff had also begun to criticise the organisation's independence and further a report by Criminal Justice Inspection

Northern Ireland (CJINI 2011) found failings relating to independence and inconsistent investigation. A study by the Committee on the Administration of Justice (CAJ 2011) – a human rights-based NGO (non-governmental organisation) – also raised questions over the OPONI conduct in relation to historical cases. Soon after the publication of these reports, Al Hutchinson resigned. His successor, Michael Maguire, reviewed the original report into the Loughinisland killings and dismissed its findings on the basis that 'the specific circumstances of [the] case were not adequately pursued in the earlier investigation (quoted in Cobain 2012b). At the time of writing, OPONI has re-opened the investigation into events at Loughinisland.

The workings of OPONI in the Loughinisland case are illustrative of the nature of state power, but also of the opportunities which exist for resistance. Had it not been for the families of the deceased and for the work of community groups, it is likely that the original report would have stood and would therefore have formed the official memory of the Loughinisland killings, in the same way that the Widgery Inquiry (1972) sought to construct the official memory of Bloody Sunday. Although they differ significantly in the modes of operation and in the powers they have, courts, inquests and inquiries (official, as well as HET or OPONI-led) all contribute to the creation of a narrative about the conflict and, as such, can be seen as transitional justice mechanisms. Yet there are a number of problems with this legalistic approach. As Bell *et al.* (2007) suggest, one should 'question any idealisation of the end game of a narrow delineated "transitional justice" discourse, defined purely in terms of criminal accountability, lustration or state building, including definitions resting purely upon ... liberalisation or deterrence'. Aspects of this analysis are supported by McEvoy (2007) who critiques both the theory and practice of transitional justice for being dominated by a narrow sense of legalism. More often than not, legal mechanisms create and maintain a fractured reading of state involvement in conflict, rendering victims/survivors invisible in their final reports. The remits of inquiries can be drawn in such a way as to exclude any real discussion of the wider context of state violence, whilst at the same time emphasising the threat from non-state actors. The language of legal judgments can often seem cold and abstract at best, confusing and impenetrable at worst. State violence is portrayed as aberrant and unusual, and the active role of the state reduced down to occasional 'incidents' or 'events'. In short, 'there is no guarantee that individual prosecutions and court cases help to reveal the bigger picture of truth' (Rolston 2002). Furthermore, pursuing justice through courts and inquiries can often be a psychological and emotional ordeal (Smyth 2003). Legal avenues are ill-equipped to respond to the broader needs of victims and their families (McEvoy 2007; Simpson 2007).

An overarching strategy?

The Consultative Group on the Past (CGP) was the first major government appointed body to attempt to develop an overarching strategy on the past and

176 *Seeking accountability for state violence*

one which includes the recognition of victims' diverse needs (McEvoy 2013). In 2009 the CGP published its report, recommending 'steps that might be taken to support Northern Ireland society in building a shared future that is not over-shadowed by the events of the past' (Eames and Bradley 2009: 22). The Report included a total of 31 recommendations, which included the creation of a Legacy Commission charged with overseeing four strands of work. These are broadly linked to engaging with community issues resulting from the conflict (including the creation of a Reconciliation Forum), the review and investigation of histor-ical cases (absorbing the investigative work of HET and OPONI), the develop-ment of a process of information recovery to help families of those affected by conflict, and lastly the examination of thematic or linked cases, including what the Report deemed 'alleged collusion' (Eames and Bradley 2009: 18). The CGP somewhat optimistically suggested that these processes could all be completed within a five year timeframe with an estimated budget of £300 million.

The publication of the CGP Report (Eames and Bradley 2009) was greeted with controversy. The response of the media (and of a number of political groups) was to focus on the 'recognition payment' of £12,000 the CGP sug-gested should be paid to the 'nearest relative of someone who died as a result of the conflict' (Eames and Bradley 2009: 31). The Report's definition of a 'victim/survivor' was based on that set out in the Victims and Survivors (Northern Ireland) Order (2006). This Order stated that:

> 3(1) In this Order references to 'victim and survivor' are references to: (a) someone who is or has been physically or psychologically injured as a result of or in consequence of a conflict-related incident; (b) someone who pro-vides a substantial amount of care on a regular basis for an individual men-tioned in paragraph (a); or (c) someone who has been bereaved as a result of or in consequence of a conflict-related incident. (2) Without prejudice to the generality of paragraph (1), an individual may be psychologically injured as a result of or in consequence of (a) witnessing a conflict-related incident or the consequences of such an incident; or (b) providing medical or other emergency assistance to an individual in connection with a conflict-related incident.

This broad definition is more detailed than that contained in the Bloomfield Report (1998), which was supposed to explore 'possible ways to recognise the pain and suffering felt by victims of violence arising from the "Troubles" of the last thirty years, including those who have died or been injured in the service of the community' (Bloomfield 1998: 2). It was strongly criticised for appearing to minimise the suffering of victims of state violence and for not actively engaging in consultation with the related support groups (Healing Through Remembering 2002). It also implicitly excluded those involved with paramilitary offences from the definition of victimhood (Duffy 2010), and presented them as 'introduced into terrorism through peer pressure' (Bloomfield 1998: para. 5–8). Mostly con-cerned with bereaved victims of paramilitary violence, Bloomfield (1998) makes

Seeking accountability for state violence 177

little direct reference to the injuries and harm experienced by other families. The Report argues that it would 'be quite unacceptable to provide services for the benefit of those convicted of serious offences which are not matched in dealing with the victims of such crimes, including in particular people placed in the path of danger by service to their community' (Bloomfield 1998: para. 5.26).

Although a decade apart, complaints about both the Bloomfield Report (1998) and the CGP Report (Eames and Bradley 2009) are indicative of the depth of feeling about hierarchies of victimhood in Northern Ireland and the sense in which people are labelled as 'deserving/undeserving' victims. The CGP's 'recognition payment' element was withdrawn, but not before it had come to symbolise the entire work of the CGP. The Democratic Unionist Party (DUP) claimed that the CGP Report (Eames and Bradley 2009) had sought to create a moral equivalence between 'terrorists' and 'innocents', and argued that such things threatened the Peace Process (McEvoy 2013; Lawther 2014). The Ulster Unionist Party (UUP) dismissed much of the CGP Report (Eames and Bradley 2009) and questioned its recommendations around truth sharing, whilst the nationalist Social Democratic and Labour Party (SDLP) and cross-community Alliance Party indicated qualified support for its proposals. Sinn Féin initially criticised the CGP for failing to propose a fully independent and international Truth Commission, although as McEvoy (2013) argues, its stance towards other elements has softened in recent years.

The British response was been to reject the 'recognition payment' outright and to launch a Public Consultation about the CGP's recommendations. The resultant report (Northern Ireland Office 2010) indicated that the vast majority of participants rejected many of the recommendations made in the CGP Report (Eames and Bradley 2009) itself. The families victimised by state violence have seemingly dismissed the romantic notion that the recommendations made by the CGP Report (Eames and Bradley 2009) might hold the British State to account for its role in the conflict. The CGP's proposed 'Legacy Commission' might appear superficially attractive, but it lacks the necessary independence required in regards to state violence and overestimates the neutrality of organisations like the HET in their work with survivors.

At the time of writing, the CGP Report (Eames and Bradley 2009) has seemingly been shelved, which has done little to reduce the 'significant cynicism … about the level of political energy emanating from the British government on seeking an overarching process to deal with the past' (McEvoy 2013: 7). A lack of consensus can be seen in the failure of the Panel of the Parties of the Northern Ireland Executive (also known as the Haass–O'Sullivan talks) to reach an agreement on what it called 'contending with the past'. Its draft document (hereafter Haass–O'Sullivan 2013) noted the lack of agreement around the definition of a victim, yet called on parties involved in the conflict to acknowledge the harm they had caused and for the collection of narratives about people's experiences. It also proposed that a Historical Investigations Unit (HIU) be set up to take on the remaining caseload of the HET and the cases before the OPONI currently awaiting investigation. Cases already being investigated by the PSNI would fall

178 *Seeking accountability for state violence*

outside of the HIU's remit – a problematic recommendation given the PSNI's role in the HET and the questions levelled at that organisation regarding neutrality and independence (to say nothing of its RUC predecessor's role in state violence). The draft report also suggested that an Independent Commission for Information Recovery (ICIR) be established to try to gather information about the conflict outside of a criminal justice setting. Those who experienced violence in detention and their families might take some comfort from the pronouncement that ICIR could also collect information about particular themes, including 'detention without trial' and the 'mistreatment of detainees and prisoners' (Haass–O'Sullivan 2013: 32). Yet the Haass–O'Sullivan (2013) proposals have little to say about the problems of inquests and inquiries made clear earlier in this chapter, suggesting that the likelihood of fully bringing to light British state violence remains remote. The 'limited immunity' proposed in relation to the ICIR would render any statements made to the ICIR by state agents inadmissible in court, even if in theory 'it would not shield them from legal proceedings based on evidence coming to light from other sources or in relation to other crimes' (Mallinder 2014). As the chapter has illustrated, the list of previous failures to hold the state to account for its violence in Northern Ireland suggest that in practice this 'limited immunity' may be *less* limited for state agents than for others involved in the conflict.

The lack of consensus around the strengths and weaknesses of the CGP (2009) can therefore be seen again in the Haass–O'Sullivan (2013) negotiations which ended without agreement around the draft proposal at the end of 2013. The failure to reach agreement and to put in place an overarching response to the violence of the past is symptomatic of the degree to which truth itself is in conflict within Northern Ireland and the embedded nature of disputes around victimhood and legitimacy, which lie at the core of both the conflict and the legacy it has left behind. For survivors of state violence it is highly unlikely that the British Government will enable the creation of the fully independent, international Truth Commission called for by groups working with survivors of state violence, including Relatives for Justice (RFJ) and the Pat Finucane Centre (PFC). In the absence of any overarching truth-sharing mechanism and with the British Government keen to put an end to the use of public inquiries, former detainees and other survivors of state violence will continue to seek redress through different means. Civil proceedings have been issued by both Republican and Loyalist former internees against the British MoD, the RUC, the administrator of the estate of the late Brian Faulkner MP (as Prime Minister of the Old Stormont Government) and the British Secretary of State in relation to legality of internment (BBC 2011; Kearney 2012). At the time of writing, newly uncovered documents have also suggested that the British Government withheld evidence from the ECtHR during the *Ireland* v. *UK* (1978) case (RTÉ 2014). There is a possibility that these revelations might lead to legal action on behalf of the 'Hooded Men'. Others might continue to seek a form of justice for state violence through the mechanisms of the CCRC and OPONI. In the future, some may engage, albeit warily, with the body which might replace the now discredited HET

Seeking accountability for state violence   179

– if such a body is created. Of these organisations, the OPONI has been strongest in its critique of State agencies (O'Loan 2007), even if that critique has more often been vague or implicit, or referred to individualised acts of violence whilst ignoring the wider aspects of British involvement. As McGovern argues:

> Fragmentation and compartmentalization have characterized the approach to truth recovery processes in collusion cases in Northern Ireland.... Redrafting laws, redefining terms, restructuring the processes and procedures of investigation, inquiry and institutional interactions, retrenchment and a return of the 'old guard' have all been features of a drawn-out process of post-conflict official truth management extending back over a decade and a half.
>
> (McGovern 2013)

The CCRA has behaved similarly, offering only a limited opportunity for former detainees to overturn their convictions. State agents are still not held to account for interrogation practices or for the wider violence within the detention system. The years which have passed might make these limited options even more circumscribed, yet this piecemeal response might be the best all families can hope for at the current time in regards to legal accountability. In the medium term at least, it is likely that the 'fudging' of a detailed discussion about the legacy of state violence will continue. The British State is faced with the continued breaking through of alternative narratives about its involvement in the conflict, along with the occasional critical court ruling or investigative conclusions. The families of those killed by the State continue to pressure for greater disclosure. For Rolston (2002: 100), it is possible that the cumulative effect of these cases might eventually persuade the British State 'to concede a meaningful truth process in return for not having to face a string of court cases lasting for decades into the future', but at the time of writing, such an open and honest process seems a long way off. The British Government's response to 'making peace with the past' has been one of rejecting an overarching Truth Commission-style body, whilst at the same time carrying out consultation after consultation with local stakeholder groups (McEvoy 2013). Representatives of the British State have rightly commented on the absence of agreement on how to deal with the past in Northern Ireland, but they have failed to lead by example by 'making public' the details of their own central position in the conflict, their involvement in violence against former detainees and their role in the deaths of 1 in 10 of the conflict's victims.

Notes

1 Judith Ward was convicted in 1974 of delivering bombs which would later kill nine members of the British military and three civilians who had been travelling by coach along the M62 motorway in North West England. The conviction was overturned in 1993 after being found to be based on unreliable forensic evidence, the withholding of evidence, problems with Judith's mental health and the subsequent unreliability of her confessions.

180 *Seeking accountability for state violence*

2 James Ward was shot by a British soldier who had been 'tracing' Ward with his rifle during a Sanger patrol. The rifle's safety catch was off and the bullet in the breech was discharged, killing Ward.
3 Known as the 'Pitchfork Killings', the two Catholic men were stabbed to death by Scottish soldiers in what McKittrick *et al.* (2007: 286) describe as a 'reprisal attack for the death of a Ulster Defence Regiment soldier, John Bell, two days earlier.
4 In 1987, members of the IRA were ambushed and killed by an SAS unit as they were about to attack an unmanned RUC station in Loughgall. The SAS unit had long been aware of the IRA plans to carry out the attack, yet no attempt had been made to stop or arrest those involved. Eight members of the IRA were killed, along with one civilian, Anthony Hughes. Two other civilians were also injured. The SAS operation had seemingly been planned in minute detail, to the extent that SAS members were positioned at particular places in and around the barracks in order to add weight to legal arguments that they had acted in self-defence (Urban 1992). A prematurely leaked report of the Historical Enquiries Team (HET) in December 2011 may have stated that the IRA had fired first, but it has done little to change the perception that events in Loughgall were part of a shoot-to-kill approach against suspected IRA members. The discrediting of the HET in 2013, particularly in regards to their approach to cases involving state violence, might in theory mean that this case should be revisited, but at the time of writing it appears unlikely. In the meantime, the families of the dead are to launch a civil action against the Ministry of Defence.

References

Aiken, N.T. (2010) 'Learning to Live Together: Transitional Justice and Intergroup Reconciliation in Northern Ireland', *International Journal of Transitional Justice*, 4(2), 166–188.

BBC (2010) *Bloody Sunday Report Published*. 15 June. Available at: www.bbc.co.uk/news/10320609 (accessed 15 June 2010).

BBC (2011) *Republicans to Sue Government Over NI Internment*. 9 August. Available at: www.bbc.co.uk/news/uk-northern-ireland-14450327 (accessed 9 November 2011).

BBC (2014) 'Robert Hamill Murder:Three Accused Will Not Face Trial'. Accessed at: www.bbc.co.uk/news/uk-northern-ireland-29045759.

Belfast Telegraph (2014) 'Unsolved Troubles Murder Reports to be Withheld until Future of Historical Enquiries Team Sorted.' 15 January. Available at: www.belfasttelegraph.co.uk/news/local-national/northern-ireland/unsolved-troubles-murder-reports-to-be-withheld-until-future-of-historical-enquiries-team-sorted-29919175.html. (accessed 15 January 2014).

Bell, C. (2002) 'Dealing with the Past in Northern Ireland', *Fordham International Law Journal*, 26(4), 1095–1147.

Bell, C. and Keenan, J. (2005) 'Lost on the Way Home: *The Right to Life in Northern Ireland' Journal of Law and Society*, 32(1), 68–89.

Bell, C., Campbell, C. and Ní Aoláin, F. (2007) 'Transitional Justice: (Re)Conceptualising the Field', *International Journal of Law in Context*, 3(02), 81–88.

Bennett Inquiry (1979) *Report of the Committee of Inquiry into Police Interrogation Procedures in Northern Ireland*, [Cmnd 7497]. London: HMSO.

Bishop, P. and Mallie, E. (1988) *The Provisional IRA*. London: Corgi.

Bloomfield, K. (1998) 'We Will Remember Them: Report of the Northern Ireland Victims Commissioner'. Belfast: The Stationery Office Northern Ireland.

Boyle, K., Hadden, T. and Hillyard, P. (1975) *Law and The State: The Case of Northern Ireland.* London: Martin Robertson.

Seeking accountability for state violence 181

Boyle, K., Hadden, T. and Hillyard, P. (1980) *Ten Years on in Northern Ireland: The Legal Control of Political Violence*. London: Cobden Trust.

CAIN (2012) *List of People Killed by Plastic Bullets.* Available at: http://cain.ulst.ac.uk/issues/violence/rubberplasticbullet.htm (accessed 14 October 2012).

Campbell, C. (2005) '"Wars on Terror" and Vicarious Hegemons: The UK, International Law, and the Northern Ireland Conflict', *International and Comparative Law Quarterly*, 54(02), 321–356.

Campbell, C. and Connolly, I. (2006) 'Making War on Terror? Global Lessons from Northern Ireland', *The Modern Law Review*, 69(6), 935–957.

Cobain, I. (2010) 'Inside Castlereagh: "We Got Confessions By Torture"'. *Guardian*. 11 October. Available at: www.guardian.co.uk/uk/2010/oct/11/inside-castlereagh-confessions-torture (accessed 1 December 2013).

Cobain, I. (2012a) *Cruel Britannia*. London: Portobello Books Ltd.

Cobain, I. (2012b) 'Northern Ireland Police Ombudsman Quashes Loughinisland Massacre Report'. *Guardian*. 12 December. Available at: www.theguardian.com/uk/2012/dec/20/northern-ireland-police-loughinisland-massacre-inquiry (accessed 12 December 2012).

Committee on the Administration of Justice (2011) *Human Rights and Dealing With Historic Cases: A Review of the Office of the Police Ombudsman for Northern Ireland*. Belfast: CAJ.

Connolly, C.K. (2007) 'Seeking the Final Court of Justice: The European Court of Human Rights and Accountability for State Violence in Northern Ireland', *San Diego International Law Journal*, 9(1), 81–134.

Cory, P. (2004a) *Cory Collusion Inquiry Report: Patrick Finucane*. London: HMSO. Available at: www.nio.gov.uk/ cory_collusion_inquiry_report_(with_appendices)_pat_finucane.pdf (accessed 12 December 2012).

Cory, P. (2004b) *Cory Collusion Inquiry Report: Rosemary Nelson*. London: HMSO. Available at: www.nio.gov.uk/ cory_collusion_inquiry_report_(without_appendices)_rosemary_nelson.pdf (accessed 12 December 2012).

Cory, P. (2004c) *Cory Collusion Inquiry Report: Robert Hamill*. London: HMSO. Available at: www.nio.gov.uk/ cory_collusion_inquiry_report_(without_appendices)_robert_hamill.pdf (accessed 12 December 2012).

Cory, P. (2004d) *Cory Collusion Inquiry Report: Billy Wright*. London: HMSO Available at: www.nio.gov.uk/cory_collusion_inquiry_report_(without_appendices)_billy_wright.pdf (accessed 12 December 2012).

Council of Europe (1950) European Convention for the Protection of Human Rights and Fundamental Freedoms, as amended by Protocols Nos 11 and 14, 4 November.

Criminal Justice Inspection Northern Ireland (2011) *An Inspection Into The Independence Of The Office Of The Police Ombudsman For Northern Ireland*, Belfast: CJINI.

Criminal Law [Northern Ireland] Act 1967. London: HMSO.

De Silva, D. (2012) *The Report of the Pat Finucane Review*, London: HMSO. Available at: www.gov.uk/government/publications/the-report-of-the-patrick-finucane-review (accessed 5 January 2013).

Dickson, B. (2010) *The European Convention on Human Rights and the Conflict in Northern Ireland*. Oxford: Oxford University Press.

Duffy, A. (2010) 'A Truth Commission for Northern Ireland?' *International Journal of Transitional Justice*, 4(1), 26–46.

Eames, R. and Bradley, D. (2009) *Report of the Consultative Group on the Past*. (HC171) London: HMSO. Available at: www.cgpni.org/fs/doc/Consultative%20Group%20on%20the%20Past%20Full%20Report.pdf (accessed 7 January 2013).

182   *Seeking accountability for state violence*

Finucane v. *United Kingdom* [2003] 37 EHRR 29.

Gawn, R. (2007) 'Truth Cohabitation: A Truth Commission for Northern Ireland?', *Irish Political Studies*, 22(3), 339–361.

Haass, R. and O'Sullivan, M. (2013) *Proposed Agreement 31st December 2013: An Agreement Among The Parties of the Northern Ireland Executive on Parades, Select Commemorations and Related Protests, Flags and Emblems, and Contending with the Past.* [Panel of the Parties of the Northern Ireland Executive]. Available at www.northernireland.gov.uk/haass.pdf.

Healing Through Remembering (2002) *Report of the Healing Through Remembering Project.* Belfast: Healing Through Remembering.

Hegarty, A. (2002) 'Government of Memory: Public Inquiries and the Limits of Justice in Northern Ireland', *Fordham International Law Journal*, 26(4), 1148–1192.

Her Majesty's Inspectorate of Constabulary (2013) *Inspection of the Police Service of Northern Ireland Historical Enquiries Team.* London: HMIC. Available at: www.hmic.gov.uk/media/inspection-of-the-police-service-of-northern-ireland-historical-enquiries-team-20130703.pdf p. 83 (accessed 12 December 2013).

Jamieson, R. and Grounds, A. (2002) *No Sense of An Ending: The Effects of Long Term Imprisonment amongst Republican Prisoners and Their Families.* Monaghan: SEESYU Press.

Jamieson, R., Shirlow, P. and Grounds, A. (2010) *Ageing and Social Exclusion Among Former Politically Motivated Prisoners in Northern Ireland and the Border Region of Ireland.* Belfast: The Community Foundation of Northern Ireland.

Jordan et al. v. *United Kingdom* [2003] 37 EHRR 2.

Jowitt, E., Richardson, K. and Evans, J. (2010) *Robert Hamill Inquiry Interim Report.* Available at: www.roberthamillinquiry.org/content/interim/ (accessed 5 January 2013).

Joyce, P. (2013) *Criminal Justice* (2nd edn). London: Routledge.

Kearney, V. (2012) *Protestant Man Jailed During Internment Suing Government.* 7 June. Available at www.bbc.co.uk/news/uk-northern-ireland-18355090 (accessed 7 June 2014).

Kelly and Others v. *United Kingdom* [2001] Application no. 30054/96 ECHR.

Lawther, C. (2014) *Truth, Denial and Transition: Northern Ireland and the Contested Past.* London: Routledge.

Leckey, J. (2005) *Inquests and Human Rights in Northern Ireland.* Belfast: Northern Ireland Human Rights Commission. Available at www.nihrc.org/documents/research-and-investigations/death-investigations-right-to-life/inquests-and-human-rights-in-northern-ireland-2005.pdf (accessed 14 June 2012).

Lundy, P. (2009a) 'Can the Past Be Policed: Lessons from the Historical Enquiries Team Northern Ireland', *Journal of Law and Social Challenges*, 11, 109–156.

Lundy, P. (2009b) 'Exploring Home-grown Transitional Justice and its Dilemmas: A Case study of the Historical Enquiries Team, Northern Ireland', *International Journal of Transitional Justice*, 3(3), 321–340.

Lundy, P. (2011) 'Paradoxes and Challenges of Transitional Justice at the "Local" Level: Historical Enquiries in Northern Ireland', *Contemporary Social Science*, 6(1), 89–105.

Lundy, P. and McGovern, M. (2006) 'The Ethics of Silence: Action Research, Community "Truth-telling" and Post-conflict Transition in the North of Ireland', *Action Research*, 4(1), 49–64.

Lundy, P. and McGovern, M. (2008) 'Truth, Justice and Dealing with the Legacy of the Past in Northern Ireland, 1998-2008', *Ethnopolitics*, 7(1), 177–193.

MacLean, L. (2010) *Report of The Billy Wright Inquiry*, London: HMSO. Available at:

http://cain.ulst.ac.uk/issues/collusion/docs/wright_140910.pdf (accessed 12 December 2012).

Mallinder, L. (2014) 'Dealing with Northern Ireland's Past: A Guide to the Haass - O'Sullivan Talks', *Open Democracy*. 8 May. Available at www.opendemocracy.net/5050/louise-mallinder/dealing-with-northern-ireland%E2%80%99s-past-guide-to-haasso%E2%80%99sullivan-talks.

McCann and Others v. *The United Kingdom* [1995] 21 ECHR 97 GC.

McEvoy, K. (2000) 'Law, Struggle, and Political Transformation in Northern Ireland', *Journal of Law and Society*, 27(4), 542–571.

McEvoy, K. (2001) *Paramilitary Imprisonment in Northern Ireland: Resistance, Management and Release*. Oxford University Press: Oxford.

McEvoy, K. (2007) 'Beyond Legalism: Towards a Thicker Understanding of Transitional Justice', *Journal of Law and Society*, 34(4), 411–440.

McEvoy, K. (2013) *Dealing with the Past in Northern Ireland: An Overview of Legal and Political Approaches*. Belfast: Healing Through Remembering.

McEvoy, K. and McConnachie, K. (2013) 'Victims and Transitional Justice: Voice, Agency and Blame', *Social and Legal Studies*, 22(4), 489–513.

McEvoy, K., Shirlow, P. and McElrath, K. (2004) 'Resistance, Transition and Exclusion: Politically Motivated Prisoners and Conflict Transformation in Northern Ireland', *Journal of Terrorism and Political Violence*, 16(3), 246–270.

McGovern, M. (2013) 'Inquiring Into Collusion? Collusion, the State and the Management of Truth Recovery in Northern Ireland', *State Crime Journal*, 2(1), 4–29.

McGrattan, C. (2009) ' "Order Out of Chaos": The Politics of Transitional Justice', *Politics*, 29(3), 164–172.

McKerr v. *the United Kingdom* [2001] Application no. 28883/95 ECHR.

McKittrick, D., Kelters, D., Feeney, B., Thornton, C. and McVea, D. (2007) *Lost Lives: The Stories of the Men, Women and Children Who Died as a Result of the Northern Ireland Troubles*. London: Mainstream Publishing.

McShane v. *United Kingdom* [2002] 35 EHRR 23.

Morland, M. (2011) *The Rosemary Nelson Inquiry Report*. London: HMSO. Available at: www.gov.uk/government/uploads/system/uploads/attachment_data/file/247461/0947.pdf (accessed 12 December 2012).

Ní Aoláin, F. (2000) *The Politics of Force: Conflict Management and State Violence in Northern Ireland*. Belfast: Blackstaff.

Northern Ireland Office (2010) *Dealing With the Past in Northern Ireland: The Recommendations of the Consultative Group on the Past Summary of Responses to Consultation*. Belfast: NIO. Available at http://cain.ulst.ac.uk/issues/politics/docs/nio/nio190710cgp.pdf (accessed 14 January 2014).

Nunca Más (1984) *Report of CONADEP: National Commission on the Disappearance of Persons*. Available at: www.nuncamas.org/index2.htm (accessed 29 March 2010).

Pantazis, C. and Pemberton, S. (2009) 'From the "Old" to the "New" Suspect Community: Examining the Impacts of Recent UK Counter-terrorist Legislation', *British Journal of Criminology*, 49(5), 646–666.

Office of the Police Ombudsman for Northern Ireland (2011) *Relating to the Complaint by the Victims and Survivors of The Murders at The Heights Bar, Loughinisland on 18 June 1994*. Belfast: PONI.

O'Loan, N. (2007) *Statement by the Police Ombudsman for Northern Ireland on Her Investigation into the Circumstances Surrounding the Death of Raymond McCord Junior and Related Matters*. Belfast: OPONI.

184 *Seeking accountability for state violence*

Pringle, P. and Jacobson, P. (2002) *Those Are Real Bullets: Bloody Sunday, Derry, 1972*. London: Fourth Estate.

Punch, M. (2012) *State Violence, Collusion and the Troubles*. London: Pluto.

Quirk, H. (2013) 'Don't Mention the War: The Court of Appeal, the Criminal Cases Review Commission and Dealing with the Past in Northern Ireland', *The Modern Law Review*, 76(6), 949–980.

R v. *Livingstone* [2013] NICA 33.

R v. *McCartney and MacDermott* [2007] NICA 10.

R v. *Mulholland* [2006] NICA 32.

Re McCaughey [2011] UKSC 20.

Reilly, R. (2014) 'Torture Retold: How the Hooded Men Case Has Come Back Under the Spotlight'. *The Irish Times*. 12 June. Available at: www.irishtimes.com/news/crime-and-law/torture-retold-how-the-hooded-men-case-has-come-back-under-the-spotlight-1. 1829676 (accessed 13 June 2014).

Relatives for Justice (n.d.) '"Victims" Groups Unite to Call for Truth Commission'. [Online] Available at: http://relativesforjustice.com/victims-groups-unite-to-call-for-truth-commission/ (accessed 14 January 2014)

Requa, M. (2014) 'Considering Just-World Thinking in Counter-Terrorism Cases: Miscarriages of Justice in Northern Ireland', *Harvard Human Rights Journal*, 27, 71–134.

Robinson, P. (1981) *Self Inflicted: An Exposure of the H-Blocks Issue*. Belfast: Democratic Unionist Party.

Rolston, B. (2002) 'Assembling the Jigsaw: Truth, Justice and Transition in the North of Ireland', *Race and Class*, 44(1), 87–106.

Rolston, B. (2005) '"An Effective Mask for Terror": Democracy, Death Squads and Northern Ireland', *Crime, Law and Social Change*, 44(2), 181–203.

Rolston, B. (2011) *Review of Literature on Republican and Loyalist Ex-Prisoners*. Jordanstown: University of Ulster. Available at: www.ofmdfmni.gov.uk/final_literature_review.pdf (accessed 12 April 2013).

Rolston, B. (2014) *Relatives' Views of the Historical Enquiries Team*. Belfast: Relatives for Justice. Available at: http://relativesforjustice.com/wp-content/uploads/2014/01/HET-research-Relatives-Views-by-Prof-Bill-Rolston.pdf (accessed 14 June 2014).

Rolston, B. and Scraton, P. (2005) 'In the Full Glare of English Politics: Ireland, Inquiries and the British State', *British Journal of Criminology*, 45(4), 547–564.

RTÉ Investigations Unit (2014) 'The Torture Files'. Broadcast 4 June 2014. Available at: www.rte.ie/news/player/prime-time/2014/0604/ (accessed 4 June 2014).

Saville Report (2010) *Report of the Bloody Sunday Inquiry*. London: HMSO.

Shanaghan v. *the United Kingdom* [2001] Application no. 37715/97 ECHR.

Shirlow, P., Graham, B., McEvoy, K., Ó hAdhmaill, F. and Purvis, D. (2005) *Politically Motivated Former Prisoner Groups: Community Activism and Conflict Transformation*. Belfast: Northern Ireland Community Relations Council.

Simpson, K. (2007) 'Voices Silenced, Voices Rediscovered: Victims of Violence and the Reclamation of Language in Transitional Societies', *International Journal of Law in Context*, 3(02), 89–103.

Smyth, M. (2003) 'Truth, Partial Truth, and Irreconcilable Truths: Reflections on the Prospects for Truth Recovery in Northern Ireland', *Smith College Studies in Social Work*, 73(2), 205–225.

Steiner, H.J., Alston, P. and Goodman, R. (2000) *Human Rights in Context*. Oxford: Clarendon Press.

Stevens, J. (2003) *Stevens Inquiry: Overview and Recommendations*. Available online at http://cain.ulst.ac.uk/issues/collusion/stevens3/stevens3summary.htm (accessed 14 January 2014).

Tomlinson, M. (1998) 'Walking Backwards into the Sunset: British Policy and the Insecurity of Northern Ireland', in Miller, D. (eds) *Rethinking Northern Ireland: Culture, Ideology and Colonialism*. Harlow: Longman.

Urban, M. (1992) *Big Boys Rules*. London: Faber.

Walker, C. (2002) 'Miscarriages of Justice' in McConville, M. and Wilson, G. (eds) *The Handbook of the Criminal Justice Process*. Oxford: Oxford University Press.

Widgery Report (1972) *Report of the Tribunal Appointed to Inquire into the Events on Sunday, 30th January 1972, which Led to Loss of Life in Connection with the Procession in Londonderry on that Day*. London: HMSO.

9 The problems and possibilities of talking about violence

By exploring both original narratives and the motivation, significance and consequences of 'truth sharing', this book has found that former detainees in Northern Ireland utilised a range of semantic devices to describe their experiences of state violence during internment, interrogation and formal imprisonment. The terms 'torture' and 'brutality' are often used interchangeably by former detainees, particularly in relation to allegations relating to internment in the early 1970s. They do so in ways which reject Compton's (1971) claim that brutality requires some element of a sadistic intent on behalf of the perpetrator. Equally significant are findings which show that experiences from the interrogation centres at Castlereagh, Gough and Palace Barracks are usually, but not exclusively, described by former detainees as torture. This pattern is reversed in narratives from the H-Blocks in which the language of brutality is dominant. In each of these three phases of state violence, the restrictive definitions of torture and brutality employed by the official discourse of public inquiries, legal judgments and the resulting case law are largely irrelevant to former detainees and the legacy which they have attached to their narrative, and to the personal and subjective nature of 'truth sharing'.

The book has also shown that a 'need' for healing was not a primary motivation behind former detainees 'making public' their experiences of state violence. For some detainees, there were indeed consequences desired from their narratives, but these were linked more to the educative potential of their accounts, rather than to a much sought after catharsis. Furthermore, only a minority of former detainees felt strongly that their experience of narrating state violence had been a positive experience. Most were nonchalant. At the other extreme, rather than helping them to heal from their experience, two former detainees recalled how 'going public' had been difficult and traumatic and that this discomfort had remained to the present day. The wider impact of the time which has passed since detainees first 'went public' with their accounts of state violence is difficult to measure. It is also possible that the ongoing political shifts within Republican discourses and the changing political landscape of Northern Ireland influenced how former detainees view both their experience of state violence and also its narration. What is clear throughout these research findings, however, is that an understanding of the diverse motivations for 'making public' private experiences of violence and the recognition that the lived reality of notions such as 'revealing as healing' are best analysed in depth alongside those who have previously made public their experiences (Stanley 2002, 2005, 2009).

Through an analysis of the significance of gender in relation to 'truth sharing', this book explored how former detainees utilised a range of techniques to downplay the tension between the 'Rough Tough Provo' imagery and the often vivid and vulnerable recollections which formed their narratives of state violence. Some of those interviewed portrayed the violence they had experienced as being so extreme that it fell *outside* of *any* masculine ability to endure. In this way, masculinity could be preserved and their narration of suffering would not challenge the imagery of the 'Rough Tough Provo', precisely because their experience of state violence had been so extreme. Jim's account evidences Seidler's (1994, 2007) theoretical claim that men can sometimes discuss suffering violence and still retain the imagery of the invulnerable male, even when their narratives are about pain and fear. The imagery could also be preserved through the downplaying of past experiences of victimhood and this was frequently observed throughout the interview process with Harry and Michael in particular.

For other former detainees, their victimhood was transformed, not through the excessive nature of the violence they experienced, nor through the dismissal of the violence they once detailed, but through their use of 'dark' humour. This process of reconceptualising experiences of violence so that masculinity could be retained was further made possible through the collective nature of state violence, a finding which supports Feldman's (1991) claims about the importance of shared experiences in the detention system of Northern Ireland. Narratives of former detainees suggest that this sharing became a way of 'negotiating' gender in an otherwise oppressive environment. Yet at times, the focus on the collective experience also meant that individual men's stories became lost and a number of former detainees hinted that any attempt to bring attention to their *individual* suffering was met with hostility from other members of the Republican movement. The romanticised imagery of collective suffering and of equal capacity to resist that suffering, meant that the personal, individual dimension of pain was largely excluded from the discourse around imprisonment.

The relationship between narratives of state violence, victimhood and masculinity is therefore a complex one and this should be borne in mind within the discourse of transitional justice (Hamber 2007). In relation to state violence in the H-Blocks, masculinity was closely tied into the prison struggle and this resulted in the transformation of narratives of pain into communal narratives of resistance, both symbolic and actual. The public suffering of prisoners became a source of strength rather than passive victimhood, and as such, the production of narratives of state violence became a further way in which former detainees could continue the struggle. The 'invulnerable male' concept of masculinity was popular amongst former detainees and significant in their 'making public' their accounts of pain, but only to the extent that some were now keen to locate their narratives firmly within the imagery of the 'Rough Tough Provo'.

188 *Problems of talking about violence*

In addition to the socio-cultural significance of masculinity, a socio-political understanding of narratives as propaganda also shaped elements of former detainees' narratives of state violence. This book analysed former detainees' understanding of the propaganda value of their narratives and deconstructed the significance attached to their accounts by the Republican movement. By exploring the meaning of propaganda alongside those who have made public their contested narratives, the book builds on the theoretical work done by Pratkanis and Aronson (1991), Jackall (1995), and Jowett and O'Donnell (1999). The persuasive elements of the definitions employed by these authors were reflected in former detainees about their narratives, albeit to different degrees. Some of those interviewed suggested that the motivation behind their narrative of state violence was to persuade an audience of the legitimacy of both the ideology and means of violent Republicanism. Others sought more clearly defined 'military' actions as a consequence of their 'truth sharing'. This finding parallels with the definition of agitative propaganda employed by Jowett and O'Donnell (1999) in framing narratives not simply as persuasion but as actively encouraging some form of action.

Many of those who did make public their experiences had given little if any thought to the possible audiences and to the possible political consequences of 'making public' their experiences of state violence. Former detainees attached different levels of significance to their narratives as propaganda for the Republican movement. Though some recognised that their stories could be used to recruit volunteers to armed Republicanism, few stated this was their explicit intention and some, such as Laurence and Michael, cautioned against exaggerating the power of narratives in this regard. Such findings suggest that former detainees possess diverse reasons for 'making public' their experiences and that each viewed the significance of their narrative as propaganda through sometimes conflicting lenses. Michael stated that rather than bringing people into the Republican movement and persuading them to act against the state, his stories of state violence might actually lead people to turn away from armed insurrection. The reputation for state violence in relation to e.g. Castlereagh Interrogation Centre may have had a deterrent effect on potential IRA recruits, which further complicates the perception of Republican(s') narratives as agitative propaganda.

Even when the persuasive power of their narratives was recognised by those who 'made public' their stories of state violence, former detainees were reluctant to label this as propaganda, possibly due to the stigma of untruth and exaggeration which surrounds such terms. Chapter 6's findings suggest a need for further research into the impact of labels like propaganda upon those who make their private memories of pain part of a contested public history, particularly when powerful official discourses seek to deny or downplay allegations of state violence.

The impact of these official denials upon former detainees who challenged the depiction of the benign British State was explored in depth in Chapter 7. The chapter provides clear and detailed examples of Cohen's (2001) literal, interpretive

Problems of talking about violence 189

and implicatory denials found within the official discourse of the Northern Ireland conflict. Many of the former detainees interviewed felt that the state denials were inevitable and suggested that they had expected nothing less from the British State. They argued that they had *expected* to be disbelieved, not only by members of state agencies, but also by what was falsely perceived as a homogeneous Unionist community. Former detainees were also dismissive of discourses which portrayed their visible physical injuries as being self-inflicted, with Interviewee 'F' labelling such claims 'daft'.

Yet not all former detainees were so unconcerned by the denials proclaimed and maintained through the official discourse about their experiences. Jim and Tommy remained deeply frustrated that their testimonies had been subjected to a process of interpretive denial. This meant that their experiences were framed as something 'other' than state violence, illustrating what Smyth (2007: 22) labels as the 'different conceptualisation of truth' common throughout the Northern Ireland conflict. Within the official discourse, Jim and Tommy were cast as deserving of ill-treatment akin to punishment for their transgressions in being a 'suspected terrorist'. These findings about detainees' experiences of denial build on work by Kelman (1995: 31) who argues that victims of state violence are often portrayed as 'menacing, destructive elements' within official discourse. They are denied victimhood and thus labelled as somehow deserving of violence, which itself becomes reconstituted as justified punishment. Part of this process also involves the valorisation of state forces, noted by Yúdice (1991) and observed throughout this book in relation to the Bennett Inquiry (1979).

There was a feeling of resignation amongst detainees that the British State could operationalise implicatory denials around their experiences of state violence. Yet, equally significant for some detainees was the wider conflict in which their experiences had taken place. Tommy, in particular, was stoical about his experiences and about the violence that the IRA had inflicted on members of state forces. Furthermore, Laurence's compassion for the wife of police Doctor Robert Irwin, whose experiences of rape were used to condemn her husband's support for detainees' allegations of state violence, sharply contrasts with the dehumanised and demonised imagery of IRA members portrayed in publications such as Robinson (1981). The chapter illustrates how former detainees experienced the full range of state denials contained within the official discourse and shows that they responded to these denials with a diverse mix of indifference, frustration, stoicism and compassion.

Non-state actors and truth sharing

Tommy's recognition of IRA violence carried out against the agents of the British State offers another avenue through which a greater understanding of 'truth sharing' can be sought. The Republican post-'Peace Process' narrative of the twenty-first century has partially moved towards the 'balanced view' that Tommy desires and has offered some recognition of Republican violence during

190 *Problems of talking about violence*

the conflict, as evidenced by the text of the IRA's (P. O'Neill in BBC 2002a) press release:

> While it was not our intention to injure or kill non-combatants, the reality is that on a ... number of occasions that was the consequence of our actions. It is therefore appropriate ... that we address all of the deaths and injuries of non-combatants caused by us. We offer our sincere apologies and condolences to their families. There have been fatalities among combatants on all sides. We also acknowledge the grief and pain of their relatives. The future will not be found in denying collective failures and mistakes or closing minds and hearts to the plight of those who have been hurt. That includes all of the victims of the conflict, combatants and non-combatants. It will not be achieved by creating a hierarchy of victims in which some are deemed more or less worthy than others. The process of conflict resolution requires the equal acknowledgement of the grief and loss of others ... we are endeavouring to fulfil this responsibility to those we have hurt.... This includes the acceptance of past mistakes and of the hurt and pain we have caused to others.
>
> (P. O'Neill cited in BBC 2002a)

The sincerity of the statement has been disputed by the families of some of the IRA's victims (BBC 2002b) and critiqued as opportunistic by Unionist politicians, such as David Trimble (*The Newsletter* 17 July 2002). Others have recognised the statement as meaningful, including Reverend Joe Parker, whose fourteen-year-old son Stephen was killed by IRA bombs in Belfast on 'Bloody Friday', 21 July 1972 (BBC 2002c). Although the statement clearly sets out an apology for the harm caused to non-combatants such as Stephen, its approach to combatants in Northern Ireland[1] is more ambiguous. It appears to recognise their suffering and that of their families, but does not explicitly apologise for it. Instead, the statement calls for the broadening out of the notion of victimhood, so that it includes both non-combatants and combatants (including IRA members).

Also missing from this Republican narrative is an apology for violence committed against its own members who were 'turned' by British agencies, or for the suffering of suspected informers who were subsequently tried in kangaroo courts and often killed by members of the IRA's 'Internal Security'. Although the violence meted out against suspected informers is complicated somewhat by allegations that some of those responsible for the killings were *also* British State agents, the cases of 'The Disappeared'[2] clearly illustrate the violence of the IRA against its own movement and against the community from which many of those involved were drawn. That said, there have been attempts made to provide families with the details of their loved ones and what happened to them. There is an acknowledgement that the IRA was involved in a number of deaths of 'The Disappeared', and to 'regret' regarding the suffering caused to families, most famously in relation to the Jean McConville case (O'Neill 2006). Just as the British State denies victimhood to paramilitary prisoners, the Republican movement has long denied victimhood to

Problems of talking about violence   191

those it labelled as offenders within its own regime. There is thus a need for greater research into these experiences of violence, in order to understand how the Republican movement today frames not just its own victimhood at the hands of the British State, but the victimhood of its own community under a form of Republican violence that remains somewhat taboo (Lundy and McGovern 2006). There is an uncomfortable parallel here, as the IRA's kangaroo trials, forced disappearances and executions share some commonalities with many elements of state violence. Researching and recognising the violence of IRA members during the conflict need not negate former detainees' stories and their own victimhood, but it instead represents the desire hinted at by Tommy to explore victimhood in all of its forms.

As Lundy and McGovern (2008) and Lawther (2011, 2013) have shown, the exploration of victimhood in all its forms would also ask difficult questions of Loyalist paramilitary groups, who were responsible for approximately 1,026 deaths during the conflict (Sutton, 'Index of Deaths' n.d.). The Loyalist Combined Military Command (LCMC) issued a ceasefire[3] statement on 13 October 1994 stating that 'in all sincerity, we offer to the loved ones of all innocent victims over the past twenty years, abject and true remorse. No words of ours will compensate for the intolerable suffering they have undergone during the conflict'. At the time, the LCMC represented the Ulster Defence Association (UDA), Ulster Volunteer Force (UVF) and its related Red Hand Commando (RCH). Rather than show remorse for all deaths caused by members of these groups during the conflict, the statement links it only to 'innocent victims'.

Despite this selective representation of victimhood, the statement is still an acknowledgement of Loyalist violence. Unionists have largely not shared in acknowledging their own role in the conflict. Within the context of Northern Ireland, Unionist politicians – including central members of the DUP – have been linked to paramilitary groups. Ian Paisley was heavily involved in the setting up of the 'Ulster Resistance' and its predecessor the 'Third Force'. These were armed paramilitary groups set up to prevent co-operation between the Governments of the UK and Ireland (*Time* 1981). The current First Minister of the Northern Ireland Assembly, Peter Robinson, was also involved. Though their official existence was short lived, the military trappings of these organisations and the inflammatory speeches of Ian Paisley in particular add weight to the arguments made by many Loyalist paramilitaries that the Unionist middle class played a role in bringing many Protestants into violence whilst publicly denying any responsibility. The representation of blamelessness is central to Unionist discourse on the conflict and this is also linked to a reluctance to apportion any blame on to the predominantly Protestant RUC for its actions during the conflict (Lawther 2011, 2014). The mechanisms of denial explored in Chapter 7 of this book are therefore frequently employed in relation to Unionist attitudes towards state violence.

The complex relationship between Loyalists, Unionists and the British State has been explored in a number of texts (e.g. Bruce 1992, 1994; McAuley 2004). Both Loyalist and Unionist groups have displayed significant hostility to the idea of an overarching truth-sharing mechanism, choosing instead to give qualified

192 *Problems of talking about violence*

support to small, intra-community projects and archives. As Lundy and McGovern (2008) have shown Loyalist and Unionist approaches to 'making peace with the past' are therefore more complex than a total lack of faith in the possibility of narrating experiences. There are benefits to such approaches in that they allow communities to retain ownership of their stories (see Chapter 1 for examples of this). For Loyalists in particular, these local community projects may be 'the means by which people from their own areas might give voice to their experiences and in so doing, combat social and historical marginalisation' (Lundy and McGovern 2008: 61). However, when these narratives remain in such silos of remembering, they lack the ability to tell the wider story of the conflict and to 'bring in' the experiences of others. Leading Unionist politicians (the DUP in particular) seemingly do 'not welcome the stories of the "other" being told in anything other than local-level initiatives, nor will they be willing to listen to them' (Lawther 2011: 366).

Both Lundy and McGovern (2008) and Lawther (2011, 2014) link Loyalist and Unionist hostility to a number of underlying factors which have affected the perception of truth sharing in these communities. Telling the story of the conflict and hearing of the lived reality of others' suffering (such as that of the Republican detainees in this book) would begin to challenge the Unionist myth of blamelessness. There is also a fear that any criticism of the British State's role in the conflict calls into question their loyalty (Lundy and McGovern 2008) and brings them uncomfortably close to the criticisms made by Republicans regarding the British State's role in the conflict. This wariness was also common during the conflict itself, as Loyalist prisoners attempted to find a balance between protesting against prison conditions and criminalisation, whilst at the same time rejecting (in public at least) any similarity with the prison struggle of Republicans (Crawford 1999). According to primary research by Lundy and McGovern (2008) and Lawther (2011, 2014) both Loyalists and Unionists also share the belief that 'truth sharing' about victimhood is somehow tied up with the nature of Irish Catholicism, suggesting that sectarian stereotypes play a role in attitudes towards discussing the past. The perception that nationalist/Republican areas have greater social capital and that there is greater interest in the experiences of Republicans – who are seen as better able to get their stories out – remains a barrier for Loyalist/Unionist support for truth sharing about their own role in the conflict (Lundy and McGovern 2008).

Perhaps most importantly, Loyalists and Unionists in particular fear that Republican and nationalist groups will be able to control the narrative legacy of the conflict. As Lawther (2014) illustrates, there is a perception that 'truth sharing' is a Republican project with the sole of aim of casting Republican violence as somehow legitimate. They distrust Republicans' commitment to full disclosure and refer to Martin McGuinness's refusal to answer all questions posed to him during the Saville Inquiry (2010). His statements indicating that he *would* disclose everything about his involvement in the IRA if and when an international and independent Truth Commission was established have been disregarded by Loyalists and Unionists (McEvoy 2013).

Problems of talking about violence   193

Unionists and Loyalists also appear to doubt the value of truth sharing in contributing to 'the reconstitution of the social and political environment and [the] forging [of] "shared narratives" of the past to make future agreement possible' (Lundy and McGovern 2008: 44). Whether this is a genuinely held belief or the result of discomfort around what truth-sharing mechanisms might reveal is unclear and difficult to measure. For Loyalist paramilitaries and/or detainees, the forging of a 'shared narrative' would also involve the breaking down of particular obstacles, including their demonisation and scapegoating by the wider Unionist community and their complicated relationship of accommodation and criminalisation by the British State. The overwhelming consensus amongst Loyalist paramilitaries is that their narratives would 'not be seen as legitimate or truthful by unionists and would be manipulated to further their stigmatisation and criminalisation' (Lawther 2011: 369). There is a belief that only particular forms of victimhood will be recognised and that even within Unionist/Loyalist communities, truth-sharing mechanisms will perpetuate a divide 'between "respectable" (meaning security forces) and "non-respectable" (paramilitary) victims', leading to the further isolation of former paramilitaries (Lundy and McGovern 2008: 57).

As this book has shown, the exploration of all forms of victimhood would not be complete without the examination of the role of all paramilitary groups alongside the role of the British State, whose violence forms the focus of this book. Whilst illustrating the violence of the British State ties into Republican arguments about its illegitimacy, for Loyalist and Unionists such discussions are more difficult, as they 'would contradict their historical reticence ... to criticise the state and its institutions' (Lawther 2011: 375). Despite the promise that all are equal before the law, the low number of prosecutions and convictions illustrate that the (overwhelmingly Catholic/nationalist) families of those killed by state forces did not have the same opportunities as other victims for formal 'justice' during the conflict. Some of the strongest calls for an official truth-sharing mechanism have emerged from those families who were most affected by state violence, as the criminal justice system has been less willing or able to bring to account state agents in comparison to its approach to paramilitary perpetrators of violence.

Yet amidst the transitional discussions about the past's role in the future of Northern Ireland, the words of former detainees who have *previously* 'gone public' during the conflict about the state violence they have experienced is largely missing. What was the motivation, significance and consequences of truth sharing about state violence in the years whilst it was ongoing, or in the early years of the so-called 'Peace Process'? This aspect of the legacy of state violence does not usually form the basis of transitional justice literature in Northern Ireland and it is this lacuna that this book has tried to address. Experiences of similar acts of violence rarely fit easily into a homogeneous meta-narrative. There is a greater diversity in the motivation, significance and consequences of making public accounts of state violence than might be expected from a political movement that promotes a communal, shared experience. What

194 *Problems of talking about violence*

the research indicates is that there is no one Republican meta-narrative and that the institutionalisation of violence within the detention system had an impact on former detainees in very different ways. The individual experience has often been secondary to the communal narrative and the findings contained in this book shed light on the discomfort experienced by some detainees regarding the loss of ownership of their story under the influences of the British State, but also under the wider influences of the Republican movement. The significance of hindsight and the shifts in the dominant Republican discourse may have influenced former detainees to recall their experiences differently, or at least to put a different value on those experiences. Yet what remains is a distinct lack of homogeneity in former detainees' experiences of narrating state violence and in the motivations, significance and consequences of 'making public their accounts'.

The central message of this book is therefore that transitional justice mechanisms in all of their shapes and forms must recognise that not all who take part will share the same motivation, give the process the same significance or experience the same consequences. This book has shown how a multiplicity of forces and factors interact when subjugated knowledges become part of a contested history. Hegemonic discourses exist which suppress other interpretations and state power often works to subjugate alternative narratives, and yet these narratives are never entirely destroyed and often live on in the words and worlds of those who 'make public' their experiences. Although primarily rooted in Criminology in its exploration of former detainees narratives of state violence, this research has added to the literature across a range of disciplines: by deconstructing the language of state violence used in legal discourse; by incorporating an awareness of the problems and possibilities of healing into the literature on 'truth sharing' and by building upon work in gender studies to examine the meaning and significance of masculinities for men who narrate pain. It has also engaged in the deconstruction of the label of propaganda as often used in political studies and brought a detailed understanding of victimhood for those who have experienced the denials of state violence into the discourse of Criminology itself. Lastly, the book has also drawn on a socio-legal approach to critique the lack of accountability for state violence which continues to emerge as a legacy of the conflict.

Thus, as political engagement continues to lead Northern Ireland into peace, albeit in a gradual and sometimes piecemeal manner, the memoirs and narratives published by former detainees who experienced state violence represent a way of giving meaning to the past and to its place in the present. By understanding the motivation, significance and consequences of 'making public' private experiences of violence, it is hoped that Northern Ireland might one day find a way to construct a narrative of the conflict in which *all* can tell their stories and have their experiences of the conflict recognised. If such things can 'face down' the 'formidable challenges' shown in this book and become part of an ambitious move to also address the structural contexts which fuel conflict (Stanley 2009) and continue to fracture Northern Ireland's society, then sharing narratives of violence and victimhood can become more than 'political

Problems of talking about violence   195

window dressing' (Lundy and McGovern 2008: 60–62). The arguments featured in this book have shown how and why an understanding of former detainees and the motivation, significance and consequences of their narratives can make a real contribution to transitional justice and the legacy of state violence in Northern Ireland.

Notes

1 The issue has been given further complexity by statements made in the Dail in 2013 during which Sinn Féin TD Gerry Adams appeared to apologise for Republican violence against Irish State forces – though it was unclear on whose behalf such an apology was being made (Reilly 2013).
2 'The Disappeared' refers to Joseph Lynskey, Seamus Wright, Kevin McKee, Jean McConville, Peter Wilson, Eamonn Molloy, Columba McVeigh, Brendan Megraw, John McClory, Brian McKinney, Danny McIlhone, Eugene Simons and the British soldier Robert Nairac who are known to have been abducted and killed by the IRA. It also includes Seamus Ruddy, killed by the INLA, and Gerard Evans and Charles Armstrong, although no paramilitary groups have claimed responsibility for what might have happened to Gerard and Charles. Established in 1999, the Independent Commission for the Location of Victims' Remains is currently tasked with locating the bodies of 'The Disappeared'. The IRA has provided the Commission with some information about the dead and has encouraged those with information about their whereabouts to pass it on to the victim's families (see McKevitt 2013).
3 The nature of the 'Loyalist ceasefire' has been the subject of some dispute. Shirlow and McEvoy (2009) have suggested that Loyalist paramilitaries have carried out 89 killings, mostly of other Loyalist paramilitaries. The existence of these so-called 'Loyalist feuds' prior to the ceasefire and following its announcement are explored in depth by Bruce (1994, 2004), Gallaher and Shirlow (2006) and Gallaher (2007).

References

BBC (2002a) *IRA Statement in Full*. Available at: http://news.bbc.co.uk/1/hi/northern_ireland/2132113.stm (accessed 31 December 2012).
BBC (2002b) *My Tears for Brian*. Available at: http://news.bbc.co.uk/1/hi/northern_ireland/2132113.stm (accessed 1 June 2013).
BBC (2002c) *IRA Apology A 'Tremendous Stride'*. Available at: http://news.bbc.co.uk/1/hi/northern_ireland/2141931.stm (accessed 1 June 2013)
Bruce, S. (1992) 'The Problems of "Pro-state" Terrorism: Loyalist Paramilitaries in Northern Ireland', *Terrorism and Political Violence*, 4(1), 67–88.
Bruce, S. (1994) *The Edge of the Union: The Ulster Loyalist Political Vision: The Ulster Loyalist Political Vision*. Oxford: Oxford University Press.
Bruce, S. (2004) 'Turf War and Peace: Loyalist Paramilitaries Since 1994', *Terrorism and Political Violence*, 16(3), 501–521.
Cohen, S. (2001) *States of Denial: Knowing About Atrocities and Suffering.* London: Polity Press.
Compton Report (1971) *Report of Inquiry into Allegations Against the Security Forces of Physical Brutality in Northern Ireland Arising out of Events on the 9th August 1971* [Cmnd 4823] London: HMSO.
Feldman, A. (1991) *Formations of Violence: The Narrative of the Body and Political Terror in Northern Ireland*. Chicago: University of Chicago Press.

196 *Problems of talking about violence*

Gallaher, C. (2007) *After the Peace: Loyalist Paramilitaries in Post-Accord Northern Ireland*. Ithaca: Cornell University Press.

Gallaher, C. and Shirlow, P. (2006) 'The Geography of Loyalist Paramilitary Feuding in Belfast', *Space and Polity*, 10(2), 149–169.

Hamber, B. (2007) 'Masculinity and Transitional Justice: An Exploratory Essay', *International Journal of Transitional Justice*, 1(1), 375–390.

Jackall, R. (ed.) (1995) *Propaganda*. London: Macmillan.

Jowett, G.S. and O'Donnell, V. (1999) *Propaganda and Persuasion*. London: Sage.

Kelman, H.C. (1995) 'The Social Context of Torture: Policy, Process and Authority', in Crelinsten, R.D. and Schmid, A. (eds) *The Politics of Pain: Torturers and their Masters*. Boulder: Westview Press.

Lawther, C. (2011) 'Unionism, Truth Recovery and the Fearful Past', *Irish Political Studies*, 26(3), 361–382.

Lawther, C. (2013) 'Denial, Silence and the Politics of the Past: Unpicking the Opposition to Truth Recovery in Northern Ireland', *International Journal of Transitional Justice*, 7(1), 157–177.

Lawther, C. (2014) *Truth, Denial and Transition: Northern Ireland and the Contested Past*. London: Routledge.

Lundy, P. and McGovern, M. (2006) 'The Ethics of Silence: Action Research, Community "Truth-telling" and Post-conflict Transition in the North of Ireland', *Action Research*, 4(1), 49–64.

Lundy, P. and McGovern, M. (2008) 'A Trojan Horse? Unionism, Trust and Truth-telling in Northern Ireland', *International Journal of Transitional Justice*, 2(1), 42–62.

McAuley, J. (2004) '"Just Fighting to Survive": Loyalist Paramilitary Politics and the Progressive Unionist Party', *Terrorism and Political Violence*, 16(3), 522–543.

McEvoy, K. (2013) *Dealing with the Past in Northern Ireland : An Overview of Legal and Political Approaches*. Belfast: Healing Through Remembering.

McEvoy, K. and Shirlow, P. (2009) 'Re-imagining DDR: Ex-Combatants, Leadership and Moral Agency in Conflict Transformation', *Theoretical Criminology*, 13(1), 31–59.

McKevitt, G. (2013) 'The Disappeared: The Hidden Story of Northern Ireland's Troubles', BBC, 4 November. Available at: www.bbc.co.uk/news/uk-northern-ireland-24765480 (accessed 13 June 2013).

The Newsletter (2002) 'Mixed Reaction to IRA Apology'. 17 July. Available at: www.highbeam.com/doc/1G1-89134780.html (accessed 1 June 2013).

O'Neill, P. (2006) *IRA Statement on the Abduction and Killing of Jean McConville in December 1972*. Available at: http://cain.ulst.ac.uk/othelem/organ/ira/ira080706.htm (accessed 1 June 2013).

Pratkanis, A. and Aronson, E. (1991) *Age of Propaganda: The Everyday Use and Abuse of Persuasion*. New York: WH Freeman and Company.

Reilly, G. (2013) 'Adams Apologises to Family of Jerry McCabe and Others Killed by Republicans', *The Journal*. Accessed at: www.thejournal.ie/gerry-adams-apology-jerry-mccabe-774648-Jan2013/.

Saville Report (2010) *Report of the Bloody Sunday Inquiry*. London: HMSO.

Seidler, V.J. (1994) *Unreasonable Men: Masculinity and Social Theory*. London: Routledge.

Seidler, V.J. (2007) 'Masculinities, Bodies and Emotional Life', *Men and Masculinities*, 10(1), 9–21.

Smyth, M.B. (2007) *Truth Recovery and Justice after Conflict*. London: Routledge.

Stanley, E. (2002) 'What Next? The Aftermath of Organised Truth Telling', *Race and Class*, 44(1), 1–16.

Stanley, E. (2005) 'Truth Commissions and the Recognition of State Crime', *British Journal of Criminology*, 45(4), 582–597.

Stanley, E. (2009) *Torture, Truth and Justice: The Case of Timor Leste*. London: Routledge.

Sutton, M. (n.d.) 'Index of Deaths from the Conflict in Ireland: Summary of Organisation Responsible for the Deaths'. Available at: http://cain.ulst.ac.uk/sutton/tables/Organisation_Summary.html (accessed 15 June 2013).

Time (1991) 'Northern Ireland: Unleashing the Third Force', 7 December. Available at: http://content.time.com/time/magazine/article/0,9171,953237,00.html (accessed 21 December 2013).

Yúdice, G. (1991) 'Testimonio and Postmodernism', *Latin American Perspectives*, 18(3), 15–31.

Index

accountability 18; British Government 36; civil proceedings 178; Criminal Cases Review Commission (CCRC) 160–3; criminal courts 170–1; European Court of Human Rights (ECtHR) 171–2; inquests 168–70; legacy of violence 165–8; limitations of inquiries 165–8, 176–7; overarching strategy 175–9; overview 160; post-conflict mechanisms 173–5; resistance by British Government 178

agitative propaganda 105, 113, 188

Agnew, Paddy 41

Ainsworth, J. 102

Alonso, R. 102, 105

alternate reality 145

Amnesty International 36–7, 111

An Phoblacht 105, 110

apologies 153, 166, 190

Ardoyne Commemoration Project (ACP) 2

Aronson, E. 16, 101, 104, 121, 188

audiences 188; choices 121; extending 110–13, 118, 119; harmonising with 113; importance of 11; role of 72–3; targeting 108–10

Auld, Jim 29–31, 50–1, 61, 62–3, 64, 72–3, 86, 104, 107–9, 131–2, 141, 187, 189

authoritarianism 146

awareness raising 110

Bairner, A. 14, 83, 93

Bandura, A. 147

Barrett, F.J. 81

Barsamian, D 121

Bean, K. 118

bearing witness 71–3

Bell, C. 175

Bennett Report 37, 69, 129, 137, 142, 144, 148, 189

Bernays, E. 120

Billy Wright Inquiry 167

Birmingham Six 160

Blain, M. 17

blamelessness 192

blanket protest 38, 84

Bloody Sunday 104–5, 165–6

Bloomfield Report 176–7

Bowyer Bell, J. 114, 115

Boyle, K. 34, 68, 170

Bradley, D. 176

British Army: deployment 8; representation of 144–5; War on Terror 164–5

British Broadcasting Corporation (BBC) 151; allegations of violence 110; censorship 32

Brown, Lord Justice 169

brutality 29–31, 33–4, 36–7, 40; defining 49–51; use of term 186; *see also* defining experiences

bullets, plastic and rubber 171

Burton, F. 145, 152, 153

Campaign for Social Justice in Northern Ireland 31

Campbell, B. 54, 85, 87, 94–5

Carlen, P. 13, 145, 152, 153

Carrabine, E. 14

Carrington, Lord Peter 32, 141

Castlereagh Holding Centre 36–7, 107, 152, 186

catharsis 12, 64, 65, 67, 75

Cavanaugh, K.A. 148

censorship 31–2, 119, 151

Challis, J. 149

Chomsky, N. 121

Christie, N. 144

Civil Authorities (Special Powers) Act 1922 28

Clarke, L. 117
Cobain, I. 161
Cohen, S. 16, 18, 61, 65–6, 127, 134, 136, 137, 143, 145, 148–9, 150–1, 188–9
Coles, T. 91
collective experience, vs. individual 89–92
Collier, R. 13
collusion 26, 167
communality of victimisation 88–90
communities, conceptualising 130–2
Compton Report 32–3, 34, 49, 50–1, 55, 132, 135, 136, 144–5, 146, 147, 186
condemnation of condemners 150–3
conflict: causes of 8; context of 14–15; and truth 151–5
conflicts, stereotypes and symbols 115
Connell, R.W. 14, 80–1, 82
Connolly, C.K. 172
Conroy, J. 135
Consultative Group on the Past (CGP) 18, 75, 175–7, 178
convictions: rate 39, 160, 170; unsafe 160–1
Coogan, T.P. 106, 120, 152
Corcoran, M.S. 38
Cory Reports 167
Crawford, C. 130
Crelinsten, R.D. 16, 31, 143, 145–6
crime control model 68
Criminal Cases Review Commission (CCRC) 160–3, 178, 179
criminal courts 170–1
Criminal Justice Inspection Northern Ireland (CJINI 2011) 175
Criminal Law (Northern Ireland) Act 170
criminalisation: and legitimacy 39; politics of 35–7; in prisons 37–42; resistance of 90
crisis of masculinity 96
CS gas 35
Culbert, Michael 37, 53, 64, 65, 72–3, 74, 88, 91, 106–7, 109, 113, 128, 187, 188
Cullen, A. 57
Curtis, L. 32, 100, 119

de la Calle, L. 102
De Silva Review 167
Deahl, M. 62
defining experiences: defining brutality 49–51; labelling 57; overview 49; summary and conclusions 55–7; torture 51–5
dehumanisation 16, 34, 39–40, 53, 72, 140, 189

delegitimisation 39, 103
Della Porta, D. 90, 91
denial 18, 188–9; Cohen's framework 150, 188–9; condemnation of condemners 150–3; idealised images 144–5; implicatory 145–50, 189; interpretive 134–8, 141–2, 143, 144–5, 150, 188; literal 126–30, 143, 150, 188; overview 126; process of 142; reactions to 130–2; of responsibility 132; of victimhood 190–1;
depoliticisation 38
Devlin, Bobby 29
Diani, M. 90, 91
Diplock Courts 28, 35, 36, 106–7, 133; acquittals 170; conviction rate 39, 160, 170
Diplock Report 35
disorder, suppression of 26–7
Doherty, Kieran 41, 114
Dowler, L. 89
'Dúchas: Living History' 2

Eames, R. 176
Einolf, C. 53
elections: hunger strikers 114, 120; participation 41
emotional literacy 85
empowerment, through testimony and storytelling 63–4
European Convention for the Prevention of Torture and Inhuman or Degrading Treatment or Punishment 10
European Court of Human Rights (ECtHR) 34, 51–2, 55–6, 153, 169, 171–2, 178
European Human Rights Commission 33–4, 40
Evans, T. 88
exemplary masculinity 84, 86
experiences of imprisonment, recasting 94

Falls Community Council 2
Fattah, E.Z. 138
Faul, Fr Denis 37, 40, 151
Feeney, B. 117–18
Feldman, A. 16, 71, 84, 89, 94, 115, 187
female detainees 3
femininity 81
Field, S. 66–7
Finucane, Pat 166–7
Fírinne (Truth) 2
Fisher, James 170
Five Demands 40–1, 119
Five Techniques 29, 32, 33, 51–2, 55, 151

200 *Index*

forgetting and remembering 41
Foucault, M. 27

Gardiner Report 36, 37, 136, 151
gender: and detention 15; of experiences
  12–13; and experiences of imprisonment
  13, 14; in going public 85–6; not
  homogeneous 80; participants' 5; and
  power 82–3; significance 187; and
  violence 13–14
Gilligan, G. 134
Girdwood Park 31
Godwin Phelps, T. 10–11
Goffman, E. 84
going public 1–2; choice to 4–5;
  consequences 188; as gendered 85–6;
  see also revealing
Gormally, B. 3
Government of Ireland, prosecution of UK
  51–2
Gramsci, A. 27
Graybill, L.S. 12, 66
Grounds, A. 83
Guildford Four 160

Haass–O'Sullivan talks 177, 178
Hamber, B. 65, 66, 75–6, 80–1, 96, 187
Hamill, Robert 168
hard men 84
hatred 54–5
Hayes, G. 63–4, 68, 75
Hayner, P.B. 66
healing 10–12, 186; assumptions of 65–6;
  bearing witness 71–3; construction of
  meaning 61; defining 61; evidence of
  66; expectations of 73; experience of
  63–5; as motivation 61–2; moving on
  73–6; overview 60; as problematic
  74–5; remaining silent 68–71; risks of
  revealing 65–8; summary and
  conclusions 74–6; in truth sharing
  process 61
'Healing Through Remembering' 3–4
health effects 161–2
Hegarty, A. 152
hegemonic masculinity 82–3
Heidensohn, F. 13
Herman, J. 11, 12, 75
Hillyard, P. 28, 57, 142
Historical Enquiries Team (HET) 18,
  173–4, 176, 177, 179
Historical Investigations Unit (HIU)
  177–8
historical lineage 114, 115–16

Hobdell, K. 83, 86
Holding Centres 36–7, 107
human rights: respect for 16; as theoretical
  instrument 9–10
human rights audiences, communication
  with 118
humiliation 84
humour 87, 187
hunger strikes 40–2, 119–20; propaganda
  113–17; representation of 91
Hutchinson, Al 174

iconography 115
idealised victim 144
identities: collective 89–90; institutional
  27; not fixed 96
images: idealised 144–5; preserved 96–7
implicatory denial 145–50, 189
incarceration, masculinity of 83–4
individuals, marginalisation 91–2
inevitability of violence 149–50
informers: state use of 9; treatment of 2–3
inhuman treatment 51–2
injuries, self-inflicted 132–4
International Covenant on Civil and
  Political Rights 10
internees, representation of 141–2
internment 28–34, 35–6, 104–5, 106
interpretive denial 134–8, 141–2, 143,
  144–5, 150, 188
interrogation 29–31, 36–7; Compton
  Report 32–3; in depth 51–2; use of
  threat 107
Interrogation Centres 36–7, 39, 107, 186
Interviewee F 56–7, 67–8, 69, 74, 82–3,
  85, 91, 92, 94, 109–10, 128, 130–1, 133,
  139, 140, 142, 143, 147, 152, 163
Interviewee P 50, 53–4, 67, 73, 87, 94,
  103–4, 128, 140, 163–4
Interviewee PJ 52, 63, 64, 75, 90, 104,
  109, 111–12, 129, 131
Iraq 164–5
Ireland v. *UK* (1978) 51–2, 55, 178
Irish News 31
Irish Republican Army (IRA) 191;
  legitimacy 119; propaganda 106–7;
  propaganda aims 120
Irwin, Dr Robert 37, 189

Jackall, R. 16, 101, 116, 188
Jamieson, R. 83
Jasper, J. 89
Jefferson, T. 83
Jewkes, Y. 85, 87

journalists: accounts of violence 4; collection of testimonies 32–3
Jowett, G.S. 101, 102, 104, 105, 106, 108, 111, 121, 188
just deserts 140–3
justice system: adaptations to 39; role of 18

Kauzlarich, D. 146, 147
Kelly, G. 2
Kelman, H.C. 141, 142, 146, 189
Kerr, R. 61
Kitson, F. 68
Korn, A. 146
kriegsgreuelpropaganda 102–3

Larkin, John 169
Laswell, H.D. 101, 102–3, 104, 108, 115, 116, 119
Laub, D. 67
Lawther, C. 191, 192, 193
Leckey, J. 169
Legacy Commission 176, 177
legitimacy 193; and criminalisation 39; Irish Republican Army (IRA) 119; official discourse 136; and propaganda 102–5; of state 17; state violence 27, 170; of violence 148
Levi, P 10, 11
Linfield, S. 71–3
literal denial 126–30, 143, 150, 188
Livingstone, S. 56
Lloyd, D. 116
Longhurst, B. 14
Loughinisland killings 174–5
Loyalist Combined Military Command (LCMC) 191
Loyalist paramilitaries 191; and State forces 166–7; truth sharing 193
Lundy, P. 2, 3, 173, 191, 192, 193

Maguire Seven 160
Maillot, A. 118
Mallinder, L. 178
manipulation, propaganda as 101
marginalisation: of experiences 165; of individuals 91–2
martyrdom 94
masculinity: cultural construction 80–1; culturally acceptable 85; defining 80–1; exemplary 84, 86; expectations of 96; gendered power 82–3; as goal 80–1; hegemonic 82–3; humour 87; ideology of 96; of incarceration 83–4; macho 86;

norms 83; overview 80; preserved images 96–7; preserving 187; recreation of 90; as resistance 92–5; and struggle 187; support networks 87–92; and victimhood 83; and vulnerability 82–3, 84, 85, 89
Mason, Roy 120
Matza, D. 16, 127, 134, 143, 145, 147, 150
McAuley, J.W. 139
McBride, Peter 170
McCann v. *UK* 172
McClean, P.J. 29–30
McElhone, Patrick 170–1
McEvoy, K. 3, 9, 35, 36, 39, 95, 105, 117, 118, 162, 165, 169, 175, 176, 177, 192
McGovern, M. 2, 3, 168, 179, 191, 192, 193
McGuinness, Martin 192
McKearney, Tommy 37, 50, 53, 62, 63, 64, 74, 82–3, 102, 106, 108, 112, 113, 133–4, 143, 149–50, 151, 152–3, 163, 164, 189, 191
McKeown, Laurence 35, 40, 50, 73, 87, 89, 92, 93, 119, 121, 133, 152–3, 163, 188
McKittrick, D. 7–8, 26, 28, 93, 171, 172
McLean Inquiry 167
McVea, D. 7–8, 28, 93
media: accounts of violence 4; allegations of violence 110–11; censorship 31–2; collection of testimonies 32–3; relationships with Republicans 118–19
memories: official 175; repression of 62–3
mental health 133, 161–2
Messerschmidt, J.W. 12, 13, 86
methodology 5–7
militarism phase 165
Miller, D. 100, 121
Mobekk, E. 61
Moloney, E. 107
Morgan, R. 16, 140, 146
Morland Inquiry 167
motivation 96, 111–13, 186–7, 188
Mousa, Baha 164–5
moving on 73–4
Murray, Andrew 170
Murray, Fr Raymond 37, 40, 151
Murray, Harry 41, 54, 64, 65, 70, 71, 73–4, 87, 88, 95, 96, 103–4, 109, 118, 121, 132, 139, 149, 187

Naan, Michael 170
narrating violence, lived experience 61
narration, significance 64

Index

narratives: communal 90; as communal resistance 15; constructing legitimacy 102–5; counter narratives 136; discrediting 16; educational function 106, 119; forms of 4; framing 118; H-Block cells 40; heroic struggle 89; heterogeneity 193–4; legacy of 163–4; meta-narratives 138; number of 69; omissions 107–8; public inquiries 136–7; publication outlets 110; re-coding/re-ordering 135; recasting of experiences 94; representation of 'enemy' 103–4; resistance of 90; *see also* official discourse; revealing; storytelling
National H-Block/Armagh Committee 118
Neier, A. 11
Nelson, Rosemary 167
Newburn, T. 96
Ní Aoláin, F. 28, 165, 166, 169, 170, 171
non-jury courts 28, 35, 36, 106–7, 133; acquittals 170; conviction rate 39, 160, 170
normative approach, definition of masculinity 80–1
Nugent, Kieran 38

Ó Fiaich, Cardinal Thomas 38, 119
O'Donnell, V. 101, 102, 104, 105, 106, 108, 111, 121, 188
Office of the Police Ombudsman for Northern Ireland (OPONI) 18, 176, 177, 178–9; Historical Investigations Directorate 174–5
official discourse: conceptualising communities 130–2; condemnation of condemners 150–3; and control of information 151–2; defining and labelling 134–5; deserved punishment 140–3; idealised images 144–5; implicatory denial 145–50; inter-state discussion 153; interpretive denial 134–8; legislative change 153; literal denials 126–30; overview 126; peace with the past 173; Royal Ulster Constabulary (RUC) 144; self-inflicted injuries 132–4; social control 137–8; summary and conclusions 153–5; truth in conflict 151–5; understanding of 136; victimhood 138–40
official memory 175
official silence 70
officials, attacks on 95
O'Hearn, D. 89, 90

O'Loan, N. 167, 179
O'Malley, P. 115, 116
O'Neill, P. 190
Operation Demetrius 28–9, 32
O'Rawe, Richard 31, 50, 53, 54, 62, 74, 75, 84, 88
O'Shaughnessy, N.J. 115, 117, 120, 121
othering 39, 53, 130, 140, 149–50

Paisley, Ian 191
Panel of the Parties of the Northern Ireland Executive 177
Parachute Regiment 31
Parker Inquiry 33, 34, 136, 146–7, 148, 151
peace with the past 173, 192
peacekeeping 9
persuasion 16, 101–2
Poggi, G. 27
politics of criminalisation 35–7
Polletta, F. 89
positivism, definition of masculinity 80–1
post-conflict mechanisms of accountability 173–5
power: and agency 92–3; displays of 94–5; gendered 82–3; of language 120; and masculinities 96; negotiation 95
Pratkanis, A. 16, 101, 104, 121, 188
Pratt, J. 134
preparedness, for imprisonment 106
preserved images 96–7
press, allegations of violence 110–11
prison staff: attacks on 95, 104, 105, 139, 144; modes of reference to 103; representation of 144
prison violence 14
prisons, criminalisation in 37–42
propaganda 188; agitative 105, 113, 188; aims of 103, 109, 116; allegations as 128–30; defining 100–2; educational function 111; as exploitation 117, 118; extending audiences 110–13; hunger strikes 113–17; intentions 120; and legitimacy 102–5; meaning and use 15–16; overview 100; pejorative labelling 129–30; pluralism 120; re-imagining 120–1; reformulation of perceptions 104; and Republicanism 105–8; as social control 115–16; stigmatising 120–1, 129; summary and conclusions 120–2; targeting of audience 108–10; truth of 121; War of Ideas 117–20
public inquiries 134–7, 165–8, 176–7

Public Inquiries Act 2005 168
Public Interest Immunity Certificates 169
punishment 84, 104, 140–3

Quirk, H. 160–1

reactive containment 165
reactive violence 102
reasonableness 170–1
recognition, of violence 130, 189–90
recognition payment 177
recruitment, effect of internment 104–5
Reilly, Thomas 170
Relatives Action Committee (RAC)
 117–18
Relatives for Justice 178
religious symbolism 115–16
Report of the Police Ombudsman 167
Republic of Ireland v. *UK* (1978) 153
Republican discourse, portrayal of 90–1
Republican News 105, 110
Republican Press Centre 106
Republicanism: discourses 152; and
 propaganda 105–8
Requa, M. 161, 162
resistance 84, 90, 91, 93–4; death as 115;
 displays of 94–5; manifestations 95;
 masculinity as 92–5; of narratives 90;
 and propaganda 109
responsibility: denial of 132; shared 146
restoration 61
revealing: as dehumanising 72; as harmful
 67–8, 186–7; as healing 63–5, 186–7;
 hopes for 103–4; motivation for 11–12,
 96, 111–13, 186–7, 188; opportunities
 for 70; reactions experienced 72–3; risks
 of 65–8, 69, 72; role of audience 72–3;
 and understanding 71; *see also* going
 public; narratives; storytelling
rights-based discourse 9–10
risks, of revealing 65–8, 69, 72
Robinson, Peter 139–40, 191
roles, victim vs. perpetrator 138–9
Rolston, B. 17, 135, 136, 137, 141, 146,
 152, 162, 166, 168, 169, 174, 179
Ross, F.C. 66
Roth, B. 56
Royal Ulster Constabulary (RUC) 139,
 191; attacks on 144; complaints against
 69, 128; primacy 36; representation of
 144; violence 8
RTÉ Investigations Unit 161
rubber bullets 171
Ryder, C. 34

sampling 5–7
Sánchez-Cuenca, I. 102
Sands, Bobby 41, 91, 114
Sangster, K. 66
Saville Inquiry 153, 166, 168, 192
Scraton, P. 17, 27, 83, 135, 136, 137, 141,
 146, 152, 168
sectarian stereotypes 192
security community: killings 26;
 prosecutions of 170
Seidler, V.J. 14, 82, 86, 88, 187
self-defence 147
self-inflicted injuries 132–4
self-representation 40
shame 83
Shannon, Liam 29–30, 50, 52, 55, 63, 64,
 72–3, 75, 109, 111, 112, 132, 135
Shirlow, P. 9, 35
Shivers, Patrick 32
silence 68–71
Sinn Féin 117–18
sliding scale, inhuman treatment/torture
 52, 55, 56
Smith, T.J. III 100–1
Smyth, M.B. 17–18, 134, 189
social control 115–16
South African Truth and Reconciliation
 Commission (SATRC) 12, 61, 66
Special Category Status 34–5, 36, 37
Special Powers 28, 133
'Squeaky Booters' 84
Stalker Inquiry 168
Stanko, E. 83, 86, 96
Stanley, E. 138, 148, 152, 187
State forces 189; and Loyalist
 paramilitaries 166–7
state of exception 142–3
state violence 9; brutality 29–31; context
 of 26–8; deaths from 165; as deserved
 punishment 140–3; in detention 4–5;
 forms of 4–5, 26–7; legacy of 18, 163;
 legitimacy 27, 170; plastic/rubber
 bullets 171; re-conceptualising 16;
 reconstruction 135; subjugated
 knowledge 17; uses of 84; *see also*
 accountability; defining experiences
stereotyping 115, 130, 192
Stevens Inquiry 167
Stewart, Brian 171
stigma 66, 83; propaganda 120–1, 129
storytelling: exclusion 3; imperative 10;
 individual vs.collective 91–2;
 mechanisms 73; modes of 61;
 motivation for 11–12, 96, 111–13;

204 *Index*

storytelling *continued*
  as resistance 95; state violence in detention 4–5; tactical 148; *see also* narratives; revealing
storytelling projects 2–3
Stover, E. 62
subjugated knowledge 17
suffering: as resistance 93; and strength 94
Summerfield, D. 75
support networks 87–92
suppression of disorder 26–7
survivors: construction of meaning 10; defining 176
suspect communities 146
Sykes, G. 16, 127, 134, 143, 145, 147, 150
symbolism 115–16

taboo issues 2–3
tactical storytelling 148
talking: benefits of 62; safe 87–8
Taylor, P. 32, 40
techniques of neutralisation 16, 127, 134, 145, 150
testimony: as empowering 63–4; reactions to 141
Thain, Ian 170
Thames Television, allegations of violence 110
The Disappeared 190–1
The Green Book 106–7
threats, in interrogation 107
threats to national security 147–8
Tomlinson, M. 166
Tonge, J. 28–9, 130
torture 29–31; defining 51–6; prohibition of 9–10; as punishment 143; use of term 186; *see also* defining experiences
total institutions 84
transitional justice 12–13, 161–2, 175, 187
Trimble, David 190
tripartite framework of denial 18
truth: in conflict 151–5; as fluid 101; uses of 126
Truth Commissions 11, 178, 179, 192
truth sharing 2–3; attitudes to 191–3; during conflict 4–5; mythology of 75; and non-state actors 189–95; time and place 60; veneration of 61

Ulster Resistance 191
United Kingdom, prosecution 51–2, 55
Universal declaration of Human Rights 9–10

unsafe convictions 160–1
utilitarianism 147–8

valorisation, of State forces 189
vengeance 104, 143
victimhood: denial of 190–1; gendered experiences 12–14; and masculinity 83; official discourse 138–40
victimisation: communality of 88–9; reframing 88
victims: defining 176; idealised 144
Victims and Survivors (Northern Ireland) Order (2006) 176
Villani, Mario 11–12
violence: accountability 36; and criminalisation 39–40; as deserved punishment 140–3; as discipline 148–9; evidence of 152; experience of narration 61; and gender 13–14; H-Block cells 40; inevitability of 149–50; justification 148; legacy of 165–8; legitimacy 148; legitimate/illegitimate 17; outside prisons 95; against prison staff 95, 104, 105, 139; in prisons 14; reactive 102; recognition of 130, 189–90; reconceptualisation 187; retaliatory 104; against RUC 139; as self-defence 147; shared responsibility 146; uses of 84; *see also* defining experiences
vulnerability, and masculinity 82–3, 84, 85, 89

Walklate, S. 138, 140, 144
Wallace, P. 88
war atrocity stories 103
War of Ideas 117–20
War on Terror 164–5
Ward, James 170
Ward, Judith 161
Weber, M. 26–7
Wessely, S. 62
Whitehead, S.M. 81
Widgery Inquiry 165–6
Wilcox, F.O. 102
women: experiences of imprisonment 13; as victims 13–14
women's narratives, scarcity 3
Worrall, A, 13
Wright, Billy 95
Wright, Mark 170

Yúdice, G. 189